Getting MORE *Excited* About USING Data

Third Edition

This book is dedicated to
my husband Lee Olsen,
because he is totally dedicated to me.

Getting MORE *Excited* About USING Data

Third Edition

Edie L. Holcomb

Foreword by Shirley Hord

CORWIN
A SAGE Publishing Company

FOR INFORMATION:

Corwin
A SAGE Company
2455 Teller Road
Thousand Oaks, California 91320
(800) 233-9936
www.corwin.com

SAGE Publications Ltd.
1 Oliver's Yard
55 City Road
London EC1Y 1SP
United Kingdom

SAGE Publications India Pvt. Ltd.
B 1/I 1 Mohan Cooperative Industrial Area
Mathura Road, New Delhi 110 044
India

SAGE Publications Asia-Pacific Pte. Ltd.
3 Church Street
#10-04 Samsung Hub
Singapore 049483

Executive Editor: Arnis Burvikovs
Senior Associate Editor: Desirée A. Bartlett
Editorial Assistant: Kaitlyn Irwin
Production Editor: Amy Schroller
Copy Editor: Megan Markanich
Typesetter: C&M Digitals (P) Ltd.
Proofreader: Dennis W. Webb
Cover Designer: Anupama Krishnan
Marketing Manager: Anna Mesick

Printed in the United States of America

Library of Congress Cataloging-in-Publication Data

Names: Holcomb, Edie L., author.

Title: Getting more excited about using data / Edie L. Holcomb; foreword by Shirley Hord.

Description: Third edition. | Thousand Oaks, Calif. : Corwin, 2017. | Includes bibliographical references and index.

Identifiers: LCCN 2016053729 | ISBN 9781506357256 (pbk. : alk. paper)

Subjects: LCSH: Educational indicators—United States. | Educational evaluation—United States. | Education—United States—Statistics. | School improvement programs—United States. | Academic achievement—United States.

Classification: LCC LB2846 .H56 2017 | DDC 379.1/58—dc23
LC record available at https://lccn.loc.gov/2016053729

This book is printed on acid-free paper.

17 18 19 20 21 10 9 8 7 6 5 4 3 2 1

Contents

List of Figures

Foreword

Data! Data!! Data!!

Few leaders and teachers in schools, and administrators at district office, have not been besieged for several decades by the topic of data and its use in district, school, and classroom improvement efforts. Nonetheless, the matter of educators using data with meaningful knowledge and effective efficiency and skills remains another matter. Developing such content and skills requires more than the typical daylong workshop or a faculty meeting devoted to the topic.

More recently, schools have been pushed in the direction of standardization and one size fits all. Most assuredly, if performance data are collected from and about individual teachers and students, we become aware of the vast differences across these populations—and the levels to which they are able to perform well in their respective roles. Employing the use of data to this problem is widely understood but not so well demonstrated.

Fortuitously, yet again Edie Holcomb in her third edition has engaged her exemplary skills in creating a significant new volume—*Getting MORE Excited About USING Data.* This third volume conveys for us rich new ideas, understandings, and insights in providing the culture, content, and processes that lead our data use to increased teaching quality and enhanced or expanded outcomes for our students. We have a moral imperative to use data tools and strategies well, to powerfully support improved classroom practice.

There is no one more critical of a body of work than the author herself. In the years since the second edition on the topic, Holcomb has given the scissors to some of the earlier strategies for engaging data for improvement purposes, while expanding and introducing more current topics and their applications.

She has given us a rich array of new ideas, materials, and activities whereby district and classroom data practice are more powerful and productive. I am particularly, but not exclusively, drawn to a number of these:

- New material on issues of morale such as teacher sense of efficacy, individually and collectively across the school, and cultures of trust, critically important for adults and connected by evidence to student learning. This links directly to the next four:
- More inclusive leadership and its various models, including descriptions of Shared Leadership Teams, Data Teams, and use of data in these groups

- Increased attention to the role of students, and engaging them with their own data
- Identification of technological advances that facilitate use of data
- Use of data to differentiate professional learning and development among and within schools

These are but a few of the new additions. Like all new ideas, processes, and practices, they are of no value unless carefully planned and consistently implemented. To emphasize this issue, a few findings from change process research can inform us.

A simple axiom frames this work: improvement requires change learning. <u>Improvement</u> (of any kind, whether it is increased competency in teaching "new math," singing a newly published hymn, computing long division, throwing complete passes on the football field, making a yummy chocolate angel food cake) <u>requires change</u> of some feature or factor that is not contributing to a factor potentially more effective and <u>learning</u> what the new factor is and how to use it.

This means that much learning about data use will be required, including its multiple kinds for multiple purposes, when and how it is collected, and other related issues. Research on implementation identifies six strategies (Hord & Roussin, 2013) required for successful implementation:

1. Create a shared vision of the change (in this case, using data) when it has been integrated into practice in a high-quality way. This means knowing *with precision* and being able to articulate what the use of data will look like in its desired environments. *Holcomb provides multiple real-life examples in words and figures so readers can envision powerful data work.*

2. Plan for implementation and its required resources based on the vision. This plan provides clear, explicit, and orderly steps for reaching implementation. Budgets, time, staffing, material, and human resources will be considered. Collaborative planning conversations with staff are done by wise leaders. *This third edition adds protocols and guiding questions for those critical conversations.*

3. Invest in professional learning. The enormous value of this learning is reflected in the term *invest.* This learning is provided on an ongoing basis as novice implementers develop expertise in using the innovation, the new way of doing things. Getting MORE Excited About USING Data *describes skills and concepts needed by data users as they shift their focus from compliance to commitment.*

4. Monitor progress. Learning facilitators (coaches) will observe and interact with each implementer to determine his or her status in implementing the vision (noted in strategy 1). *Holcomb emphasizes the need for proactive identification of sources that will generate evidence of both implementation by the responsible adults and impact on the learning environment and learning results for students.*

5. Provide ongoing support and assistance. Monitoring and supporting are like the proverbial hand in glove. There is little reason to monitor without addressing what the implementer needs as revealed in the monitoring. *Holcomb provides useful guidance about appropriate support for skills, time, technological resources, and professional learning provided by building and district administrators.*

6. Create a context conducive to change. While the first five of these six strategies are implicitly sequential, this strategy covers all and should be present before implementation begins. If this culture or climate reflected in the five strategies already cited is not present, it must assuredly be cultivated and developed as new practices are being implemented. Getting MORE Excited About USING Data *can be useful for diagnosing cultural factors such as beliefs and structures and creating readiness for attention to data that leads to change.*

In this context conducive to change, participants must celebrate—in large and small ways, publicly and privately, both individual and collective progress. This action is so often forgotten but is a powerful "intervention" and motivation for the implementers.

Powerful also describes Holcomb's current gift to us, *Getting MORE Excited About USING Data*, which is so helpful for us in learning about this topic. Such learning can be accelerated through employing this volume, so well developed and presented. Engage your team with this book so that your data use becomes a powerful means to improved practice and successful student learning.

—Shirley Hord, PhD
Scholar Laureate
Learning Forward

Preface

In the seventeen years since the first edition of *Getting Excited About Data*, I've heard the word *data* described in various ways as dangerous, threatening, "the dreaded *D*," and even "the four-letter *D* word." I've found two other words to be far more risky: *always* and *never*. I eventually learned to avoid *always* because as sure I would say "I always use data," someone—usually a friend or family member and in jest—would say something like "Then why do you always buy red cars even when you know the data about odds of being pulled over?" (Because candy apple red makes me happy and I like to *beat* the odds.) I've had more trouble avoiding the word *never*. There was "I'll never leave the classroom [to be a principal] because I care too much about the kids" and "I'll never leave the building level [for central office] because I don't want to lose touch with kids" and "I'll never work at a university because it's too far from kids."

More recently, working with a school leadership team, a teacher leader who was checking something on the Internet blurted out, "What?! You've written these books? When are you doing the next one?" "I'm done writing . . . (aka never)." Two days later, in another school, a team member said, "This was a classic example. You should put us in your next book." "I'm not writing books anymore . . . (aka never)." Before the day was out, I got an e-mail from Corwin asking me to consider writing a third edition. The idea kept growing on me, so when I talked with editor Arnis Burvikovs on the phone, I agreed to at least pull my thoughts together on what I *would* change if I *did* revise the second edition. During that "think about it" time, I accidentally went to the wrong file cabinet looking for some tax information and found my hand on a folder labeled "If Data 3e." So at some point, I must have already been thinking about things I might want to add—or subtract. And I began.

WHY ANOTHER BOOK

So why this third edition? For one thing, in the past year, professors preparing principals and principals leading schools have said, "My students reference you" and "I still use your book to help me." It seems there's still value in a simple, straightforward approach to the challenges of sharpening our practice by checking the facts about our realities and our results. For another, over the last decade of working with professionals at the district, school, and classroom level, I've come across unintended negative consequences of a few of my earlier recommendations, and

I value the chance to set the record straight. As a third reason, I've struggled alongside educators bombarded by external mandates that have actually detoured them from the most important work and mission of our schools. The expectations I set for professionals are just as high as they have been for two decades, but my empathy for their reality is even higher. No Child Left Behind (NCLB) has been replaced, and I want to reflect on its impact—leaving most, but not all, of it behind. Finally, as I reread the two previous editions, they seem aimed mostly at administrators, though that was not the intent. I am a passionate believer in shared or distributed leadership as the only way new practices can be implemented and sustained. I am reviewing and rewriting portions of earlier work and adding new content with a deep desire to convey *that* and *how* it is critical for individuals at all levels of an organization to kindle the excitement for continuous improvement based on real evidence of results.

WHAT'S NEW HERE IN THE THIRD

The most enjoyable part of rewriting this book was the chance to **delete** so many passages that reflected the increasing sanctions of NCLB and replace them with newer, more exciting, more educator-friendly material. Connections are made to ESSA, the Every Student Succeeds Act, and its potential to restore energy for the real mission of our schools. But it has left its scars, and one of my greatest hopes in writing anew is to help educators heal and renew hope. To that end, here is what this edition provides:

- Frequent references to changes in the law and their potential to redirect our focus and improve our outlook
- Realities of how NCLB affected teachers—from fears of sanctions on their schools to use of test scores to evaluate their performance and in turn threaten their employment, which for most is also their mission in life
- New material on tender morale issues—teacher sense of efficacy individually, collective sense of efficacy throughout a school, and cultures of trust—critically important for the adults *and* linked by evidence to student learning
- Identification of technological advances that facilitate use of data, along with needed steps to counter the realities of threats to privacy and security
- A more inclusive approach to discussions of leadership—shared, distributed at all levels, drawing on personal influence as well as position power
- Refined descriptions of the work of Shared Leadership Teams and Data Teams, with an entire new section on the use of data in Teaching Teams
- Attention to the concepts and balance of formative, benchmark, and summative assessments and their appropriate uses in school-wide planning and instructional design
- Increased attention to the role of students—resurrecting other sources of data that reflect the whole child and engaging students with their own data

- Updated sources of best (evidence-based) practices
- Redefined roles of the central office in support of schools
- Use of data to differentiate professional development among schools and individual teachers and the positive impact that teacher evaluation rubrics *could* provide
- New tools for team productivity, including the use of norms and protocols
- Current case studies from a diverse set of schools not present in former editions

WHAT THIS BOOK IS *NOT*

Even with the new material, there are still a number of things this book is not.

This is not a statistics book. The uses of data recommended in this book require the ability to count, calculate averages and percentages, and construct simple graphs. Students who meet the sixth-grade Statistics and Probability standards of the Common Core State Standards would be able to assist with the data work discussed here. Regression formulas and correlation coefficients are omitted. Here, the term *significance* isn't represented as $p < 0.05$. It refers instead to what the *school* defines as significant—that is, as important, relevant, and useful to know.

This book is not comprehensive. If psychometricians describe this book as simplistic and basic, we will know we've been successful. There are legitimate reasons why most educators are uncomfortable with the use of data. The purpose of this book is to raise comfort and interest levels so readers will become ready, willing, and able to explore more sophisticated uses of data. My intent is simply this: to meet people where they are and help them take their next steps forward in this standards-based, data-driven age of accountability.

This book is not bureaucratic and impersonal. Reading it and implementing its recommendations won't turn anyone into an accountant or auditor. Its purpose is to affirm and build on the nurturing nature of teachers, adding the support of objective information to their usually accurate professional intuition. Stories from the trenches illustrate how the use of data can stimulate greater sensitivity to the needs of students, not turn them into faceless numbers.

This book is not a quick fix for the achievement gap. Almost every chapter highlights some equity issue I have experienced myself or encountered in schools and districts—urban, rural, and suburban—in over thirty states and several countries. These experiences began over forty years ago, when I taught in an Alabama school that had just experienced forced desegregation, and my class of third graders spanned eleven reading levels. The experiences became even richer some thirty years ago, when I became principal of a school with racial and socioeconomic diversity. The state Department of Education came to conduct an audit of our Title I program, because the fall-to-spring normal curve equivalent gains we reported were suspect. The gains were validated, and state officials described our elementary school as "the best kept secret in the state."

More recently, I worked with urban schools in Seattle, Washington, including those with a majority of students of color, large numbers of

English language learners (ELLs), and 70 percent or more qualifying for free or reduced-price lunches. I learned with pride that the best of classroom teaching and assessment most dramatically impacts challenged learners and accelerates their progress. I learned with frustration that schools most in need of stability and sophisticated instructional expertise suffered constant teacher turnover due to rigid salary schedules, seniority-based transfer policies, and the sheer enormity of the task at early career stages. I learned with humility that I needed to partner with leaders of color, because learning cognitively, listening compassionately, and becoming culturally competent are not the same as "knowing" the realities of the achievement gap. In this book, I share what I can say with confidence from my own experience and observation. And I embed findings from organizations like the Center for Educational Leadership (CEL) and the Education Trust, who relentlessly pursue the mission of gap-closing.

This book is not written in jargon. For this book, I have intentionally chosen a casual, conversational style. My purpose is to use plain English to describe simple things that have created interest and opened doors with real people. Because these activities have helped my colleagues and clients, I hope you will find them useful also.

WHAT THIS BOOK *IS*

The purpose of this book was captured in the subtitle added to the second edition: *Combining People, Passion, and Proof to Maximize Student Achievement*. Collecting more data for the sake of having more data is an exercise in futility unless it engages people by connecting to their deep and authentic passions for teaching and learning. People who work incredibly hard because they care need the proof of their efforts to encourage and sustain them and to help them gain the respect they so deserve. The goal is not to be a more research-based, data-driven school. The goal is to increase student success.

The focus of *Getting **More** Excited About **Using** Data* is the human element—hopes and fears, prior knowledge, beliefs about student potential and professional practice, and current needs. This book offers a variety of tools and group activities to create active engagement with data and interaction with peers that will build more collaborative cultures with a shared sense of collective responsibility for all students' learning.

HOW THIS BOOK IS ORGANIZED

The previous edition of *Getting Excited About Data* was organized sequentially. It began with a knowledge base and rationale for data use, followed by discussion of barriers to use of data that are embedded in the reality of school life. A synthesis of research on how high-performing schools use data was introduced. It is updated here in Chapter 1, and Figure 1.5 (p. 17) guides you to the chapters that provide more detail and examples. A school improvement framework was provided at the beginning, and ensuing chapters discussed how data would be used and people engaged at each significant stage in the process: creating readiness, gathering baseline data, displaying the data and interpreting the results, establishing priorities and setting goals, studying best practices that would address the goals, planning and monitoring implementation, and documenting the bottom line impact on learning.

From my point of view now, the field doesn't need another school improvement planning guide. Things are way more complicated than following a series of steps. A greater need is for an honest look at the barriers faced by committed professionals willing to courageously confront their reality and challenge themselves and their colleagues. But such people do not focus on barriers; they focus on possibilities. So the third edition has been organized around factors that help people get excited about using data—or interested anyway—or at least willing to look. For readers who are anxious to look at data use in the context of the school improvement process, it's still here, somewhat condensed in Chapter 7, with references to related sections throughout the book. For readers who are just seeking ideas and support to ignite data use, read Chapter 1 as a foundation, and then start with any chapter that resonates with what you hear, see, and experience in your own setting. It's easier to get excited about data when it fits your beliefs, when it feels safe, when you're not in it alone, when you see faces in it, when it's easy to get, when it fits a bigger picture, when it helps save resources, when you can do something about it, when you have time to deal with it, when you have appropriate support, and when it shows you've made a difference. There's a chapter to help address each of those conditions. Each chapter includes related concepts and background information, activities that may engage you and your colleagues, and at least one real-life "for instance" example.

NCLB may be replaced, but the critics of public education are not silenced. For public education to survive—and it *must* because it is the last, best hope for success for so many young people—all schools and districts must develop the will and skill to gather, display, analyze, interpret, make decisions, and take action with data. We must be able to tell our stories and state our case not just for the outside world but so that we can strengthen the faith, the fervor, and the force within us by focusing on our own proof that we have made a difference.

Acknowledgments

Thank you to Shirley Hord for being my personal friend and mentor over these many years—and for impacting our entire profession through your vast body of work on the change process, professional development, effective schools, the role of central office, and professional learning communities of continuous improvement and inquiry,

Thank you to my friends Kathy Crossley, Gloria Tuggle, Sharon Green, and June Rimmer. These brilliant, courageous African American educators have intersected my life, generously shared their journeys, and patiently forgiven my shallow understandings. You are my angels of conscience.

Thank you to my coaches Judy Heinrich and Kathy Larson. You have both sharpened and softened my judgment and decision-making.

Thank you to the late Dave Pedersen, who compensated for my technological inadequacies in previous editions. Through his role with instructional technology, he worked to close the digital divide for his students and initiated a scholarship fund to support others to continue his mission.

Thank you to Beth Wallen, Cara Haney, and Emily Coleman of Panther Lake Elementary School in Kent, Washington. Your determination to make data work for your staff and students will inspire many.

Thank you to Darren Benson, principal of Blaine Middle School in Blaine, Washington. Your journals helped chronicle a multiyear story of change for many who need to know that small steps and persistence will win the day.

Thank you to Matt Jensen, Brenda Clarke, Amy Bessen, and Bridget Martel of Bigfork School District in Bigfork, Montana. Your voices from the district, school, and classroom speaking in harmony assure us that collective responsibility and efficacy can cross all levels.

Thank you to Arnis Burvikovs and Desirée Bartlett at Corwin. Your patience reenergized my passion for this work.

Thank you to countless educators—including you, the reader—who pursue equity and excellence for our students, constantly challenging and checking yourselves . . . with the data.

PUBLISHER'S ACKNOWLEDGMENTS

Corwin gratefully acknowledges the following reviewers for their editorial insight and guidance:

Jane Chadsey, Vice President
Educurious
Seattle, WA

Eva Kubinski, School Administration Consultant
American Indian Student Issues
Special Education Team
Wisconsin Department of Public Instruction
Madison, WI

Pamela H. Scott, Associate Professor
Educational Leadership and Policy Analysis
East Tennessee State University
Johnson City, TN

Megan Tschannen-Moran, Professor of Educational Leadership
College of William & Mary
Williamsburg, VA

Jennifer Wilson, Third Grade Teacher Leader
University Park Elementary
Denver, CO

About the Author

 **Edie L. Holcomb** has experienced the challenges of improving student achievement from many perspectives:

- From classroom teacher to university professor
- From gifted education coordinator to mainstream teacher of children with multiple disabilities
- From school- and district-level administration to national and international consulting
- From small rural districts to the challenges of urban education

She is highly regarded for her ability to link research and practice on issues related to instructional leadership and school and district change—including standards-based curriculum, instruction, assessment, supervision, and accountability.

Edie has taught at all grade levels, served as a building principal and central office administrator, and assisted districts as an external facilitator for accreditation and implementation of school reform designs. As associate director of the National Center for Effective Schools, she provided training and technical support for school improvement efforts throughout the United States and in Canada, Guam, St. Lucia, Hong Kong, and the Philippines. She led development of a comprehensive standards-based learning system in the Seattle, Washington, school district and has supervised K–12 clusters of schools and evaluated principals.

Edie received the Excellence in Staff Development Award from the Iowa Association for Supervision and Curriculum Development (ASCD) and the Paul F. Salmon Award for Outstanding Education Leadership Research from the American Association of School Administrators. She served as an elected member-at-large on the Leadership Council for ASCD International and as a mentor in Learning Forward's Academy.

Since retiring from full-time work as executive director of curriculum and instructional services for Kenosha Unified School District No. 1 in Wisconsin, Edie has served as senior consultant with the University of Washington Center for Educational Leadership. Her work also includes coaching with principals and school leadership teams. Holcomb is the author of eight previous books and numerous articles and reviews.

Chapter 1

Excited About Data–Really?!

When the first edition of this book was published, who knew that so many people would get excited about data—thinking it means more stuff on their phones? Or that "We do data differently" would be an annoying advertising slogan on television?

As noted in the Preface, the "*D* word" has had many connotations over the years. To avoid the negative ones, advocates have switched emphasis to synonyms like *results* and *evidence* and *outcomes*. Various adjectives have been substituted as attempts to make "data-driven" processes sound less threatening by calling them *data-guided, data-enhanced, data-enriched,* or *data-informed.* Recommendations from studies have been parsed into those that are *scientifically based* versus *evidence-based* versus *sound theories*— somewhat in relationship to how "hard" their data are. Now that the word *data* is used to refer both to sets of information and the amount of capacity to access, store, or use the information, perhaps the advice that "you need to add to your data plan" is more exciting than "we need to add data to your planning."

In this chapter, we'll review critical sources and uses of data and celebrate those that are more common now. We'll also explore the degree to which the progress made has been from a mindset of compliance and/or commitment. The chapter title "Excited About Data—Really?" prompts reflection on whether we've looked at data for our own real, authentic purposes—or because we did want to act as professionals in response to external mandates—or because we feared for our job security if we didn't. And any of those responses is understandable. What this third edition hopes to do is add *more* excitement by providing examples of real school people *using* a variety of data based on a shared commitment to learning— of *course*, for our students . . . *all* of them . . . and for ourselves . . . **and** for our colleagues. At the time of the second edition, the strategic plan of the

Association for Supervision and Curriculum Development (ASCD) included a goal about developing educators' capacity to address complex problems with this description:

> The 21st century educator will thrive in a work culture that stresses collaboration, knowledge creation, and a respect for diversity. No longer working in isolation, teachers and administrators will . . . examine ways to meet individual needs through the sophisticated and recurrent analysis of data. School communities will commit to long-term, ongoing, school-specific professional development that builds both individual and community capacity. Wisdom, after all, develops only when knowledge is viewed through the lenses of keen judgment, insight, interwoven relationships, and wide experiences.

There's been a lot of progress, but I'm not convinced we're quite there yet. But, then, I never expected to be excited about data *myself* either.

UNEXPECTED EXCITEMENT

I had just been appointed to my first principalship. I stopped at the district office and asked for any materials I could pick up that would help me prepare for the coming school year. I was given a large wad of keys of all sizes and three notebook binders of district policy and procedures, each four inches thick, covered with light blue canvas cloth, threadbare at the corners, unraveling along the spine (that's how it was done before flash drives). As I headed for my car, the heavy, pointed keys tore through the lining of my suit pocket and fell to the ground. As I bent to retrieve the keys, the stack of notebooks in my arms became unbalanced, and they tumbled to the ground; nine rings popped open, fanning their contents across the parking lot like a deck of cards in the hands of a gambler. I was not off to an auspicious beginning. I never found the locks to match some of those keys, and the time it took to reassemble the policy notebooks exceeded the total number of times I opened them in the next three years.

The only other thing the district gave me was a registration form for some training called Effective Schools. That small brochure turned out to be the real key that unlocked doors for me and provided principles of leadership that have guided me for many years. My school served students who were Caucasian, Native American, Vietnamese, Cambodian, Hmong, and African American. Their parents were blue-collar workers at the nearby meatpacking plant or state prison. Many lived with assistance in low-income housing projects and some alternated time in town and on the reservation. Their test scores were second lowest of the elementary schools in a district of 47,000 students. I was delighted to learn that Ron Edmonds and other researchers in the United States and England had found schools where student achievement exceeded the levels typically associated with their demographic profile. These schools that defied the findings of the Equality of Educational Opportunity report, or the Coleman Report, were characterized by seven factors that became beacons to light my way:

- Strong instructional leadership
- A clear, focused mission
- A safe, orderly environment
- Teaching oriented to time-on-task and opportunity-to-learn
- High expectations for student success
- Frequent monitoring of student progress
- Home-school communication and parent involvement

I was excited about the potential for strengthening these characteristics at my new school, but I was the only one who knew about them. I lacked an ally, and I had a Title I certificated position to fill. With only three days to go until the start of school, my yet-unknown ally fortuitously moved into town and applied. We began to study together and to look at how Title I services had been delivered in our school. It was a typical program, with small groups of students pulled out of the classroom for remedial skill drill, delivered by instructional aides, and supervised by the certificated teacher. There was almost no interaction between the Title I aide and the classroom teacher, except an occasional note in the staff mailbox that would read this way: "Suzie Student needs to work on . . . " or "Peter Pupil is failing in . . . "

With varying degrees of support, we changed from "pull-out" to "push-in" and assigned the aides to work in the classrooms. We identified a set time each week for the classroom teacher to conference with the Title I teacher about the content that would be taught in the *coming* week. We switched from "fix after failure" to "prime the pump" and helped students review their prior knowledge and practice prerequisite skills in advance of the whole class instruction.

Some teachers were resistant to having another adult in the room, or, as some admitted, didn't like having "those children" in their rooms the whole day without a break from them. Some students became uneasy because their stereotypes were being challenged. One day, a sixth grader made an appointment with me to discuss the cheating that was going on. He claimed to be representing a "lot of us" who think the teachers are giving away the tests to certain kids. His evidence of this crime was this: "There's some kids who never got anything but Ds and Fs and now they're getting Bs, and there's no way that could be." Even the state Department of Education became suspicious when we reported our standardized test score gains from fall to spring a year after the changes. They came for an audit, validated the gains, and a state department newsletter declared Bancroft Elementary "the best kept secret in the state."

That is the simple story of how I got excited about the power of data. How could staff, students, or the state argue with the evidence? Our results allowed us to continue with our change process and, in turn, raised our expectations of student capability—and our own efficacy. Being a "best" kept secret in a state was a lot more exciting than being the "worst" performer in the district.

THE URGENCY REMAINS

Since that early experience, some things have stayed the same while others have changed immensely. The underlying need for use of data continues to be emphasized. A review of twenty-five national and state studies is synthesized in Figure 1.1. Some were reviews of other research conducted over a period of years on the same topic. Others examined high-performing schools with specific populations and settings. Nine characteristics emerged as themes in multiple studies:

- Clear and shared focus
- High standards and expectations for all students
- Effective school leadership
- High levels of collaboration and communication
- Curriculum, instruction and assessment aligned with standards
- Frequent monitoring of teaching and learning
- Focused professional development
- Supportive learning environment
- High levels of family and community involvement

One of the studies reported on sixteen elementary schools outperforming schools with similar levels of poverty and mobility, proportion of English language learners (ELLs), and other factors. Those schools that beat the odds had four things in common:

- A caring and collaborative professional environment
- Strong leadership
- Focused, intentional instruction
- The use of assessment data to drive instruction

When I first reviewed these findings—and on many occasions since—I am struck by the similarity between these characteristics and those seven correlates of Effective Schools that first began to light my way. Strong instructional leadership has grown into shared instructional leadership. A clear, focused mission has evolved into being equity-minded. A safe, orderly environment has expanded into the realization that it's about relationships as much as routines, and new resources have been created to help educators adopt culturally responsive practices. Opportunity to learn is still just that—made clearer with references to guaranteed, viable curricula and access to skilled, experienced teachers and up-to-date materials and technology. High expectations for student success are stated more overtly (but still too often questioned covertly). Frequent monitoring of student progress has surged for some students and been replaced by once-a-year high-stakes testing for many. And the need for home-school communication and parental involvement remains a huge challenge.

From all three research sources, use of assessment and data to drive instruction and monitor student progress frequently (not annually) emerge as critical. The bottom line is the importance of data—up close, formative assessment data that teachers can use to make decisions about student learning and plan instruction that meets their needs.

More recently, as part of the waiver process from the worst sanctions of the No Child Left Behind Act (NCLB), many states have adopted teacher and principal evaluation systems based on years of solid research on effective teaching. Three common models arise from the work of Marzano, Danielson, and the Center for Educational Leadership (CEL) at the

Figure 1.1 Synopsis of National Research Reports

Research Base
Summary

Characteristics of High Performing Schools

National Reports	Clear & Shared Focus	High Standards & Expectations	Effective School Leadership	High Levels of Collaboration & Communication	Curriculum, Instruction & Assessment Aligned with Standards	Frequent Monitoring of Teaching & Learning	Focused Professional Development	Supportive Learning Environment	High Levels of Family & Community Involvement
Comprehensive School Reform	X			*	X	*	X		X
Dispelling the Myth		X			X	X	X		X
Educational Reform and Students at Risk	X		*	X	*	X	X	X	*
Hawthorne Elementary School	X	X	X	X	*		X		X
Hope for Urban Education	X	*	X	X	X		X	X	X
Key High School Reform Strategies		X		X			X		X
Leave No Child Behind	X	X	X	X	X	X	X		X
Org. Characteristics of Schools that Successfully Serve . . .	X	X	X	X	X		X	X	X
Profiles of Successful Schoolwide Programs	X	*	X	X	X	*	X	*	X
Promising Practices Study of High-Performing Schools	X	*	X	*	*	X	X		
Promising Programs for Elementary and Middle Schools	X				X	X	X		
Schooling Practices That Matter Most	X		X		*	X	*	X	X
Schools That Make a Difference	X	X	X	X	X	X	X	X	X
Stories of Mixed Success	X		X	X	X		X		X
Successful School Restructuring	X	*	X	X	X	*	X	X	*
Toward an Understanding of Unusually Successful . . .	X	X	X	X	X	X	X	X	X
Turning Around Low-Performing Schools	X	X	X	X	X	X	X	X	X
Washington Reports									
Bridging the Opportunity Gap	X	X	X	X	*	X	X	X	X
Make Standards Meaningful	X	X						*	
Make Standards Stick	X	X	*	X	X	X	X		X
Make Standards Work	X			X	*		X		X
Organizing for Success	X	X	X	X	X	*	X		X
Reality of Reform			O	*				O	O
School Restructuring and Student Achievement in WA	X			X			X		X
Washington State Elementary Schools on Slow Track . . .	O		O	O	O		O		
Total	22	16	18	21	21	15	23	12	21

X　Explicitly identified as key finding, or in discussion of findings
*　Inferred or identified indirectly in descriptions
O　Identified as important by noting the absence or lack thereof

Source: Shannon, G. S., & Bylsma, P. (2003). Nine characteristics of high performing schools. Olympia, WA: Office of Superintendent of Public Instruction.

University of Washington. Two elements in the Marzano Teacher Evaluation Model refer to tracking student progress and providing students with recognition of their status on learning goals. Danielson's Framework for Teaching Evaluation Instrument refers to assessment or data in three of its four domains, including components based on knowledge of students' skill levels, designing student assessments, using assessment in instruction, and maintaining accurate records. One of the 5 Dimensions of Teaching and Learning (5D) undergirding the CEL Teacher Evaluation Rubric is completely devoted to Assessment for Student Learning with six indicators reflecting both teacher and student use of data. In Washington State, principals evaluate teachers in the model chosen by their district and are in turn evaluated under The AWSP (Association of Washington School Principals) Leadership Framework. Thirteen of the twenty-eight elements in their rubric refer to use of data.

The importance of data remains unchanged—with increased accountability for its use. But the context has shifted dramatically.

EXCITEMENT–KILLED BY COMPLIANCE

In the intervening years since the second edition, educators have lived through increasing levels of sanctions of NCLB. They have "raced to the top." They have hoped their states sought waivers. They have adopted Common Core State Standards. They have implemented high-stakes tests—sometimes several different ones in just a few years. Amidst these external mandates, many have sincerely sought to create professional learning communities. And they have been impacted by new technologies for instruction, assessment, and data management. *Some* have lived through these challenges, but some have left the profession in despair. I feel this keenly. A close family member—exactly the type of person we most need in the profession—was among the departing.

The basic components of NCLB included annual testing of reading and math for all students in Grades 3 to 8 and once in high school, plus science at one Grade 3 to 5, 6 to 8, and 10 to 12; identifying rigorous standards for those assessments; and setting targets on a pace for 100 percent proficiency by 2014. Nonparticipation would essentially mean no federal funding. But not meeting the annual targets also raised the spectre of an escalating set of sanctions. Parents had to be given the option to attend another school. Principals and teachers could be replaced. Eventually the state or a designated entity could take over the school or district. As it became clear that the goal of 100 percent proficiency by 2014 would not be met, a process was created to seek waivers from the most draconian sanctions. These waivers focused attention on the educators themselves by requiring new teacher and principal evaluation systems based on research and including links between teacher performance and student growth.

The impact on schools and teachers will be explored in more depth in subsequent chapters. Some aspects of the requirements had positive potential, which will also be noted. But in general, priority was shifted to focus on "THE TEST" itself. As states developed or adopted new academic standards, time and energy was devoted to curriculum realignment. Explicit instruction in the necessary knowledge and skills was replaced by "test prep." As new assessments were piloted and flaws were discovered, tests were revised or replaced—keeping educators in a state of uncertainty and making use of longitudinal data difficult and suspect. The sheer management of the testing requirements required so much time and energy that designated assessment coordinators at the school and district levels spent weeks away from their usual roles of instructional coaching, curriculum work, professional development, and other supports to teachers. On a recent day in a high school, the professional in this role had over 6,000 steps on her fitness bracelet by 9:15 a.m. The test with all its technical and accommodations requirements had resulted in the necessity for 88 separate testing groups—and none could be conducted in the same room at the same time. The hyperemphasis on preparing for and being judged by results of one high-stakes assessment contributed to a jaundiced view of assessment and data in general. Serious attempts to incorporate and use formative assessment faced increased competition for time and motivation.

The mandates did include some components with promise that should not be left behind as NCLB is replaced by the Every Student Succeeds Act (ESSA). Common Core State Standards, while vague in some areas and overwhelming in sheer numbers, did—at least—become common. Thus, they had some potential for equity of expectations for learning across states. Disaggregation of data by student subgroups forced all stakeholders to be aware of gaps in student success. Development of teacher and principal evaluation systems based on instructional frameworks grounded in years of research provided rubrics showing growth paths in critical teacher behaviors. In states that did not link student growth to once-a-year scores on a fluctuating series of high-stakes tests, many educators were prompted to work on collaborative student growth goals using benchmark assessments and common formative assessment that more directly measured, and could more promptly guide, their instructional decisions.

Concurrent with the timing of NCLB, the Individuals with Disabilities Education Improvement Act (IDEIA) was reauthorized and introduced the term *Response to Intervention (RTI)*. Both NCLB and RTI require research-based models that include reliable screening and progress monitoring of student responses to evidence-based instruction. They also require the use of data to match instructional interventions to areas of specific student need as soon as those needs become apparent. Data-based decision-making is the essence of good RTI practice; it is essential for the other three components: universal screening, progress monitoring, and multileveled intervention. This last component evolved as tiers of intervention and then levels of support with a newer acronym MTSS: Multi-Tiered System of Supports. All components must be implemented using culturally responsive and evidence-based practices.

During the intervening years, two other aspects of teacher practice grew in strength voluntarily. More and more schools aspired to become professional learning communities, building on the original research of Shirley Hord and expanding through the auspices of the Learning Forward organization and other consultants and publications. Fidelity to critical components of the research is mixed but can grow forward in a less punitive, more authentic environment. A second factor affecting teacher practice has been increasing use of technology in instruction, assessment, and data management. The quality of decisions about data management systems and the amount and type of implementation support have resulted in these products being perceived as valuable tools or inflexible tyrants.

Meanwhile, as NCLB ruled at the macro level and classroom teachers served valiantly at the micro level, two national professional organizations pushed for change. ASCD launched its Whole Child initiative to maintain visibility and advocacy for the student as more than a test score, with her future dependent on a broader range of knowledge, skills, and experiences than reading and math proficiency. Learning Forward pursued an agenda of supporting student learning through powerful professional learning opportunities for educators. One clear result of their efforts is the inclusion of this definition of professional development in the full text of ESSA itself: "activities that are *sustained* (not stand-alone, 1-day, or short term workshops), *intensive, collaborative, job-embedded, data-driven* and *classroom-focused*" (p. 205, italics mine). Many of those adjectives stand in sharp contrast to what teachers experience as well-meaning attempts to help them improve student learning.

EVERY STUDENT SUCCEEDS ACT ENTERS AMID CONTINUING CHALLENGES

This new federal act contains many familiar requirements, while leaving more autonomy to states and districts and strictly prohibiting some powers of the U.S. Department of Education. (A detailed chart comparing components of NCLB and ESSA is available on the ASCD website.) Annual testing of all students in reading and math will still occur in Grades 3 to 8 and once in high school, plus science once at each school level, but states may select interim benchmark tests instead of one annual megatest, may allow districts to choose their high school test, and may limit the total amount of time for mandated testing at each grade level. The secretary of education may *not* specify any aspect of assessments. Results from assessments will still be disaggregated by socioeconomic status (SES), limited English proficiency, diagnosed disabilities, and racial and ethnic group. Three additional subgroups include homeless students as well as those in foster care or with parents in the military. In response to curricular areas and programs that had found themselves left behind in NCLB, districts must use 10 percent of any Title IV funds to support counseling, music and arts, foreign languages, history and environmental education—and another 20 percent for nutrition, physical education, bullying and harassment prevention, and similar needs. This review of disaggregation requirements and recognition of whole child needs raises the gut-wrenching question of where we now stand on those criteria—and what data should be collected and used as we move forward.

The ASCD Whole Child initiative provides a yearly national and state-by-state snapshot of related indicators. The most recent report described 22 percent of America's children living in poverty but only 14 percent of white children compared to 39 percent of black children, 37 percent of American Indian children, and 33 percent of Hispanic children. About one-third of high school students are overweight or obese, and 20 percent were bullied at school in the past year. Only 52 percent of children surveyed reported that they always cared about doing well in school. Thirty-four percent of fourth-grade students had scored proficient on the most recent National Assessment of Educational Progress (NAEP), and the same percentage of eighth graders reached proficiency in math. Clearly, NCLB did not achieve its targets.

The distribution of poverty among racial groups reflects recent findings about achievement gaps in America—narrowing somewhat by race and ethnicity but widening by income level. Synthesizing twelve nationally representative studies, Reardon (2013) noted that the income achievement gap has grown 40 percent larger over the past three decades. The college completion rate for higher-income students has grown sharply, but the completion rate for students from low-income families has barely moved. Taking a longitudinal look at student data, Reardon reported that the income achievement gap is wide when students enter kindergarten but changes little during the K–12 years, prompting recommendations to invest more heavily in preschool and the earliest grades and "ensure that all students have equal access to high-quality teachers, stimulating curriculum and instruction, and adequate school resources (computers, libraries and the like)."

Rimmer (2016) referred to these factors as opportunity gaps, noting that "a quality education is for many, particularly our most vulnerable students, the *only* pathway out of poverty" but that these students "often don't have full access to such resources as quality pre-school education, the highest quality teachers, maximum amounts of instructional time, enriching life experiences, college preparatory curriculum, engagement with rigorous content and authentic learning" (p. 1).

When Kati Haycock (2016), CEO of the Education Trust, testified on ESSA implementation before the Senate Committee on Health, Education, Labor, and Pensions, she reported that during the NCLB years, "achievement among black, Latino and low-income students has improved." Haycock reported the percentage of fourth graders below basic proficiency in math was reduced by more than half between 2000 and 2015, with similar improvement among students of color. At the high school level, graduation rates improved from 59 percent of black students to 73 percent and from 66 percent of Latino students to 76 percent. However, she also emphasized that ". . . elementary reading is one of the most important predictors of high school life opportunities, yet almost half of our black, Latino, and Native children are still reading below the basic level" (p. 2). Like Rimmer, Haycock spoke about teacher quality, citing a pattern in which low-income students and students of color are assigned to ineffective, out-of-field, or inexperienced teachers. In a similar vein, Sparks (2015) referred to a thirty-three-country study of 15-year-olds' scores on the Program for International Student Assessment (PISA), which specifically identified unequal access to rigorous math content as a driving force behind performance gaps. In spite of various gains in other measures and grade levels, Hanushek's analysis of 2013 NAEP data (Camera, 2016) revealed that the average twelfth-grade black student placed only in the 19th percentile in reading and at the 22nd percentile in math. Looking back over the fifty years since the Coleman Report, he predicted that—at the current incremental rate—"it will be roughly two and a half centuries before the black-white math gap closes and over one and a half centuries until the reading gap closes."

The Coleman Report did not shock the nation into adequate voluntary action. NCLB, with its mandates and sanctions, had some positive effects but mixed with other kinds of losses noted in this and subsequent chapters. ESSA will not be a panacea either. That is why this chapter title challenges readers to get excited about data "real-ly" . . . from real commitment, compassion, and curiosity and not from a focus on how much or little can be done to comply with a newer federal act.

WHAT DATA MATTERS *NOW*

The data that matters now is—as it has always been—much more than the state test scores that have taken center stage in recent years. Previous editions of *Getting Excited About Data* included a list of sources of data available in most settings and useful for addressing important aspects of teaching and learning, the staff and school culture, student engagement, and family and community involvement (see Figure 1.2). The only category no longer in widespread use is national norm-referenced achievement tests. Italicized items in the figure show the few additions that have emerged in the past ten years. The increase in use of benchmark (or interim) assessments has been a response to the focus on RTI and the inability to use changing state assessments in any legitimate way to track longitudinal progress of individual students. Common formative assessments have gained visibility through the work of Doug Reeves, Larry Ainsworth, and Solution Tree's trademarked model of "PLCs at Work." The bolded bullets under Demographics represent the three new categories for disaggregation included in ESSA.

Findings from these multiple sources are often compiled into categories that represent a balance of focus: on academic and cultural conditions, on both cognitive and affective domains of students' experiences, and on staff characteristics and community involvement. In Chapter 7, Figure 7.1 (p. 108) displays four bullet points in the section "School Portfolio." These bullet points represent use of four types of data: Academic Student Data, Nonacademic Student Data, Staff Data, and Parent/Community Data. The last three sections should incorporate both quantitative (or objective) data and perceptual (or subjective) data that provides insight into how students, staff, and stakeholders experience that school. Writing about a school system change in Hawaii, Victoria Bernhardt (2015) refers to four data types as Demographics, Perceptions, Student Learning, and School Processes. In his article on data dashboards, Rothman (2015) reports that Monroe County, Georgia, organizes data around student learning outcomes, organizational effectiveness, public engagement, and professional learning while California tracks eight categories that include student achievement, student engagement, college and career readiness, school climate, parent involvement, basic services, implementation of state standards, and access to rigorous coursework. In Alberta, Canada, the six categories are safe and caring schools; student learning opportunities; student learning achievement; preparation for lifelong learning, the world of work, and citizenship; parental involvement; and continual improvement.

Figure 1.2   Sources of Data

- College Entrance Tests
  - SAT
  - ACT
  - Other

- Criterion-Referenced (Standards-Based) Tests
  - Mandatory State Assessments
  - National Assessment of Educational Progress
  - *Benchmark/Interim Assessments (e.g., MAP, AimsWeb, STAR)*

- Beginning- and End-of-Year Tests

- Midterm, Semester, and Course Exams

- Local Unit Tests

- *Common Formative Assessments*

- Grades and GPA

- Graduation Rates

- Status of Graduates
  - 2 years out
  - 5 years out

- Local Unit Tests

- Team Projects/Exhibitions

- Performance Checklists

- Individual Student Work

- Homework Monitoring

- Student Attendance Data

- Student Participation Data
  - Extracurricular activities
  - Community service

- Student Behavior Data

- Student Demographics
  - Gender
  - Racial/ethnic group
  - Home language
  - Socioeconomic status
  - Mobility
  - **Homeless**
  - **In Foster Care**
  - **Parents in Military**

- Climate/Perception Surveys
  - Staff
  - Students
  - Parents
  - Community

- Career Interest Surveys

- Questionnaires

- Focus Groups

- Interviews
  - Staff
  - Students
  - Parents
  - Community

- Checklists, Rating Scales, and Inventories

- Observation Logs

- Journal Entries, Anecdotes
  - Staff
  - Students

- Staff Attendance

- Staff Qualifications
  - Teaching in area of major
  - Graduate degrees
  - Years experience
  - Students

- Professional Development Participation

- Parent Involvement Data
  - Conference attendance
  - Volunteer participation

But there is a difference in motivation between a mandated list and a collection of data chosen by the school as having significance for students, staff, and constituents. An alternative to organizing data under headings or categories is to raise critical questions that matter to the participants and provide the data needed to address them, as in Figure 1.3. However the data is organized, decision-making and planning must be based on a combination of data sources: information on outcomes achieved, as well as the conditions and opportunities provided, and feedback from those involved.

PROGRESS IN DATA USE

In their mega-study for the Wallace Foundation, Louis and colleagues (Louis, Leithwood, Wahlstrom, & Anderson, 2010) reported that all districts and schools now have adequate and similar data sources *and* that the greatest variability occurs in the way those data are used. Over the past thirty years, through various official and unofficial roles and channels, I've been privileged to work with schools in over thirty states and several countries. I have reviewed successful and unsuccessful applications for grants and awards and noted the differences in responses related to assessment and data use. The previous edition outlined eighteen critical tasks that differentiated the extraordinary from the ordinary based on the perspective of my observations and study.

Figure 1.3   Critical Questions and Data Sources

Are students learning?

- State assessment data
- Districtwide assessments
- Curriculum-based classroom assessments
- Collaborative analysis of student work

Are students connected and engaged?

- Disciplinary actions
- Attendance
- Truancy
- Graduation/dropout rates
- Co-curricular participation
- Survey results

Are teachers/staff engaged and productive?

- Teacher attendance
- Professional development participation
- Survey results

Are parents and community confident and supportive?

- Parent-teacher conference participation
- Survey results

Those eighteen uses continue to surface as descriptors related to high data-use schools. The good news is that progress has been made on all! Figure 1.4 reviews the list and adds an informal reflection on whether the progress has been limited or laudable. Developments on each data use are briefly discussed next, followed by additional points of emphasis from recent studies. These are tasks that high-performing schools do with data:

Create a culture of collective responsibility for all students. Progress: Limited. NCLB and RTI have increased awareness of student needs, but changing a culture is more difficult than adding a structure or activity, because it's about beliefs and a history of "how we've always done things

Figure 1.4 Progress in Data Use	Limited	Laudable
Create a culture of collective responsibility for all students	X	
Understand that assessment is an integral part of the instructional process	X	
Test their results against their espoused mission	X	
Make clear distinctions between inputs (by adults) and outcomes (for students)		X
Use both objective and subjective (perceptual) data appropriately	X	
Focus on most critical priorities to conserve time, energy, and money		X
Drill down for student- and skill-specific data in priority areas		X
Plan forward as students rise—to respond to individual skill gaps	X	
Plan backward to fill gaps in the instructional program	X	
Look around at research, best practices, and exemplary schools		X
Look within to analyze curriculum and instructional strategies	X	
Select proven strategies for implementation		X
Identify and plan for student populations with specific needs		X
Identify formative assessments to balance large-scale, high-stakes tests	X	
Monitor rates of progress over time—student and cohort	X	
Gather evidence of both implementation and impact of improvement strategies	X	
Consolidate multiple plans	X	
Take the initiative to tell "the rest of the story"	X	

around here." A laudable rating would include a total absence of comments about "those kids," or "they're not my kids," or "Mr. Smith's kids." Coteaching models would not create a single section of each course in which every student with an individualized education program (IEP) is placed. Chapter 2 explores more about beliefs and efficacy, and Chapter 5 emphasizes collective action on behalf of struggling students.

Understand that assessment is an integral part of the instructional process. Progress: Limited. The emergence of instructional frameworks and common formative assessments has increased the focus on assessment as an early part of unit planning instead of the last step. Educators understand in theory that curriculum, instruction, and assessment are an interrelated set of constructs and that assessments should be developed based on the established learning targets. In reality, the term *assessment* still brings a first reaction related to the implications of a high-stakes test.

Test their results against their espoused mission. Progress: Limited. Through various school improvement initiatives dating back decades now, schools have been "writing" mission statements. It's still hard to find a setting where conversations are frequent around what the mission (or vision or beliefs or collective commitments, etc.) would look like and sound like and what would be changing in measures of learning and satisfaction.

Make clear distinctions between inputs (by adults) and outcomes (for students). Progress: Laudable. A decade ago, reports of success in school improvement efforts too often focused on what the adults had done, such as trainings provided and attended. NCLB did provide momentum to focus more on student results.

Use both objective and subjective (perceptual) data appropriately. Progress: Limited. Objective data tell us *what* needs attention. Very often, excellent ideas for *how* to resolve concerns are embedded in responses from students, staff, and other stakeholders. Unfortunately, many schools and districts are reducing their use of surveys and interviews because they "already have more data than we can deal with."

Focus on most critical priorities to conserve time, energy, and money. Progress: Laudable. As more schools strive to become professional learning communities, "staff members, with their school leaders, are using data to make decisions about what to learn, how to learn it, how to transfer and apply it to their classrooms, and how to assess its effectiveness" (Hord, 2009, p. 43). However, the reality is that high-stakes testing in reading and math has defined those as the "priority areas," when the intention of this data use is for educators to determine *their* priority areas—which might include needs like student engagement that cross content areas and also impact nonacademic measures like attendance and discipline.

Drill down for student- and skill-specific data in priority areas. Progress: Laudable. The emphasis of RTI on use of data for screening and progress monitoring has been a (mostly) positive force in progress, with a few unintended consequences pointed out in subsequent chapters.

Plan forward as students rise—to respond to individual skill gaps. Progress: Limited. This data use focuses on moving individual student data from grade to grade so there can be seamless focus on the support that struggling students need. Because it relies on more local data than state tests, it has not received as much attention.

Plan backward to fill gaps in the instructional program. Progress: Limited. Both of these data uses have been impacted by the NCLB-era focus on high-stakes tests, which have not remained the same year to year. The result has been an annual review of areas of low performance at each tested grade level, with less time for vertical articulation.

Look around at research, best practices, and exemplary schools. Progress: Laudable. Emphasis in recent years on implementing research-based practices has contributed to more use of clearinghouses that vet research studies and the emergence of publications and consulting services that provide information and training on effective strategies—the first two parts of this statement. Exemplary schools in terms of their results on state tests can be found on state websites. It can still be very difficult to identify the top-performing schools with similar size and demographics— "schools like ours"—in order to learn from their practices and progress.

Look within to analyze curriculum and instructional strategies. Progress: Limited. It is now fairly common practice to study best practices, but progress is limited in the rigor applied to analyzing what is actually occurring in classrooms. To what degree has the curriculum realigned to standards resulted in a realignment of unit plans? To what degree have the strategies "taught" in professional development been effectively and consistently added to student experiences? The promising practice that will move this forward is use of a research-based instructional framework to conduct learning walk-throughs, gather and analyze the data, and provide both feedback and targeted support based on the data (Rimmer, 2016).

Select proven strategies for implementation. Progress: Laudable. As noted in the previous paragraphs, it has become easier and more common to access sources that describe strategies with evidence to support their value and *select* one. As also noted previously, the necessary follow-up and support for consistent *implementation* of a proven practice is not as consistently provided.

Identify and plan for student populations with specific needs. Progress: Laudable. Screening and progress monitoring in RTI has increased the use of data to identify specific needs of students. Multidisciplinary MTSS teams plan interventions for struggling students and monitor their progress. Although laudable, these endeavors do not seem to include systemwide focus on subgroups with achievement gaps based on SES and race or ethnicity.

Identify formative assessments to balance large-scale, high-stakes tests. Progress: Limited. The use of formative assessments is becoming more prevalent—but with mixed degrees of consistency and commonality. Chapter 2 will discuss how a balanced assessment system can influence beliefs about data and provide powerful information for teachers and students.

Monitor rates of progress over time—student and cohort. Progress: Limited. The primary focus on high-stakes tests, which have changed too frequently, has made it difficult to monitor longitudinal data. As schools and districts increasingly use and track their own assessments in their own data systems, this task will be more manageable.

Gather evidence of both implementation and impact of improvement strategies. Progress: Limited. Before student results change, teacher practice has to change. A school improvement plan that promises to "teach one new evidence-based practice per month" is well-intended, but if it does not provide support and data-gathering for implementation, it may also be unable to demonstrate an impact on student learning—with the unintended consequence of further discouraging the staff.

Consolidate multiple plans. Progress: Limited. More mandates have required more kinds of plans to be written and reports generated. I have seen no decrease in the number of "Now, why are we doing this?" and "So where does this fit in?" questions asked at professional development sessions and team meetings.

Take the initiative to tell "the rest of the story." Progress: Limited. This data use involves documenting, sharing, and celebrating progress that is being made locally—regardless of what the state may be reporting on a larger scale. The limited progress may be attributed to sheer fatigue and the vicious cycle of working so hard to make something happen that there's no energy left to report and celebrate it, when that very celebration could be the source of renewed energy to continue the effort.

More recent studies of data use have provided support for these eighteen data uses and added new perspectives. The Learning from Leadership studies that encompassed nine states, forty-three school districts, 180 schools, and 312 classrooms (Louis et al., 2010) described high data-use schools as those that were as follows:

- Actively using data to monitor the outcomes of school improvement plans
- Using formative assessments of student progress at regular intervals throughout the year
- Using data in making decisions about professional development plans
- Using data in conversations with parents about student performance and programming
- Using data to move beyond problem identification to problem-solving [and] gathering additional data to better understand the causes or factors related to the problems in question

Three of the previously stated findings reinforce data uses already addressed in Figure 1.4 and previous editions. Two additional uses are now added to Figure 1.5 in bold italics. Figure 1.5 also references the chapters that provide tips and examples for each data use. For example, discussing data with parents is introduced in this edition in Chapter 5. Use of data in professional development planning is described as one of the "appropriate supports" in Chapter 12.

Use of data as a critical component in professional learning has been emphasized by the Learning Forward organization, making it one of six *Standards for Professional Learning* (Learning Forward, 2011).

At the classroom level, teachers use student data to assess the effectiveness of the application of their new learning. When teachers, for example, design assessments and scoring guides and engage in collaborative analysis of student work, they gain crucial information about the effect of their learning on students. Evidence of ongoing increases in student learning is a powerful motivator for teachers during the inevitable setbacks that accompany complex change efforts. At the school level, engaging teams of teacher leaders and administrators in analyzing and interpreting data for example, provides them a more holistic view of the complexity of school improvement and fosters collective responsibility and accountability for student results . . . Ongoing data collection, analysis, and use, especially when done in teams, provide stakeholders with information that sustains momentum and informs continuous improvement.

Figure 1.5 A Further Look at Uses of Data

Use data to:	Learn how in:
Create a culture of collective responsibility for all students	Chapters 2, 3, 4
Understand that assessment is an integral part of the instructional process	Chapter 2
Test their results against their espoused mission	Chapter 2
Make clear distinctions between inputs (by adults) and outcomes (for students)	Chapters 2, 11
Use both objective and subjective (perceptual) data appropriately	Chapters 1, 5, 11
Focus on most critical priorities to conserve time, energy, and money	Chapters 8, 9, 10
Drill down for student- and skill-specific data in priority areas	Chapter 5
Plan forward as students rise—to respond to individual skill gaps	Chapter 5
Plan backward to fill gaps in the instructional program	Chapter 9
Look around at research, best practices, and exemplary schools	Chapters 8, 9
Look within to analyze curriculum and instructional strategies	Chapter 9
Select proven strategies for implementation	Chapter 8
Identify and plan for student populations with specific needs	Chapter 7
Identify formative assessments to balance large-scale, high-stakes tests; *use formative assessment of student learning at regular intervals throughout the year*	Chapters 1, 2, 7
Monitor rates of progress over time—student and cohort	Chapter 5
Gather evidence of both implementation and impact of improvement strategies	Chapters 7, 9, 11
Consolidate multiple plans	Chapter 10
Take the initiative to tell "the rest of the story"	Chapter 11
Use data in conversations with parents about student performance and programs	Chapter 5
Use data in making decisions about professional development plans	Chapter 12

The imperative features of the data we use and how we use it are these. First, we must have multiple sources of evidence that help us understand our results and our practices, our students, and the learning environment we are creating. Second, we must analyze the data to determine that all students are learning. Data must be disaggregated and the results made transparent to everyone. Names must be connected to numbers so the focus is on individual students, not categories. Third, we must take action on the data. Teams of teachers must work together at frequent intervals to assess student learning and plan classroom instruction to move all students forward and add support for those who struggle. Fourth, schools as communities must attend to the culture and conditions in which staff and students work, including the systems and processes that cross all classrooms.

EXCITEMENT EXTINGUISHERS

Every use of data outlined in Figure 1.4 has shown some degree of progress, but many are still discussed in the literature as exemplary rather than typical practice. What's been getting in the way? We've already noted the chilling effect of the sanctions in NCLB and the distraction of time, energy, and money to the logistics of high-stakes test preparation and administration. But we can't assume that the changes from NCLB to ESSA will automatically break down whatever barriers have been slowing the progress. The second edition listed six barriers, but the list is actually longer now. In my work with schools and districts, I often use an activity I learned from Bob Garmston. It is called Go for the Green and can be used to identify points of entry into a problem. It can help deepen understanding of perceptual data. It can develop greater empathy and help participants move from a "blaming" mode to a more strengths-based stance. Figure 1.6 provides an illustration that is pertinent to our question about barriers to progress with data use. The process of facilitating Go for the Green starts with large chart paper as well as black, green, and red markers. Start with a *red* circle in the middle of the paper. Let the participants know that you are using that color deliberately because this is the target. It reminds us of a stop sign because it prevents accomplishment of their task or goal. Help the group decide how to phrase the concern or problem and write it in *red*. Then switch to the *black* marker and write this at the top: Under what conditions would I . . . ? In Figure 1.6, this creates the following question: Under what conditions would I be reluctant to work with data? The usual rules of brainstorming apply: list all possibilities without judgment. In this activity, the ideas generated are placed on rays or spokes from the central question. A final stage in the process is to use the *green* marker to circle, star, or highlight the items that are within the control or influence of the group. These are the areas where energy can be spent productively and can be rephrased in positive language as actions to pursue—thus Go for the Green.

In Figure 1.6, the statements on the spokes are statements that have been made in multiple discussions in schools—even within the past few months. Those that are starred (although not green in this black-and-white

Figure 1.6   Go for the Green on Data Reluctance

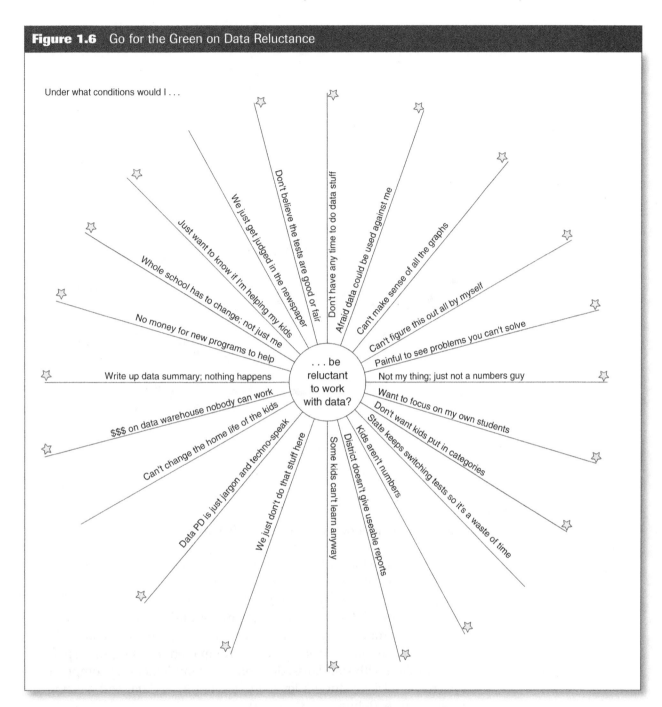

Under what conditions would I . . .

. . . be reluctant to work with data?

Don't believe the tests are good or fair

We just get judged in the newspaper

Just want to know if I'm helping my kids

Whole school has to change; not just me

No money for new programs to help

Write up data summary; nothing happens

$$$ on data warehouse nobody can work

Can't change the home life of the kids

Data PD is just jargon and techno-speak

We just don't do that stuff here

Some kids can't learn anyway

District doesn't give useable reports

Kids aren't numbers

State keeps switching tests so it's a waste of time

Don't want kids put in categories

Want to focus on my own students

Not my thing; just not a numbers guy

Painful to see problems you can't solve

Can't figure this out all by myself

Can't make sense of all the graphs

Afraid data could be used against me

Don't have any time to do data stuff

format) are within the scope of influence of a school and district. They are combined and turned into positive statements that frame each of the next twelve chapters. People get excited about data work when it fits their beliefs, feels safe, is a collaborative effort, reflects their own students, is accessible and understandable, fits a bigger picture, saves resources, is actionable, is given time and support, and yields the satisfaction of having made a difference.

Chapter 2

You Get More Excited About Data When . . . It Fits Your Beliefs

Imagine your school being described this way:

> Teachers, counselors, administrators and parents came to understand the power of data to make improvements in the achievement of all groups of students. They began to "own" the data and to take leadership in the use of data at their sites. Some results included upgrading curriculum, strategically focusing on students' academic needs, highlighting institutional barriers and discrimination, revising the report cards to align with standards, designing and implementing computer systems to retrieve student-level and teacher-level data, and creating a data culture. (Johnson, 2002. p. 34)

An organization's culture has been described as "the way we do things around here," and patterns of behavior are based on shared beliefs—spoken and unspoken. These beliefs and patterns did not coalesce from thin air but from individual and shared experiences that were repeated until they became ingrained. Surfacing, understanding, and challenging underlying beliefs are first steps toward reshaping a culture. This chapter will lead readers to examine beliefs about the purpose of schooling, beliefs about students, and beliefs about assessment(s) and then provide some strategies for addressing those beliefs and moving mindsets from compliance to commitment.

ESPOUSED SCHOOL BELIEFS

The now-common practice of articulating shared beliefs is referred to using the terms *belief statements* and other nouns like *mission, vision,* and *values.* Others have written lengthy descriptions parsing the differences in definitions and advocating for creation of three or four unique documents. In my experience, repeating the development process multiple times and sorting out what should be in each document has been frustrating and increased the feeling that this is an externally required, redundant exercise. I've also observed that even *one* document—thoughtfully created *and used* skillfully and constantly—can be a valuable tool to surface contrary beliefs, change behavior, and gradually shift the culture of a school or district.

Unfortunately, the mission is too often on the wall but missing in action. When I ask a group, "How many of your schools have a mission statement?" almost all of the hands go up. But when I ask, "Who will tell us what your mission statements says?" no hands go up and eyes drop to the table. When I follow up in a soft, gentle, puzzling tone with "If you don't know what it says, how do you know you have one?" the answers are usually as follows:

"We did one in an in-service once."

"The Board went on a retreat and did one for the district."

"It's on the bottom of our letterhead."

Saying we have a mission statement but don't know what it says is like trying to convince the highway patrol that I'm a good, careful, safe driver but just don't exactly know what the speed limit is.

If so many mission statements are lying around on letterheads without making a difference, why devote this section to it? Because a mission statement is one of the ways we can articulate the common core values of an organization, and it has the *potential* to make a radical difference. In his study *Peak Performers,* Charles Garfield (1987) noted the passion that some individuals have for their endeavor. He described their sense of mission as "an image of a desired state of affairs that inspires action, determines behavior, and fuels motivation." That's how you know if your school really has a mission statement. Does it inspire action? Does it determine behavior? Does it fuel motivation?

In *Asking the Right Questions* (Holcomb, 2001), I described an affinity process for developing a mission statement that has been used by schools that don't have one or believe they need to try again. In Chapter 7 of this book, I point out the need for alignment between our mission statement and all of our data work and planning—what we say we're all about and the evidence of what we really do. Colloquially, it's expressed as "putting our money where our mouth is."

I believe that almost all teachers chose their careers based on a sense of mission. I also believe that at least an ember of that passion still smolders somewhere deep inside the most burned-out veteran in the profession. I've discovered, somewhat to my surprise, that getting engaged with data can help rekindle that passion. Here's one way.

Some mission statements just float out there with nothing to grab on to. Some data just sit and stagnate because they don't seem to connect with anything meaningful. The simple form in Figure 2.1 can help people make those connections. Before using this activity, verify that the school has a mission statement and have it ready to project. If you are working with a group of people from various schools, use a sample mission statement like the one in the next paragraph so that participants can use it for practice if they don't have one or can't remember it. Some may be frantically tapping on their devices to find their own on their school websites.

Begin with the first column of Figure 2.1. Our mission is what we say we will do as a school. It's a set of commitments. Ask the participants to look at their mission statement, and circle the words or phrases that represent key components or commitments. Here's an example:

> The mission of Our Town School is to provide a safe, orderly environment where students master their academic skills and become productive citizens and lifelong learners.

> The key components of this mission statement are

> - safe, orderly environment,
> - mastery of academic skills,
> - productive citizens, and
> - lifelong learners.

Have the participants write these words or phrases in the boxes in the first column because they are "What We Say" we will do.

Next, tell them you assume that considerable time and energy probably went into development of this mission statement and that there was strong support that Our Town School should accomplish these things. If so, we need to provide evidence that the mission is being fulfilled.

Figure 2.1 Monitoring Our Mission		
What We Say	**Evidence We Have**	**Evidence We Need**

In the second column—Evidence We Have—the task is to consider the types of data already available somewhere in the district and school that are relevant to that aspect of the mission. If the group appears stuck, project the list of possible data sources from Figure 1.2. As participants identify indicators for components of the mission statement, there may be comments like "We should be keeping track of that" or "We don't have any way of knowing" or "That can't be measured." These ideas go into the third column, where participants record types of data that will be needed. For example, many classroom teachers keep track of student behaviors that are related to employability skills, such as tardiness, materials ready to work, and homework completion. This data may never have been compiled on a schoolwide basis, but it could be. We'll discuss other values that can't be as readily measured later in this section.

After the groups have worked a while, ask them to take a look at the Evidence We Have column, and put an *S* by the items they've listed there that are student results and an *A* by those that are adult activities. The significance of the coding is to remind us that the evidence we need to produce is that something more or better is occurring for children. Traditionally, we have reported things like "We have DARE and peer mediation and conflict resolution" as evidence that we provide a safe, orderly environment. They are programs we offer—which is not the same as results we achieve. If the participants have listed types of data that are all adult activities, programs, and practices, encourage them to be sure that the Evidence We Need column will eventually provide indicators of results for students.

The completed product fulfills several purposes. First, the process of discussing the headings on this form reconnects people to their mission statement. Sometimes it makes them decide to revise their mission or start over completely. Second, connections are made between what we believe is important to do and how we will know we're doing it. Third, the Evidence We Have column prioritizes these types of data as being available and being of importance to the school. Fourth, the Evidence We Need column generates awareness of information that should be gathered for next steps planning and added to the school's data portfolio as it is continually updated.

Including the Unmeasurables

I've been told on occasion that nothing should be put in a mission statement that isn't measurable. So participants shy away from things like character education and creativity. In the previously given example, "productive citizen" and "lifelong learning" might be considered unmeasurable if we think only of formal tests and numerical scores. But there *is* much more to what we accomplish as a school than just content and skills, and sometimes those are the things that inspire us most. If they speak to our hearts, we should keep them in the language of our mission and goals. We just need to stretch our vocabulary from measurable to observable and identify evidence that can be gathered.

For the previously given example, challenge participants to reflect silently and identify a person they know and regard as a lifelong learner. Ask them to jot down the things they *see that person do* or *hear that person say* that add up to their impression of lifelong learner. Then record a general list from the group. Prompt as needed to be sure the factors are all observable. For example, "He's a risk taker" needs the clarification of "What do you *see* him do that you call taking risks?" A typical list includes items like these:

- Gets interested in something and wants to know more
- Goes to the library and gets books and gets on the Internet
- Reads a lot
- Shares new ideas and knowledge
- Tries to get other people interested
- Takes courses and workshops that aren't required
- Likes to figure out his own way to do things
- Sets goals for himself

These are indicators of lifelong learning in an adult. We work with children to develop these characteristics. Now ask participants to link up with two or three others who teach (or parent) students of about the same age. Their task is to take this list and discuss, "What do each of these behaviors look like at age seventeen? At age eleven? At age seven?"

Two observations usually emerge when groups report out. The first is the conclusion that most of those behaviors look pretty much the same at any age and could be observed in the school setting. The second is a realization that many of the school's own practices limit the opportunity to observe these characteristics and may thus be inhibiting rather than nurturing their development.

Figure 2.2 provides an example of the Monitoring Our Mission activity completed for both the measurable academic skills and the observable characteristics of citizenship and lifelong learning.

Making the Mission Visible and Meaningful

There is power in language. If not, we would be unmoved by Abraham Lincoln's Gettysburg Address or Martin Luther King Jr.'s "I Have a Dream" speech. There is also power in the process of collectively articulating what is important, what is nonnegotiable, and what is essential to our professional spirit. There is even greater power when the result of that collaborative product is actually used to ground and filter discussions and actions.

Just as we need people who are by nature number crunchers to play a vital role in our work with data, we need people who are by nature cheerleaders and zealots to keep our mission alive. Conscious planning should go into ways of referencing the mission frequently during faculty meetings and other events. Here are a few ideas I've learned from school "mission-"aries:

- When new staff members are hired, be sure that a presentation on the mission of the school is part of their orientation.
- When a tough decision is being made, ask the staff to complete statements like these: "This fits our mission because . . ." or "This doesn't fit our mission because . . ."

Figure 2.2 Monitoring Our Mission: A Completed Example		
What We Say	**Evidence We Have**	**Evidence We Need**
Safe, orderly environment	• Discipline referrals • Expulsion/suspensions • Vandalism	
Mastery of academic skills	• Scores on state assessments • Percentage of students passing district criterion-referenced tests • Degrees of Reading Power test • ACT scores	• Desktop access to individual student records of mastery • Performance assessments (portfolios, exhibitions)
Productive citizens	• Attendance/truancy • Tardiness • Homework completion • Percentage of students in leadership roles (clubs, council, peer mediators, etc.) • Number participating in co-op work experiences • Graduation/dropout rate	• Participation in community service activities (church, Scouts, food drives, etc.)
Lifelong learners	• Number and quality of independent projects completed • Co-/extracurricular participation • ACT participation • Feedback from local business partners	• Interview mature adults in community about what contributed to their lifelong learning habits • Survey students about learning opportunities they pursue outside of school (piano, etc.)

- Keep a Mission Box (version of a Suggestion Box) in the office. Students, teachers, and parents can drop notes in it to report actions they have seen that exemplify the mission. Some of these can be read with the announcements or shared in newsletters.
- Short scenarios of problem situations can be presented to the staff. Ask small groups to prepare or role-play responses that are consistent with the mission statement.
- Have elementary students learn the vocabulary of the mission statement and draw what they think it means.
- Have students of all ages identify what their roles are in contributing to the mission of the school.

Chapter 7 illustrates the relationship between these core beliefs and everything we do in a school. Figure 7.1 (p. 108) shows *Mission* in the upper left-hand corner, illustrating that our use of data and our focus on student achievement must come first and foremost from the core values that drive us personally and bring us together professionally. But the statement and sense of mission in the school remains under construction.

Imagine a dotted arrow on Figure 7.1 going around the entire figure, and from each component back to Mission. As we learn more about our students, we reexamine our beliefs. As we engage in deep reflection about our practices, we clarify our understanding and expectations of ourselves. And as we courageously assess the results of our common efforts, we build the culture of collective responsibility for the success of all students. As Fullan and Hargreaves (1991) reminded us, "in collaborative cultures, the examination of values and purposes is not a one-time event . . . but a continuous process that pervades the whole school" (p. 9).

BELIEFS ABOUT STUDENTS

The beliefs stated and espoused in a mission statement are, by intention, aspirational, and while they represent a consensus of the group, individual members of the group may consciously or unconsciously hold other, unspoken beliefs. When we ask educators to look at evidence of their school's effectiveness, we are not just asking them to crunch numbers and plot graphs. That's technical work, and the reality is that we are challenging the existing culture of the school. Datnow and Park (2015) pointed out,

> If you were only concerned about the achievement of the students in your classroom or if you felt competitive with your colleagues, you would have little motivation to assist your colleagues in examining data or developing new instructional strategies. School leaders play an important role in cultivating a belief that teachers share responsibility for all the students at the school, not just those in their classrooms. (p. 12)

Collaborative work with data is essential to accepting collective responsibility for the learning of students during their total time at that school. Every teacher has underlying beliefs about who "my" students are. They are often revealed in off-the-cuff comments like "We have to do something about Bill's kids." When Datnow and Park (2015) outlined five good ways to talk about data, the very first component noted was that conversations must convey the belief that students are the shared responsibility of everyone. And in her article on being "equity-centered," Rimmer (2016) stressed the need to "shape and nurture a culture that integrates an inclusive approach to schooling where collaboratively, the staff and community are all committed to *each* child's academic success" (p. 6). She added that "being able to work together using a range of qualitative and quantitative data to identify problems and strengths of student learning and support, and then to engage in collaborative reflection, problem-solving and leveraging strategies, empowers staff and can strengthen relationships, trust and the culture of learning" (p. 10).

Individuals also have beliefs about the character, ability, and innate value of the students they see each day. They should not be judged harshly for saying, "These kids aren't like the ones we used to get" because there is truth in the statement. Many experienced teachers do face a more diverse and challenging student population than when they began their careers. The difference-maker is to move that reality into the proactive "so let's figure out how to reach and teach them." And "let's discover the strengths they bring and build on them." This difference in response became so apparent that the Center for Educational Leadership (CEL) (2012) questioned whether its *own* equity mission statement was appropriately reflected in the language of its 5D+ Teacher Evaluation Rubric. In Version 3.0 (2016a), wording that referred to students' academic background, life experiences, and culture and language as "learning needs of students" has been changed to "capitalizing on students' strengths." In the webinar announcing its release, further explanation emphasized that it's "about building on their strengths as people and learners, rather than using a deficit stance."

Beliefs about students influence if and how people will engage in data work. Sometimes the reverse is true: The data forces a reexamination of the beliefs. For example, teachers in a school were concerned with declining test scores, attributing them to an influx of a new population of students. "We'd still be doing fine if we could just test our *own* students." The simple 2×2 grid in Figure 2.3 was constructed to test that assumption. I asked the group how long a student would have to be in the district before they would accept responsibility for the student's learning. The group settled on two years and quickly broke out scores into two columns. When they looked at the results, they had to move away from "student mobility" as the cause of their problems and look more deeply at why they had made that assumption and what other factors they must consider in their quest to achieve better outcomes.

Another school was on the slippery slope toward similar assumptions about their special education students. Statements were being made about how unfair it was to include their scores in state reports. "Our test scores would be fine if they didn't make us test the IEP kids or if they would just keep their scores out of the report." The stacked bar graphs in Figure 2.4 represent the percentage of students in each level of performance on a state assessment. For elementary, middle school, and high school levels, the first bar represents the distribution of all students tested. To test the statement about "keeping their scores out of the report," the second stacked bar does remove the scores of students with individualized education programs (IEPs). Before showing the resulting graph, the district's curriculum director asked, "How do you think the bars will look?" When staff saw the actual data, they were amazed that the difference was only about 1 to 2 percent at most levels of performance—whether with or without including the special education students' scores. Eventually a quiet voice said, "Then maybe we need to look for some other action."

Figure 2.3 Reading Achievement Scores Disaggregated by Mobility

	In district less than 2 years	In district 2 years or more
Proficient and above	93% (n = 28)	92% (n = 72)
Below proficient	7% (n = 2)	8% (n = 6)

BELIEFS ABOUT ASSESSMENT

When assessment is narrowly defined in terms of annual high-stakes tests like those mandated by the No Child Left Behind Act (NCLB), and especially when connected to punishments for inadequate progress, it is natural and logical to "not believe" that data can be useful in a positive sense. The PDK Gallup Poll of the Public's Attitudes Toward the Public Schools (Phi Delta Kappa, 2015) is conducted every two years. In 2015, 64 percent of public school parents said there is too much emphasis on testing.

Fortunately, the scales have begun to reach a better balance in recent years with increasing attention to benchmark (or interim) assessments and formative assessment. The large-scale standardized assessments that evaluate student learning after instruction is over are summative assessments. They include tests like the ACT and Smarter Balanced Assessment. These assessments are given very infrequently and measure overall student growth. Often, the test items are designed to measure multiple skills at the same time, so they are not very useful in crafting individual instruction strategies. Item analysis of summative assessments can be valuable in evaluating the alignment of curriculum to standards on a larger scale, but this is not typically the focus of individual teachers and teams.

Interim assessments, as the name implies, are administered more frequently, at intervals between yearly tests. They also may be called benchmark assessments, because they create benchmarks or milestones against which to measure progress over a smaller passage of time. For example, the AIMSweb test is available for all grade levels and is given three times a year in the fall, winter, and spring and its short, progress monitoring probes can be administered as frequently as weekly or monthly. The data is used to screen students for intervention and provide teachers ongoing progress monitoring for students receiving interventions. Another common interim assessment is the Measures of Academic Progress (MAP) tests, used in elementary and middle schools three times a year. Data are used for similar purposes—as an instructional tool for informing instruction, creating flexible groups, and identifying students for services or interventions. Because districts make their own decisions about what interim assessment(s) to use, they can be used over a period of years to reveal trends and help educators monitor the performance of student groups, entire classrooms, grade levels, and schools.

Formative assessments are shorter, more frequent evaluations that quickly and immediately inform instructional practices to support learning. The nature of the assessment does not make it formative. What makes it formative is that it used to in*form* instruction, *form* flexible groups for immediate support, and allow students to re*form* the grade they receive. This means that formative assessment is conducted during the instructional unit, while there is still time for students to have further support and the opportunity to improve their performance.

Formative assessment may be embedded (Wiliam, 2011) into the activities of the lesson, with a planned task or method of response that gives the teacher an immediate picture of how well students are accessing the new learning. Formative assessment may be used at the end of the

Figure 2.4 Scores on State Math Assessment: By Quartile With and Without Scores of Students With Individualized Education Programs

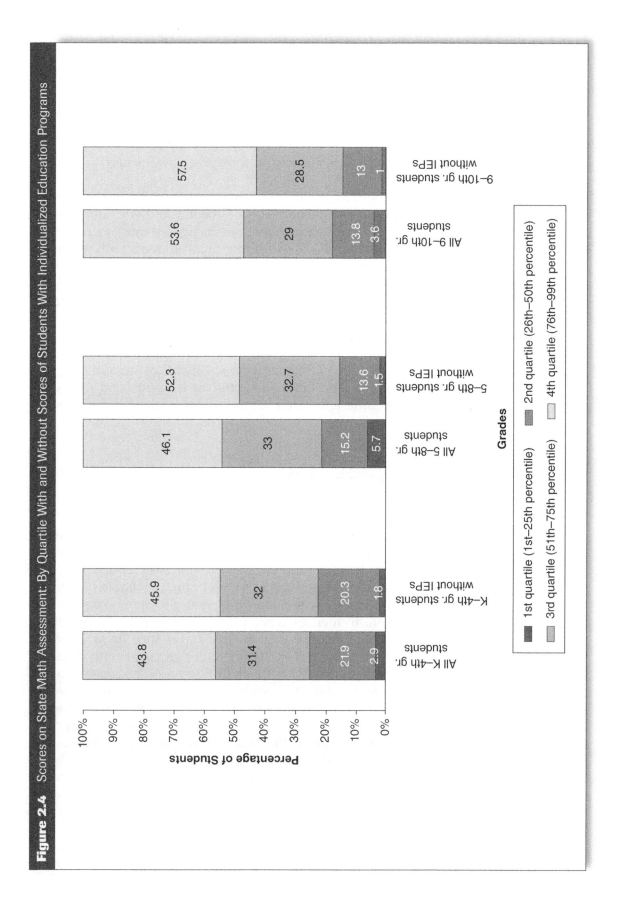

lesson, as in the use of exit slips with a sample question to determine whether today's learning target was met. Weekly quizzes may also be considered formative if they are not just entered into a student's record but inform what will happen on Monday. Formative assessments can be on paper, or demonstrated in performance, or technology-based. When a team of teachers who work with the same students on the same coursework collaborate to create, administer, and analyze these frequent assessments, they are referred to as common formative assessments (Bailey & Jakicic, 2012).

The capacity to "believe in" the assessments is greater for interim assessments, and greatest for formative assessments. And educators are dead-on to perceive that their formative assessments are most valuable. Dylan Wiliam (2011) noted in his 2004 finding that "students with which the teachers used formative assessment techniques made almost twice as much progress over the year" (p. 37). To counter all the real reasons it may be hard to have faith in the "big tests," it's important to invest in the capacity of teachers to develop quality formative assessments. Louis, Leithwood, Wahlstrom, and Anderson (2010) asserted, "One of the most productive ways for districts to facilitate continual improvement is to develop teachers' capacity to use formative assessments of student progress aligned with district expectations for student learning, and to use formative data in devising and implementing interventions during the school year" (p. 214).

SURFACING BELIEFS AND ACKNOWLEDGING DIFFERENCES

Application of the brain research to our instructional approaches is increasing and making us more effective with children. The power of the limbic system to override both rational thought and basic bodily functions is awesome. As the emotional center of our brain, the limbic system relays stimuli to the neocortex, where reasoning and planning take place. Since the limbic system influences what we pay attention to, consider important, and remember, we must ease anxiety and reduce stress when we challenge people's beliefs and ask them to get engaged with data. Facilitators of cultural change need to be skillful users of language, stories, humor, and music as ways to soothe anxiety and encourage the risk-taking necessary to explore underlying beliefs. Throughout this book, a variety of activities are provided to guide data discussion and decision-making. Some are more "formal" protocols and processes. Others are shorter, less formal, even tongue-in-cheek humorous. In *The Art of Coaching Teams*, Aguilar (2016) pointed out that play helps people become more innovative, refine skills, and increase happiness. It helps shape our brains for learning, makes us more resilient, and strengthens our connections with others.

If we can't laugh at ourselves and laugh with each other, that's data, too—it tells us something about the trust level in our culture. These "playful" activities may be introduced as and for energizers, team-builders, and even just tension relief.

The Magic of Metaphor

At the start of workshops that relate to data work, I ask people to introduce themselves with the usual name, position, and school and then complete this sentence:

When I think about data and graphs, I feel like (a)/(an) _____
_____

because _____.

Here is a sample of typical responses:

- I feel like I'm helpless because what we have is not very good.
- I feel like I'm excited because this will strengthen what we have.
- I feel like an owl because I'm wondering "who-who-who's" gonna do this.
- I feel like I'm in a stats course and wonder if I'm supposed to make the numbers lie for our benefit.
- I feel like a computer because this will be dehumanizing people.
- I feel like I'm in the wrong room because I noticed the accountants are meeting next door.
- I feel like I'm on *The Price Is Right* because something's hidden behind every door.
- I feel like a deer in the headlights because I don't know which way to run.
- I feel like I'm at the edge of a minefield with a long stick because there's so much negative reaction and doesn't seem to be much appreciation of what we do well and how hard we work.
- I feel like a professional because I can finally use the math skills I teach to help my whole school.
- I finally feel like I belong because I hate touchy-feely workshops, and it looks like we're going to do real work here.

During the introductions, capture some of these on a flip chart or jot some of them down on a notepad as you walk around the room. This allows you to observe nonverbals and chuckle to yourself at the shocked looks on many faces when someone says he or she *likes* working with data. After the introductions, respond to some of them. For example, you can reassure the less-excited that we will be doing nothing more complicated than counting, percentages, and simple graphing so if they have fifth-grade math skills, they will be fine. You will also have a chance to diagnose the levels of readiness of the group and adjust accordingly. You can also use this activity to check the composition of groups or teams. If there is just one of the "excited" type in each group, you can proceed with some degree of confidence in their collective capacity. When all the members of a team express anxiety, come back to them later and ask if they know someone back at their school who would probably answer the prompt with enthusiasm. Usually they do, so suggest that they recruit that person to help with this part of their school improvement work.

An alternative metaphor prompt is more collective since it requires a table group to create a plural response. "Based on how we treat data, our school would be a _____ because _____."

Cheers and Jeers

"Cheers and Jeers" provides an opportunity to use music and humor to relax and release tension. Ask participants to work in groups of three or four or as table groups, depending on the room setup. Their job is to create a cheer or jeer—depending on how they feel about using data—and either is fully acceptable. Their cheers or jeers can be performed all at once, or you can ask for one to be shared whenever the group needs an energizer. Shifting from the technical work to something more creative raises the level of energy throughout the room. Here are some cheers and jeers I've enjoyed!

As a rap, while snapping fingers:

Data, data, data.

Things were gettin' badda.

Data, data, data

Told us whatza matta.

Data, data, data.

Now it's goin' up the ladda.

As a cheer, with motions:

Data, data, data's

Just yadda, yadda, yadda (thumbs to fingers like lips flapping)

Be a clown! (any funny pose)

Turn it around! (twirl)

Engage them all! (point around room)

Have a ball! (arms form circle above head)

As a song to the tune of "Row, Row, Row Your Boat":

C'lect, count, graph your data

So you'll know your school.

If you don't have proof to show

You'll look like a fool.

COLLECTIVE COMMITMENTS AND COURAGEOUS CONVERSATIONS

Earlier in this chapter, the terms *mission*, *vision*, and *values* were mentioned, and readers may have wondered about the similar verbiage of norms and collective commitments. These are also discussed regularly in literature about teams and schools. Both of them refer to how people say they will *behave* in order to accomplish what they have said they *believe*. If there's a significant difference, it may be in scope—collective commitments perhaps being more schoolwide, while norms are articulated in each and every smaller team. Here I use the term *norms* for simplicity. They are typically the result of an affinity process with participants considering what they would need from themselves and the group in order to be effective and efficient. Their individual thoughts captured one per stick-on note can be combined and recombined through an affinity process to create no more than ten statements that specifically describe what they will (and will not) consider acceptable behavior from themselves and each other. As with the mission statement, norms are only powerful if taken seriously and used as a rigorous reference point. For example, a statement related to equal participation literally means that all members of the group agree to monitor their own airtime and to accept a reminder of the norm from someone designated to gently do so. (Chapter 10 includes more about the role of norms to save time, increase team effectiveness, and resolve conflict.)

The mission and norms provide an expectation about the topics and comments that will be part of teamwork, including data discussions. They also create an agreed-upon reference point for follow-up conversations that are described by various authors as courageous, crucial, critical, or downright hard. When something happens—like a negative comment about students in the teachers' lounge—it's important that something be said in response. Otherwise, the speaker feels validated; silence is consent. I encourage teams to learn all they can about courageous conversations from the author of their choice and develop a set of strategies that are comfortable for them. But this takes time, and as team members often say, "I walk away feeling guilty because I didn't say anything, but I don't feel confident yet about what to say and how."

Many have found this simple frame to be helpful when just beginning the complex and personal work of challenging beliefs: "I'm not sure I understand what you're saying (or this may be: I'm not sure why you're saying that.). I want to understand, but I need to think about it some more first. Could we talk some more a little later?" This usually works to stimulate some reflection on the part of the speaker and creates an opportunity to pursue a more extended conversation after some reflection and planning on the part of the concerned hearer.

FROM CAUTION AND COMPLIANCE TO COMMITMENT

In Chapter 1, we noted that external mandates have created a culture where data work that could be empowering is completed in a cursory manner from a sense of compliance. Earlier in this chapter, we noted that there are beliefs about students and assessment (and, therefore, data) that arise from real-life experiences. I believe there is a window of opportunity in the early years of the Every Student Succeeds Act (ESSA) to generate intrinsic motivation and move toward a culture of commitment.

This activity allows participants to choose factors that create meaning and motivation for each of them as individuals. There are two versions of the Motivation Continuum activity that can be further adapted depending on the group.

The Reflective Continuum

The first version is best suited for occasions when the audience can work in small groups and is open to reflection and serious discussion with peers. It takes about 15 to 20 minutes to complete. Ask individual participants to think about this question: Why is it important to be able to produce evidence of what the school achieves for its students? Each participant can have a supply of stick-on notes and write one of the factors he or she identifies on each note.

After generating reasons why the use of data is incredibly important, have participants arrange the factors they identified along the continuum drawn on large chart paper. (See Figure 2.5.) They should discuss the degree to which each factor is driven by outside forces or arises from internally perceived needs and desires. Figure 2.6 shows the factors identified by a recent group.

After time has been allowed for discussion, ask participants whether any of these factors seem inappropriate or unfair. Acknowledge that it's perfectly all right to feel this way, and tell them to cross out the reasons that feel *de*motivating to them as individuals. Participants then circle or star the factors on their own continuum that they find most meaningful. These are the sources that will provide motivation for their ongoing exploration of data.

Conclude the activity by asking each participant to make a one-sentence response to a prompt such as, "I can be motivated to work with our data if I remember that . . ." These statements are the first level of commitment to get engaged with data.

The "Live" Continuum

The "live" motivation continuum is a variation that takes about twenty minutes and has been used successfully with as many as 200 teachers in an auditorium setting. It even worked with a group of eighty-five high school teachers on the Friday afternoon before Christmas vacation!

Instead of having participants work in small groups to generate reasons to get engaged with data, this variation starts with factors previously identified in other groups, such as those in Figure 2.6. In preparation, these

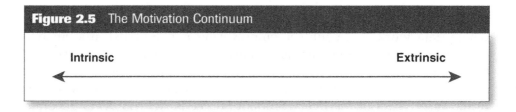

Figure 2.5 The Motivation Continuum

Intrinsic   Extrinsic

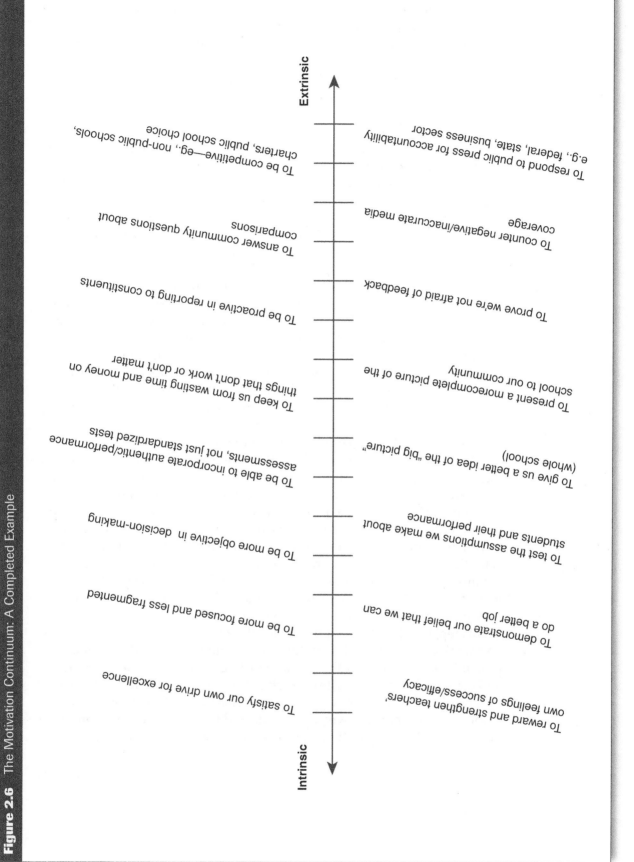

Figure 2.6 The Motivation Continuum: A Completed Example

Extrinsic

To respond to public press for accountability e.g., federal, state, business sector

To be competitive—eg., non-public schools, charters, public school choice

To counter negative/inaccurate media coverage

To answer community questions about comparisons

To prove we're not afraid of feedback

To be proactive in reporting to constituents

To present a morecomplete picture of the school to our community

To keep us from wasting time and money on things that don't work or don't matter

To give us a better idea of the "big picture" (whole school)

To be able to incorporate authentic/performance assessments, not just standardized tests

To test the assumptions we make about students and their performance

To be more objective in decision-making

To demonstrate our belief that we can do a better job

To be more focused and less fragmented

To reward and strengthen teachers' own feelings of success/efficacy

To satisfy our own drive for excellence

Intrinsic

factors are printed in bold colors on strips of chart paper. Also prepare two signs: one saying "Extrinsic" and one saying "Intrinsic."

Tell the audience that you have been working with teachers in other schools and have brought their ideas about using data to get this group's reaction. Describe this as an audience participation game show, where audience members will need to be active, loud, and demanding in order to succeed.

Recruit two volunteers to hold the Extrinsic and Intrinsic signs, and ask them to stand at opposite ends of the front of the room. Briefly review the two terms as they relate to motivation, and identify participants to hold the strips of paper on which you printed the factors from Figure 2.6. The responsibility of the audience is to scream, yell, and gesture at their colleagues to tell them where to stand so the factors they represent are in order across the room based on their extrinsic or intrinsic value. Most audiences relish the permission to be a bit rowdy at an in-service and participate readily in the true spirit of *The Price Is Right*.

After the audience members have arranged their colleagues along the live continuum, use another old game show adaptation called the Applause-o-Meter. At least a few in the group will remember winners being chosen by the length and volume of the applause. Tell the audience that they will now rate the motivational power of these factors. Participants can be silent or boo and hiss at factors they reject and clap and whistle for those they accept as meaningful reasons to get more engaged with data. As you move along the continuum, have the factors that are validated step forward.

Conclude by briefly commenting on the importance of each of the factors the group validated as meaningful. Ask the group members to get a mental picture of their colleagues holding these words, and remember that these are the real reasons they will be working more with data in the days to come. In one district, the professional development sessions were being videotaped, and the "lineup" of reasons to use data became a matter of record for future reference (and laughter) during school improvement activities. The bottom line is that people will be more likely to get excited about data when it fits their beliefs about what's important. Help them identify some aspect of the assessment and data work they do believe in, and make a commitment about how they will participate. It may be a small step, but it will contribute to development of a culture where everyone works together to understand their results, their students, and their practices—and shares in the planning of actions to take next. Mandates and competition don't kindle enough enthusiasm and energy to learn new skills and tackle different work. A more personal meaning must be created to motivate complicated work with data and to address complex problems of student achievement. It has to start with "something I believe in."

Chapter 3

You Get More Excited About Data When . . . It Feels Safe

Spring break had come and gone, and the countdown was under way. It wasn't the last day of school we were anticipating. It was the release of the test scores. Principals and teachers knew they had arrived in the district, because the corner window of the Research and Evaluation Department was lit up until the wee hours for two straight nights. It meant that the test expert was poring through the printouts, preparing them for dissemination to the buildings.

When we received them a few days later, we knew what mattered. The areas of student performance that would be listed as concerns on Figure 7.1 (p. 108) were highlighted on each report. A memo was attached directing us to study them carefully and respond within two weeks with an improvement plan. It wasn't motivating, and it didn't increase interest in working with data for several reasons:

- The implication was that staff at the school were not willing or capable to identify areas of concern for ourselves.
- The absence of acknowledgment that our students did very well in some areas created resentment and added to the emotional stress, creating an emotional barrier to dealing with the data.
- The expectation that a two-week window during the last month of school was either adequate time or the appropriate time to develop a sound improvement plan was ludicrous.

FEAR OF EVALUATION

The greatest conundrum encountered in my early attempts to help schools use data was the fear expressed in questions like, "How can I keep this from being used against me?" and "Why would I want to help create the hatchet they could use to 'give me the ax'?" This was particularly puzzling since no one could describe any example of a person dismissed from a teaching or administrative position based on performance of students. Admittedly, implementation of the No Child Left Behind Act (NCLB) raised that risk. The anxiety was much more well-founded when the lack of adequate yearly progress by any group on a single measure of reading or mathematics could lead to loss of students and thereby loss of resources, loss of staff and leadership, loss of involvement in decision-making, and eventual closure or takeover of the school. Anne Wheelock referred to "politicians with an ax to grind who then use the data, often for purposes that serve neither schools nor their schools well. As a result, many educators have come to think of data—whether couched in terms of the numbers of students passing standardized tests or student survey information gathered to determine how students view their teachers and classrooms—as the stuff that bureaucrats in faraway offices use to beat up on schools" (in Johnson, 2002, p. xii).

The threats of evaluation with negative consequences are less real under the Every Student Succeeds Act (ESSA), but stress remains and coping with the fear requires the same discipline of focusing on the goal and doing what is right for children for their own sakes, rather than seeking more politically expedient strategies. In reality, the response to my question is still the same: no one can name a specific example of a person being dismissed purely on the test results of their students.

Datnow and Park (2015) realized that "some teachers mistrust data use because they fear that the data may be used against them" (p. 13) and that "many teachers experience fear and lack confidence in their ability to change" (p. 14). They emphasized that it's crucial to establish trust between leaders and teachers and within teacher teams—and that requires having respect for all involved. "If you walk into a meeting with a feeling of respect for your colleagues, you're more likely to be nonjudgmental when you examine the data they share . . . If team members understand the challenges their colleagues are facing, they can better understand those colleagues' decisions and respond more helpfully" (Datnow & Park, 2015, p. 14).

FEAR OF EXPOSURE

In my work with data and teams in many states, I've encountered a more puzzling type of resistance that was less overtly expressed. Individuals who were recognized as "master teachers" would become enthused about using schoolwide data but shy away from discussions of individual students or classrooms. Several attempts to understand their ambivalence yielded this honest observation: "Everyone thinks I'm a great teacher. I'm three years from retirement. How would I ever recover if the data shows I'm not as good as all my friends think I am?"

The same fear of exposure surfaced in a conversation recently with a highly regarded teacher who is learning to be a peer coach. His initial training includes being intensely coached himself, which entails more rigorous self-reflection than many of us would be willing to risk. After the first few weeks of this experience, he stated, "I feel like a 'scammer.' I've been so unaware and unintentional in my teaching—it's almost like I'm a fraud." Fortunately, he has now come through the pain of that self-realization and reached a level where he is both more competent and more confident. And he has discovered that sharing his painful self-revelation makes him transparent and vulnerable and opens up relationships as the foundation for the coaching support he wants to provide.

These revelations of fear point out two important concepts about people in change.

1. Every new challenge requires a different definition of "ability" based on the knowledge and skills needed in that specific endeavor. High performers with many talents and intense dedication can still feel—and be—less prepared and enthused about new challenges in less familiar areas.

2. Leaders of change must be diligent about their own evaluations of others, or they may falsely interpret normal fear of failure as resistance and lack of commitment. Clarifying questions and needs assessments can help an organization identify and provide the human and technical supports that are needed. If we want people to move out of their comfort zones, the "new place" to which they will go must be seen and felt as "safe" and the "bridge to cross" must have a firm foundation and solid guardrails.

FEAR MASQUERADING AS RESISTANCE

Bryan Goodwin (2015) described how high-stress environments make it hard for people to reveal their struggles and work together. For example, "the longer low-performing schools faced the threat of sanctions, the less apt they were to examine their underlying assumptions and current practices—and pull together to improve them" (Goodwin, 2015, p. 79). Educators who fear being judged will be less likely to engage in the self-reflection that we found necessary to surface and change beliefs in Chapter 2.

In his article "10 Reasons Your Educators Are Resisting Your Change Initiative," Scott McLeod (2011) blogged that teachers fear loss of face and have concerns about future competence. They may perceive an implication that the way they have been doing things is in some way "wrong." They may feel embarrassed trying to tackle new ideas in front of their peers or staff. They may question whether they can be effective in a new situation. And most pertinent to our recent NCLB experiences, he pointed out that "sometimes the threat is real."

For example, Tschannen-Moran (2014) described how "one's sense of identity can be damaged as a result of receiving public criticism; being the target of wrong or unfair accusations; being blamed by another person for his or her own mistakes; or fielding insults either personal or to the collective of which one is a part. When one's dignity has been damaged, one often feels duty-bound to redress the wrong and may invest enormous energy in conjuring up a plan to do so" (p. 75). This natural urge to defend oneself and restore identity saps the individual's time, energy, and in turn, undermines the sense of collective efficacy needed throughout the school.

Aguilar (2016) also described resistance as "a camouflaged expression of underlying emotional distress" and cautions us as follows: "When you sense resistance in others, activate your compassion for them . . . make connections . . . seek understanding . . . listen. . . . Resistance in others is strengthened by anger, lecturing, counterarguments, and placating. . . . 'This person is afraid of something. I wonder what's going on?'" (p. 199). Listen for clues to whether the fear may be about the person's knowledge and skills to be able to do what is now asked of them, and respond to their needs. Figures 3.1 and 3.2 (pp. 42–43) provide another way to analyze what you hear as legitimate concerns, not outright resistance or refusal.

SURFACING THE FEARS

Just as the master teacher assesses students before planning instruction, change agents need information about the knowledge, skills, and attitudes of members of the organization. Assessments of readiness can range from the informal and humorous to very structured and formal.

Self- and Staff Rating

A lighthearted diagnosis can take place by asking staff members to give themselves a one to ten rating, from the low of one described as "scared to death of data" to a high of ten "ready to sky-dive into the data." These humorous descriptions of themselves relieve stress and the explanations they often feel compelled to give for their rating reveal questions that need to be clarified, skills that need to be learned, and supports that need to be provided.

When participants in this informal exercise are administrators or members of a leadership team, they will rate their own reactions to the use of data and may not pause to consider whether they are typical of the entire staff. In this situation, it is advisable to do a second rating in response to this stem: "The average of the rest of our staff who aren't here would probably be . . ." Sensitivity to the difference in comfort level between the leaders and the overall group is essential.

Best Hopes, Worst Fears

Use of this protocol (adapted from the School Reform Initiative) can surface expectations and concerns and help participants to see that their fears and hopes are shared by others and that they are out in the open and will be addressed. It will take twenty to thirty minutes in groups of twenty-five to thirty. In larger settings, each table group should work together and then report out to the whole. The only materials needed are individual writing materials, chart paper, and markers.

Ask participants to write down briefly for themselves their greatest fear for this meeting, group, or new project. "If it's the worst experience you've had, what will have happened (or not happened)?" And then write your greatest hope: "If this is the best meeting (or activity) you've ever participated in, what outcome(s) will have taken place by the end?" (three to four minutes). If there is time, ask participants to share their hopes and fears with a partner (three minutes). On two charts—one labeled Fears and one Hopes—list everything that participants share, asking them to listen carefully and avoid repeats. Be sure that all fears and hopes are written down, as expressed, without comment or any sense of judgment, except perhaps, "That's interesting." Do not be fearful of having folks express their worst fears; it always makes things go better once expressed. Plus, we want to know what NOT to do! If used at the start of a meeting or new team, this activity transitions very well into norm-setting. "In order to reach the outcomes we hoped for, what norms will we need?" (Norms are discussed further in Chapters 4 and 10.)

In some situations, the fear is so palpable that participants may not risk even the idea of saying *what* it is that they fear, so this modification provides greater safety in anonymity. It is very helpful where there seem to be issues of trust and safety. It is also helpful when the group includes differences in position power (e.g., superintendent, principals, teachers). Participants are provided with stick-on notes of two colors: bright yellow for "sunny" hopes and light blue for "fears." Every participant has the same two colors of stick-on notes so that color does not create an identifier. Participants write each of their best hopes and worst fears on an appropriate color stick-on note. Participants then choose a group member to collect the fears and another (if size allows) to collect the hopes. Trust is highest when the person collecting the stick-on notes is one of those with "lowest" position power (e.g., a teacher, not an administrator). The group member who collected the stick-on notes reads them aloud one at a time, so this trusted person is the only one who might recognize handwriting. A scribe can summarize on a chart or a note-taker can type into a document to preserve the comments. Briefly address any concerns for which there is an immediate reassurance or clarification, and explain how remaining questions and concerns will be answered. Never ask for subjective data like this without a commitment to return with responses.

RESPONDING TO CONCERNS

One way to analyze concerns and plan responses came from the work of Hord, Rutherford, Huling-Austin, and Hall (1987) at the University of Texas. Figure 3.1 identifies a developmental sequence of seven stages of concern through which people move as they accept and adjust to change. The first three are sometimes called Self-concerns, since they revolve around wanting to know more about the change (in this case, data use) and how it will affect them personally. As these questions are answered, Stage 3 represents Task concerns—how they will manage logistics, such as time and materials. When these concerns of self and task are addressed, teachers can become more interested in how their use of a new practice will benefit students and the school. Impact stages also include sharing their efforts with colleagues and using their own ideas to modify and improve the practice further.

Figure 3.1   Stages of Concern

Tools For Schools   February/March 2003

7 Stages of Concern

The Concerns-Based Adoption Model outlines seven Stages of Concern that offer a way to understand and then address educators' common concerns about change.

Stage 0: Awareness
Aware that an innovation is being introduced but not really interested or concerned with it.

☐   "I am not concerned about this innovation."
☐   "I don't really know what this innovation involves."

Stage 1: Informational
Interested in some information about the change.

☐   "I want to know more about this innovation."
☐   "There is a lot I don't know about this but I'm reading and asking questions."

Stage 2: Personal
Wants to know the personal impact of the change.

☐   "How is this going to affect me?"
☐   "I'm concerned about whether I can do this."
☐   "How much control will I have over the way I use this?"

Stage 3: Management
Concerned about how the change will be managed in practice.

☐   "I seem to be spending all of my time getting materials ready."
☐   "I'm concerned that we'll be spending more time in meetings."
☐   "Where will I find the time to plan my lessons or take care of the record keeping required to do this well?"

Stage 4: Consequence
Interested in the impact on students or the school.

☐   "How is using this going to affect students?"
☐   "I'm concerned about whether I can change this in order to ensure that students will learn better as a result of introducing this idea."

Stage 5: Collaboration
Interested in working with colleagues to make the change effective.

☐   "I'm concerned about relating what I'm doing to what other instructors are doing."
☐   "I want to see more cooperation among teachers as we work with this innovation."

Stage 6: Refocusing
Begins refining the innovation to improve student learning results.

☐   "I have some ideas about something that would work even better than this."

When concerns are gathered, whether through a group process or through individual compassionate listening, group the responses. Which are purely needs for factual information—or correction of misinformation? Which are expressions of internal concerns? How many are purely management concerns that can be addressed during implementation? Although

Figure 3.2   Responding to Stages of Concern

Tools For Schools   February/March 2003

Address Individual Concerns

To help bring about change, you first must know an individual's concerns. Then those concerns must be addressed. While there are no set formulas, here are some suggestions for addressing the stages of concern.

Stage 0: Awareness concerns
- If possible, involve teachers in discussions and decisions about the innovation and its implementation.
- Share enough information to arouse interest, but not so much it overwhelms.
- Acknowledge that a lack of awareness is expected and reasonable and that there are no foolish questions.

Stage 1: Informational concerns
- Provide clear and accurate information about the innovation.
- Use several ways to share information — verbally, in writing, and through available media. Communicate with large and small groups and individuals.
- Help teachers see how the innovation relates to their current practices — the similarities and the differences.

Stage 2: Personal concerns
- Legitimize the existence and expression of personal concerns.
- Use personal notes and conversations to provide encouragement and reinforce personal adequacy.
- Connect these teachers with others whose personal concerns have diminished and who will be supportive.

Stage 3: Management concerns
- Clarify the steps and components of the innovation.
- Provide answers that address the small specific "how-to" issues.
- Demonstrate exact and practical solutions to the logistical problems that contribute to these concerns.

Stage 4: Consequence concerns
- Provide individuals with opportunities to visit other settings where the innovation is in use and to attend conferences on the topic.
- Make sure these teachers are not overlooked. Give positive feedback and needed support.
- Find opportunities for these teachers to share their skills with others.

Stage 5: Collaboration concerns
- Provide opportunities to develop skills for working collaboratively.
- Bring together, from inside and outside the school, those who are interested in working collaboratively.
- Use these teachers to assist others.

Stage 6: Refocusing concerns
- Respect and encourage the interest these individuals have for finding a better way.
- Help these teachers channel their ideas and energies productively.
- Help these teachers access the resources they need to refine their ideas and put them into practice.

it would be nice if everyone could jump straight to consideration of the benefits for students and the school, we're all human and must first feel assured that we have the capacity to participate. Figure 3.2 then provides some suggestions for how responses will be different, depending on the stage of concern revealed in the comments and questions.

BUILDING TRUST

When people openly or individually express concerns, they are taking a risk. When responses are timely and appropriate, the risk is rewarded and trust is strengthened. Building trust is critical—not just about trust in data or trust for data usage but as a necessary ingredient in the culture of the school. It must be a constant focus of attention and intention because it's an essential foundation for the sense of collective efficacy discussed in Chapter 2 and for the collaborative work described in Chapter 4 and beyond. Trust is built when leadership is shared, strengths are celebrated, integrity is consistent, and sincere efforts are made to restore broken relationships.

Share Leadership and Decision-Making

Leithwood, Harris, and Strauss (2010) encountered the effects of fear in their study of how low-performing schools in Canada were transformed. One of the necessary early steps was to reduce teachers' sense of being under threat. They noted the same thing observed in U.S. schools under NCLB—that "staffs in both elementary and secondary schools were anxious about their students' performances on provincial tests, especially in light of how publicly available their scores were" (Leithwood et al., 2010, p. 52). They also articulated how such fear inhibits constructive action "when a group is confronted with a significant threat to its existence, psychological stress reaches dysfunctional levels, and this limits the ability of individuals within the group to think flexibly and innovatively about how they might respond productively to the threat. The outcome of such inflexible thinking is to reduce the flow of information, quality of decisions, and divergent views" (Leithwood et al., 2010, p. 52). In order to build trusting relationships between and among teachers, and between teachers and administrators, they recommend "increasing teachers' feelings of empowerment and involving them in more decision-making." Chapter 4 describes structures that can enhance this effort.

Of course, this involvement must be authentic. When the motivation for including staff in decision-making is to win compliance for a decision that's already been made, "teachers see through the ruse and resent how their time has been wasted (not to mention the implicit insult to their intelligence). A more authentic form of shared decision-making stems from the belief that the involvement will result in higher-quality decisions because these individuals are close to the action and have information and insight . . . When administrators share actual influence in decision-making, they demonstrate significant trust and respect for their teachers and are more likely to be trusted in return" (Tschannen-Moran, 2014, p. 31).

Take a Strengths-Based Stance

Scudelia (2016) studied veteran teachers to determine what administrators do that builds intrinsic motivation. Teachers described principals who eschewed a formal evaluation stance in favor of actions like conversations about teaching practices, feedback that allowed for personal reflection, encouragement for a job well done, and a positive and open relationship between the teacher and the administrator. In turn, teachers in these settings believed they were good at teaching, believed they were skilled as teachers, and continued to believe in their efficacy while receiving feedback and experiencing change.

In a similar vein, Tschannen-Moran described a principal who "was able to improve the quality of teaching through an artful combination of support and challenge . . . [her] affirmation and acceptance of differences in teaching style helped create an atmosphere in which teachers were willing to share with one another." A teacher commented that "Our principal . . . plays on our strengths . . . and she treats us all equally . . . that changes the whole atmosphere between staff members because you never have that sense of competition. If you need help in something, you feel comfortable going to your coworkers and asking for help—or sharing what has worked for you or what hasn't worked for you . . . Every person feels valued" (Tschannen-Moran, 2014, p. 126).

The author later generalized,

> Trustworthy leaders put the culture of trust ahead of their own ego needs. Skillful principals often earn the trust of their faculty by leading *quietly*: they are soft on people and hard on projects. They combine personal humility—exercising restraint and modesty—with tenacity and the professional will to see that the complex work of educating a diverse group of students is accomplished at a high level of quality. Trustworthy principals foster the development of trust in their school by demonstrating flexibility, adopting a problem-solving stance, refusing to play the blame game, and involving teachers in making important decisions. (Tschannen-Moran, 2014, p. 268)

Demonstrate Integrity

Based on findings from their longitudinal study of 400 schools in Chicago, Bryk and Schneider (2003) identified integrity as one of the conditions necessary for the "relational trust" that correlated with the schools making greater improvement. "The first question that we ask is whether we can trust others to keep their word. Integrity also demands that a moral-ethical perspective guides one's work' (Bryk & Schneider, 2003, p. 43). Bryk pointed out that people in an organization are constantly interpreting the intentions of others, considering how others' efforts will advance or threaten their own self-esteem. The history of previous interactions will influence these interpretations, so any breach of integrity poses a risk not only now but in the long-term.

On the other hand, the benefits of trust are many. Collective decision-making with broad teacher buy-in occurs more readily in schools with strong relational trust. Change is easier in a high-trust school because trust reduces the sense of risk. Talking with colleagues honestly about what's working and what's not working creates vulnerability, so collaborative work is far more productive in a high-trust environment.

Repair Broken Relationships

Whereas Bryk and Schneider (2003) summarized the positive interdependence of trust and collaboration, Tschannen-Moran (2014) described the opposite interaction as a spiral of distrust that can develop when teachers in a school do not trust one another, become guarded in their interactions, and divert energy from common goals into self-protection. Teachers' collective sense that they have what it takes to promote student learning is then reduced and motivation suffers. Greater collaboration, a stronger collective sense of efficacy, and constructive conflict resolution are more likely when trust is present—and these, in turn, are the very elements that foster the conditions for improving trust.

Even when trust has broken down between two individuals or two groups, it takes only one party to change the quality of the relationship. When one person begins to sincerely inquire to try to understand the other's interests, attitudes, and beliefs, the dynamic begins to shift.

Tschannen-Moran (2014) included two full chapters related to restoring trust in her book *Trust Matters*. Among her topics is the need to repair relationships, using the "four A's of absolution—Admit it, Apologize, Ask for forgiveness and Amend your ways" (Tschannen-Moran, 2010, p. 224). Admitting involves opening up the topic for discussion, noting the changes in attitude and behavior you observed that prompted you to realize there were unresolved feelings, and admitting to having caused a situation and that the result was harmful. Apologizing includes expressing regret over the harm that was done. Asking forgiveness provides an opportunity for release of feelings in both parties, and forgiveness is usually granted. The final step of amending one's ways includes being concrete and specific about what will be done differently in the future—and, of course, following through with integrity.

There is an old adage that refers to students: They won't care how much you know until they know how much you care. A paraphrase that relates to trust and feeling safe in data use might be this: They can't care what the data shows until they know where the analysis goes. It might even be stated as "unless they know where the blame will go." We can get more excited about data when we feel safe to face what it might reveal. In a safe environment, trust is increased, which then builds a stronger collective sense of efficacy and commitment to work together. Chapter 4 introduces team structures that provide opportunities for that collaboration to occur, which in turn heightens the trust level.

Chapter 4

You Get More Excited About Data When . . . You're Not Doing It Alone

A typical day in my life as a classroom teacher went something like this: get to the staff room early to make copies before the machine breaks down, runs out of paper, or the line gets too long; hurry to my classroom to make final preparations for the day and write things on the board (first black, then green, then white—now "smart"); meet students at the door; teach the large group and the small groups and work with individuals; keep some in for discipline or extra help at recess and at lunchtime and after school; recoup from today and reorganize the classroom for tomorrow; and drag my book bags to the now-empty parking lot—all with no more than a passing nonverbal smile or gesture to another adult the entire day. The system just wasn't set up to interact with my peers, except once a month at a "sit-n-get" faculty meeting. The idea of talking with other teachers about my practice or sharing the challenges of my struggling students would have been astounding. In truth, only perfect work was "shared" because it was posted on bulletin boards that were outside the door in the hallway—and the principal would compare and check to make sure visitors to the building would be impressed. I would look at students' scores from the twice-yearly tests thrice yearly. In August, I'd look at scores from the previous spring and grin or groan over whether it looked like a good year or tough year ahead. In October or November, I'd take the start-of-year scores and try to figure out how to explain them to parents at conferences. In the spring, I'd compare the test scores to the grades I was giving on report cards and be fairly sure that my professional judgments were accurate. And I'd compare back to the fall scores just because I was curious. Since they were norm-referenced tests reported in percentiles, I thought I must be doing okay if they at least stayed the same and didn't go lower. I had no idea of whether this was what I should be doing— I knew my colleagues were just filing the reports—and I wasn't sure what benefit or value could come from it. I was definitely doing data on my own.

I had nothing like this experience Shirley Hord (2008) has described:

> When staff members work together . . . the typical isolation experienced by teachers and administrators is reduced. When the staff members come together to hold conversations about teaching and learning, the participants demonstrate high commitment to the goals, mission, and vision of the school. Their energy and enthusiasm contribute to a higher probability that the vision of the school will be realized. Together the staff members engage in powerful learning that adds to their knowledge base and repertoire of technical skills that increases their effectiveness. In addition, staff gain deeper understanding and meaning related to their content area and to the curriculum. They gain an appreciation for the vertical articulation of skills and competencies expected of students across the grades. This contributes to educators' exercising their roles in helping all students meet expectations for reaching high standards of learning. The development of students in all subjects is explored and a collective responsibility for all students' successful learning is manifested. (pp. 18–19)

She described this as a professional learning community. It is surely the type of context in which educators' beliefs could be challenged and shaped, and fear could be replaced by trust and safety.

A scholar at the Southwest Educational Development Laboratory and Scholar Laureate of the National Staff Development Council (NSDC)/ Learning Forward, Hord has studied learning in schools since the 1980s. She identifies these critical components: shared beliefs, values, and vision; shared and supportive leadership; collective learning and its application to meet students' needs; supportive structural conditions that provide time, space, and resources for collaboration; relational conditions characterized by openness, truth telling, and respect and caring among members; shared personal practice with feedback for individual and organizational development. In Chapters 2 and 3, the themes of shared beliefs, shared leadership, collective learning, and relational conditions surfaced and are woven throughout. The structural conditions of time, space, and resources are explored further in Chapters 8, 10, and 12. This chapter is based on my own study and experiences working with schools to create and strengthen structures within the school that nurture use of data to address needs of students, staff, and stakeholders. The roles of students and stakeholders are considered more in Chapter 7 as part of the big picture of school improvement. In most of this book, the inclusive use of the word *staff* refers to all the adults who work in the school, whether they are licensed teachers, aides, clerical support, custodial, or other roles. Here, we look primarily at interaction among the educators as they tackle what is new, unfamiliar, and uncomfortable work for some. Whether it's the data use that is new or the collaborative process that is a challenge, educators need to work in a safe environment—not sheltered from the data but safe to risk sharing new ideas and challenging each other. All constituents have a right of access to the data and input to shape school planning (Chapter 7), but educators should have the first chance to explore and analyze and prepare to discuss the data with others.

On a balmy day in August, a California superintendent had gathered the Administrative Team to review the district's priorities for the coming year and plan opening day activities for staff. His charge was to shift attention from mediating adult issues to outcomes accomplished for students. He realized that this would require a transformation of the culture of schools and stated that "the key to changing a culture is to create structures, processes and activities that cause people to think about different things in different ways with different people than they ordinarily would." This chapter focuses on structures that include the Administrative Team, the Data Team, the Shared Leadership Team, and the staff as a whole. Throughout the book, there are activities that engage staff in looking at a "different thing" in different ways with different people. The different thing is data. The "different ways" are through planned, structured, facilitated, collaborative conversations that require careful preparation and skilled leadership. The "different people" are colleagues from other grade levels or departments engaged more intentionally than the informal contacts they may have in the normal course of the day and week.

TEAM STRUCTURES FOR COLLABORATION

Figure 4.1 represents a school as a large circle with a reminder that the whole school is always in process toward functioning as a unified learning community. The circle is divided into segments with the designation of Teaching Teams—so named because their members share responsibility for student learning in shared content areas. For an elementary school, these segments are most naturally grade levels. For a high school, they are usually subject area departments or combinations of small but related content areas. Middle schools sometimes define core areas and electives. These segments are subdivisions that house people with a common assignment. If collaboration occurs spontaneously, it is likely to be limited to members of the same segment. Depending on the culture of the school, the "walls" between these segments may be permeable and could be replaced by dotted lines—or they might have to be more accurately represented by a triple-thick line. The architecture of some high schools, for example, erects very solid walls between segments when it places traditional subject area departments in separate wings with their own entrance and exit doors to their own parking areas.

Concentric circles moving in from the Teaching Teams represent the Shared Leadership Team, the Data Team, and the Administrative Team. Their membership and roles are discussed in following sections and in the Chapter 7 discussion of the school improvement process and inquiry cycle.

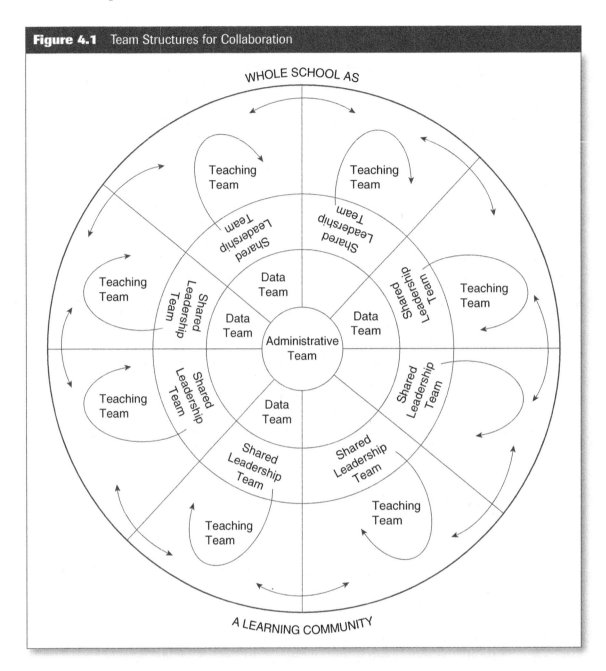

Figure 4.1 Team Structures for Collaboration

Figure 4.1 also includes two kinds of arrows. Looping arrows represent the need for feedback loops, processes by which all members of the Shared Leadership Team assure that they are sharing information with, and gathering input from, all of those they represent. The two-way arrows around the perimeter of the circle illustrate the importance of interacting "through the walls" to engage the whole staff in interactions that break down or bridge the physical configuration of the school and historical patterns of contact.

The Administrative Team

At the center of the school (and Figure 4.1), responsible for the performance of every segment, is the Administrative Team. At the elementary school, this is typically a single individual, experiencing even more isolation than a regular classroom teacher. At the secondary level, the Administrative Team may include assistant principal(s), dean(s) of students or counselors, and perhaps the activities/athletic director. Because the ultimate accountability for the school rests with the Administrative Team, the school improvement process and development of the student Action Plan must be a primary focus. Where there are multiple administrators, decisions about delegating responsibility must be carefully weighed in terms of the unspoken messages they convey. For example, an assistant principal may lead the Data Team as a component of her assigned work, but the head principal must be closely involved with the overall analysis and resulting plan development—or the implicit message may be that this work is not important enough to engage the central figure. A worst-case scenario developed in a school where an administrative intern from another building was assigned to prepare data and coordinate development of a school improvement plan. This signaled to staff that it was just a "project for a graduate course" and was not owned by the ultimate leader of the school (which was true).

The Shared Leadership Team

Moving out from the center of Figure 4.1, the next circle is the Data Team. Since it functions as a subgroup from the Shared Leadership Team, it is discussed in the next section. The word *shared* is intentionally added to "leadership team" to convey the sharing of decision-making between administrators and staff directly and through their representatives. This requires that

> the principal and other positional leaders participate with the staff as learners and contribute democratically to decision making and guiding and supporting members of the staff to develop leadership qualities and skills. Characteristics required . . . include the need to share authority, the ability to facilitate the work of the staff, and the capacity to participate without dominating . . . The staff is consistently involved in discussing and making decisions about school issues, but with the understanding that some areas must be the purview of the principal alone. The principal actively nurtures the entire staff's development as a community, but finds opportunities for the staff to perform in leadership roles. Leadership is promoted and fostered among members of the staff who have accessibility to data and key information in order to make sound decisions. (Hord, Roussin, & Sommers, 2010, p. 55)

The administrators' role of participation without domination cannot be overstated, given the importance of modeling to build the needed trust described in Chapter 3. Principals who have been in their schools a long time and have not always operated this way have a golden opportunity to share their intent and their struggles with staff as transparent learners of "different ways" themselves. (Team members may also need to actively assist their principals in making such changes—for example, by breaking their own habits of turning to the principal and waiting for him or her to expound first.) On the flip side, members of a Shared Leadership Team have to accept that there will be times when the principal may not be able to share *all* information with them or may not be able to carry out their first choice decision. In accepting that, they have the right to expect that the administrator(s) will be open to provide as much explanation as possible. While principals have a major role in building trust, team members have an obligation to presume positive intentions and extend at least preliminary trust on that basis.

In an era of collaboration and participatory decision-making, most schools have some representative group that works closely with the Administrative Team. If it has been called a Leadership Team but has dealt primarily with management details (e.g., textbook inventory, supply room raiding, schedule) or resolving interpersonal conflicts among adults (e.g., most senior teacher gets the room with most windows), another name should be chosen for the group discussed here. Some schools have chosen names like "achievement team" or "teaching and learning team" to clearly signal that this is a "different way" and that the focus will be on increasing the success of students. The Shared Leadership Team should meet at least once a month. (More detailed discussion of time considerations is in Chapter 10.)

The Shared Leadership Team should include representation from every segment of the school, as shown in Figure 4.1. Identification of members for this group should be carefully considered and not a pro forma approach, like automatically tapping department heads or most senior staff members. A useful approach is to provide an overview of the roles of the group and ask staff to consider this: Knowing the tasks they will be doing, who do you feel could best represent you?

It's fairly obvious that a Shared Leadership Team shares leadership with administrators. But it works both ways. Leadership is also shared "outward" with *all* staff, and it's important that this be obvious and intentional. In the case of developing a school improvement plan (Chapter 7), the Shared Leadership Team does not *make* the decisions about how to improve the school. Decisions made by the Shared Leadership Team are about how and when to engage peers, students, and constituents in the decision-making *processes*. Shared Leadership Team members prepare, plan, coordinate, orchestrate, and follow up on the work done with the full staff.

Creation of the culture of collective responsibility rests upon the diligence with which members of the Shared Leadership Team maintain the feedback loops illustrated by the looping arrows in Figure 4.1. Whenever the Shared Leadership Team meets, information must be shared back to all other staff members. Input should also be gathered for future discussions on ongoing issues still under deliberation. Figure 4.2 (p. 57) will provide a simple protocol that facilitates this process.

The Data Team

The circle around the Administrative Team represents the Data Team. This group should be a subset of the Shared Leadership Team, or have some members that belong to both groups in order to communicate closely and inform each other's work. Some spaces around this circle are blank to illustrate that the Data Team is a smaller group and may not include a member from every grade or department. There may, in fact, be members of the Data Team who are not members of the Shared Leadership Team, but who possess skills and interests that are needed. The Data Team may also include an administrator, especially in situations with only designated people having access to data sources. The Data Team is somewhat like an ad hoc committee in that it will meet more frequently at some times of the year and less frequently during other time spans. For example, when a new data source emerges such as a district or school climate survey, they will meet to compile results.

The Shared Leadership Team and Data Team work in tandem. For example, the Shared Leadership Team (which includes administrators) considers *what* data needs to be gathered. The Data Team determines *how* to collect it and delegates or distributes the tasks of collection and compilation. The Shared Leadership Team looks at a wide range of data sources and identifies data that is most significant for all staff to discuss. The Data Team prepares the graphics and materials. The Shared Leadership Team facilitates the group activities.

Members of the Data Team should be individuals who *do* get excited about data and are comfortable working with it. Some might not have the time or interest in the full set of responsibilities of the Shared Leadership Team but can help identify, prepare, and interpret data in preparation for consideration by the Shared Leadership Team or for sharing with the whole staff. In addition to technical skills, members of the Data Team should be individuals who have established strong relationships of trust with other staff members. Because this team will help sort out the most significant data elements for first review, they could be suspected of having power to portray a picture that highlights their personal interests and issues. They must have the respect of staff and a reputation for being totally objective.

In some settings, a district-level staff member may work with the Data Team to provide access and support. This might be a person with a title that encompasses assessment and accountability. It may be a district-deployed data coach, although few districts have resources to provide this level of support. Where there is a data coach, roles should be clearly defined so this person does not become the data guru that does all the data work. The purpose of a coach is to make a team more effective—not to play in the game. The goal should be to develop the capacity within the school so that many people can and will advocate for and facilitate use of data.

Teaching Teams

As noted earlier, Teaching Teams (grade levels, departments) are groups who teach and support students with similar content. School level and size influence the makeup of these teams. In a middle school, there may be a math team that includes all math teachers from Grades 6 to 8, whereas a large high school may have so many math teachers that they form multiple teams. One pattern might be a core math team and an advanced math team, with one group sharing strategies and assessments for the required math courses (e.g., algebra, geometry) and another sharing the higher-level and Advanced Placement (AP) math courses. Secondary schools often have a unique challenge providing team collaboration for their "singletons" who are the only ones with a specific niche of course-work. These staff members need to have a specified link into the teamwork structure, often being offered a choice of where they sense their best fit or similarity. This is to assure that they know through what "channel" their voices reach discussion in the Shared Leadership Team. (Chapter 10 points out that the district also needs to provide these teachers with inter-school connections if there is more than one high school, or opportunities for electronic networking with job-alike teachers in other districts.)

Careful thought should be given to the roles of special education teachers and others who support students. Although there are times when having an "all-SpEd" department or team is useful for program coordination, it is important that the Shared Leadership Team and the Teaching Teams include a mixture of general education and special education teachers in order to build out the reality that *all* teachers are responsible for *all* students.

Ideally, content teams would meet weekly—although having somewhat longer times every two weeks can also be effective. It's in their Teaching Teams that educators share instructional strategies, have the in-depth discussions of specific student needs (see Chapter 5), and develop formative assessments. Chapter 7 compares the overall school improvement process with the shorter, more in-depth inquiry cycle that occurs in Teaching Teams.

The Whole School as a Community

For the entire school to be a community of learners, they have to be connected through common language and communication as noted in following sections. They also have to be in the same place at the same time for face-to-face awareness of each other and active engagement in certain tasks. Hord and colleagues (2010) stressed that "all professionals at the school come together to meet as one community—comprising all staff members of the school—to share what the smaller units are learning and to carry out the specific learning that the whole school group deems important . . . Without this larger group's collegial and intentional learning, the various parts of the staff are moving in different directions that may well result in the lack of alignment of the scope and sequence of student learning" (p. 2). This is an important distinction. When people in a school state that they "have PLCs," rather than that they *are* a professional learning community, they may be in danger of such fragmentation. Chapter 7 will reiterate the importance of full engagement of all staff at critical points like these:

- Developing and affirming the school's mission
- Identifying significant, meaningful data to be compiled
- Interpreting the data, requesting the data, and identifying areas of concern
- Focusing areas of concern to a few priorities and developing goals
- Participating in study groups (Teaching Teams) to further analyze data in priority areas and recommend validated strategies
- Affirming the completed Action Plan

- Participating in staff development to learn the use of agreed-upon strategies and assessments
- Discussing evidence of progress with implementation and impact on student achievement

As Marzano (2016) also stressed, one indicator of a High Reliability School is that "teacher teams and collaborative groups regularly interact to address common issues regarding curriculum, assessment, instruction, and the achievement of all students."

The Test of Your Structures

Following on the trust theme of Chapter 3, Bryk and Schneider (2003) reiterated that every party in a relationship maintains an understanding of his or her roles and obligations and has expectations about the obligations of the other parties. In our discussion here, this means that every citizen of the school should know what the structures are, what each group does, and how to contribute their insights. If this isn't clear, the risk is that another team member will not "live up" to our expectations—which he or she may not even know we hold—and then we feel "let down" when they disappoint us.

Earlier in this chapter, the term *staff* was defined as all the adults who work in the school: licensed teachers, aides, clerical support, custodial, or other roles. Descriptions of the Shared Leadership Team, Data Team, and Teaching Teams have focused primarily on the teachers, but the measure of whether those structures can actually create community is something that should be tested. One way to do this is through a random set of brief, informal conversations or an exit slip used at the end of a staff gathering. The questions would include these: Who do you know on the Data Team? What does the Data Team do? Who do you know on the Shared Leadership Team? What do they do? Who is on your Teaching Team? How are your Teaching Team activities the same or different from what the other teams do? And the bottom line question is this: What is your route for sharing your voice in the decision-making of the school? All categories of staff should be aware of the structures in the school and should know that their voice is important and has a way to be heard. For example, the custodian who comes on shift near the end of the school day may have observations about dismissal procedures or student activity outside the building that are useful *data* for school planning.

COMMUNICATION FOR TEAM CONNECTIONS

Two interrelated considerations are important as collaborative structures are designed or refined in schools. One is that groups are formed and operate in such a way that they are trusted and earn further trust, strengthening the collaborative culture. The other is that groups are productive, accomplishing enough concrete and timely tasks to avoid being considered "all talk and no action." Both of these involve transparency through consistent, intentional two-way communication. Figure 4.2 is an example of the type of communication protocol that can support both goals. It specifically serves the purpose of the looping arrows on Figure 4.1. The creator of the document is a member of the Shared Leadership Team, and the receivers are all members of the Teaching Team (or teams) represented by that individual. So the line for "your representative" underscores that this member of the Shared Leadership Team is not there to advocate for their own preferences but as a communication loop to designated colleagues. An electronic template can be created on a shared drive or Google doc so team members are listed already and attendance can be quickly checked. This is important because if a Shared Leadership Team member is absent, someone must be designated to provide this communication to him or her and the individuals usually represented. The norms that have been identified by the team are also made a permanent part of the template. Goals or objectives for the meeting can be added to the template prior to each meeting. As each agenda item is completed, the Shared Leadership Team can jointly create a summary of key points of discussion (Section I), the decision made (Section II), and/or the task accomplished (Section III). In this way, the protocol serves as both communication and a record (minutes) of what occurred. Individual Shared Leadership Team members highlight or asterisk points they brought up on behalf of their colleagues. This holds them accountable to bring input to the meeting. Before adjournment, next steps are summarized in Section IV. The feedback loop circles back again when needs for input are identified in Section V. As with any protocol, individuals create their own meaning of whether it's "just another form to fill out" or whether their words and actions endorse its value as the transparency or glue between and among groups of staff.

COMMON LANGUAGE FOR COLLABORATION

Professionals do not come into new or refined group structures as blank slates. They bring with them a knowledge base of learning from undergrad and graduate education, professional development, and individual reading. They bring experiences with students and adults that have formed into concepts about what works and what doesn't. And they have terminology for all of these knowledge concepts, skills, and strategies. That's the good part. The challenge is that they almost surely do *not* have the *same* terminology.

To communicate efficiently and reduce conflict, we need to agree on what we will call the things that we do. We have often helped to create our own Frankenstein monster as the "last year's new thing—this year's new thing—next year's new thing" phenomenon. We bring in an additional component to strengthen an existing process, but we also transport a whole set of terms for it that make it sound like something entirely foreign. Then our colleagues wonder what happened to the other model, because it had its own separate language. We need to create a thesaurus of all the interrelated terms we have used individually and in various initiatives and then reach consensus about which of those synonyms we will strive to use consistently for clear understanding.

One way to approach this reality is to begin with whatever new task is facing the staff and record the terms on a flip chart, leaving plenty of space between them. Using this chapter as an example, some terms might

Figure 4.2   Communication Protocol for Shared Leadership Team Feedback Loops

Shared Leadership Team Meeting Date: _____

Your representative: _____

Members Present: Norms:

_____   _____
_____   _____
_____   _____
_____   _____
_____   _____
_____   _____
_____   _____
_____   _____
_____   _____

Goals for this meeting:

-
-
-
-

I. Issues Discussed (for each issue, use bullets for main points and asterisk the input you provided from your grade/department):

II. Decisions Made (list each decision, who will be affected, when it will take effect):

III. Tasks Accomplished (list project, process, or product completed and how it will be distributed and used):

IV. Next Steps, Meeting Date, and Topic:

V. Input Needed (for each topic, include method for input and deadline):

be *Shared Leadership Team, Data Team, Teaching Team, collaboration,* and *data.* The first step is to go through the list with the group, asking participants to name as many adjectives as they can for each term. Repeat each word and record it. Or ask someone else to serve as recorder so you can better observe nonverbals during this part of the process. You may note interesting reactions to words that some people assume mean the same thing and other participants don't think are the same thing at all. An example here would be various synonyms for the word *data.* If for some it's synonymous only with state test scores, the belief and safety issues explored in Chapters 2 and 3 are likely to be bubbling above or simmering just below the surface.

After the thesaurus of synonyms has been generated, go back through each term and ask the group to discuss language that has been used in the past. Encourage participants to reflect on the connotations that have become attached to certain words. Sometimes people will realize they've thought they disagreed for years when they simply had different definitions for terms they were both using. Complete the activity by asking group members to select and circle those terms that sound familiar, are accurate, and have positive connotations in their setting, and agree to strive to use them consistently. In the example in Figure 4.3, participants agreed to use *mission* as one encompassing term for many that had been bandied about by a succession of principals. They decided to refer to what they would pursue as "improvement objectives" and what they would do as "tactics" with "implementation steps." But for the word *data,* they chose to use a whole range of terms, including *proof, evidence, measures, results,* and *indicators* but not *scores.* They knew that test scores would be thought of automatically and wanted to stretch understanding by modeling other terms.

NORMS AND PROTOCOLS

The concepts of mission, vision, values, and collective beliefs were explored in Chapter 1 and encompassed in the one term *mission* for purposes of this book. The mission is a driving force for every team, group, and individual in the school. The topic of norms was briefly introduced in Chapter 3 as a way of establishing a set of agreements that can be referenced as a building block toward a trusting culture. Those would be norms that describe ways of interacting with each other and mindsets or attitudes individuals will emulate to help create a sense of safety and reduce the perceived risks of open, honest communication and discussion. Every team or group creates its own norms, based on its purpose, its members' styles and needs, and their shared (or not) history. Some norms refer to structures and procedures like the communication protocol in Figure 4.2. Here are some norm statements:

- Start and end on time; plan and take breaks.
- Come prepared with agenda, materials, and input.
- Start each meeting by updating resolution or progress.

Figure 4.3   Our Common Language

MISSION

Purpose   Function
Philosophy   Belief statements
Vision   Foundation
Trust   Commitments

GOALS

Objectives   Results
Targets   Guidelines
                           Improvement needs

STRATEGIES

Methods   Tactics
Plans   Actions
Interventions   Programs
Approaches   Techniques

DATA

Test scores   Measures
Evaluations   Performance
Criteria   Results
                           Observations
Proof
                           Indicators
Evidence   Perceptions

ACTION PLANS

Network   Road map
Details   Timelines
Steps   Implementation
Key Questions

TEAM VISIT

Collaboration   Feedback
Validation   Focus
Evaluation   Future Projections
Data   Updates

- Create a parking lot or use stick-on notes to identify things for future discussion but not detour from agenda topic.
- Clarify next steps, determine assignments, identify next agenda topics, and debrief parking lot items before adjourning.

Chapter 10 provides one complete set of working norms and some additional examples and discusses how norms support positive dynamics and productive data work.

Norms apply to every meeting of a team or group. Protocols are activities or processes used for specific purposes, depending on the agenda. A protocol is simply a process to use to achieve a purpose. The greater the history of failed initiatives or mistrust in an organization, the more valuable it is to rely on a prearranged process or activity to guide group work. Protocols can also increase equitable participation by assuring that all voices are heard. This book contains both long and short, formal and informal processes and activities that serve as protocols because they are preplanned and facilitated. Protocols like the Data Discussion Chart (Figure 4.4) are scaffolds to support the work of teams, particularly as they discuss data and share their students' work.

Data Discussion Chart

Although schools now have many kinds of data available and it is fairly common practice to summarize data for some type of plan development, there are still some challenges around "where to start" and "how to express what I want to say about the data." There are also two challenges about action related to data: discussing the situation but not taking *any* action or the converse, which is jumping to conclusions and actions too quickly. Figure 4.4 provides a template to jump-start a data discussion by reviewing where the data came from, how it was collected, why it was gathered, and the type of results that would be desirable or targets that were set.

Another purpose of a protocol is to convey or remind participants of key concepts in the work they are doing. The headings across the top stress that we must start with FACTS and constrain ourselves from immediately jumping to interpretation. In fact, there's a reminder that first review of only one set of data may *seem* to tell one story, when use of multiple sources of data and further study may challenge those initial impressions. The two columns under that first heading also make the important point that when we look at data, we must resist the tendency to jump into deficit mode. The search for results to *celebrate* is important not only for morale, but so that successful practices will be sustained and not lost in the search for new strategies to address the concerns that usually arise as well.

Part of not rushing to interpretation is acknowledging that there are limitations to any set of data. Some of the negative beliefs about data expressed in Chapter 2 can be surfaced with these questions: What do the data *not* tell us? What *else* do we need to find out? The last column provides a place to capture ideas that surface about what *might* need to change. This honors those ideas but signals the importance of further study of other data sources and comparison to evidence-based practices before committing to a course of action.

Figure 4.4 Data Discussion Chart

Before looking at our data, reflect on:

How was the data collected?

Why?

What would we want to see?

FACTS What do these data seem to tell us?		What do they *not* tell us? What else do we need to find out?	What needs for change *might* arise from these data? Possible Changes for Further Study
Celebrations	Concerns		

Sentence Stems and Question Prompts

Sentence stems can help newer team members build confidence to voice their insights and ideas. The following prompts can be useful in discussion and in summarizing academic data for others. Chapter 5 provides similar prompts for discussing other kinds of data.

- The percentage of students proficient and above in ____ on the ____ improved from ____ to ____.
- Our mean score on the ____ improved from the ____ percentile to the ____ percentile.
- The average gain per student from last fall to this spring was ____ points.

Prompts for large-scale assessments could include the following:

- On which standards are we making the most progress? Some progress?
- On which standards do we have ongoing challenges?
- Which standards do we consider most critical for long-term success in school and beyond?
- Do all of our student groups show evidence of the progress we're making? If not, describe differences.
- Do all of our student groups experience the same general challenges? If not, describe differences.

A third set of prompts can be helpful when more experienced group members and/or administrators want to focus attention on particular aspects of the data:

- Wow! I'm thrilled about the (results, gain, increase) I see in this data from the ____. What do you think made that possible?
- Did you notice ____ when you looked at this data from the ____? What are your thoughts about that?
- I'm concerned about ____ as shown by ____ and I wonder if ____. What do you think it might mean?
- I'm puzzled by this data from the ____ because it doesn't seem to match with ____. What ideas do you have about that?

These questions focus attention on the facts without blame or judgment. They solicit multiple viewpoints and ideas and strengthen trust and risk-taking by encouraging reflection and honoring all ideas and possible interpretations.

INTERDEPENDENCE OF CULTURE AND STRUCTURE

So what comes first: the culture or the structures? It's like asking the same about chickens and eggs. Structures can be created, people can show up and act nice and then go away, but nothing has changed in the culture.

On the other hand, a culture can't become more collaborative without there being settings that provide time and colleagues to work with.

In the last two chapters about beliefs and fear or safety, group activities were provided. That means this work can't be done all alone—structures are a way to bring partners to a table. Providing new structures will not guarantee a change in culture, but *not* providing structures *will* assure that no culture change occurs. One of the key findings Louis, Leithwood, Wahlstrom, and Anderson (2010) noted in their study was that leadership practices considered instructionally helpful by high-performing principals and teachers included "creating structures and opportunities for teachers to collaborate" (p. 66). Little ones do not learn how to "play nice in the sandbox" if there is no sandbox.

Chapter 5

You Get More Excited About Data When . . . You See Faces in It

"I don't want to lump kids into categories." "Students aren't just numbers." "I want to focus on my own students." These are some of the statements educators have made when asked why they might be reluctant to use data (Chapter 1). They are all expressing a common theme of knowing students as real people, being able to put faces with the numbers, and looking at results within relationships. They also represent the dual perspectives of value statements like "Every adult is responsible for every child" versus "I need to focus intently on the specific students assigned to me this year." The value statement about "every" adult and child represents the culture of collective responsibility stressed in Chapter 2 on beliefs. The second reflects the passion we want every teacher to have for the students they face each day. Collaborative structures like those described in Chapter 4 must be used effectively and consistently to keep both flames burning. The Administrative Team has a critical responsibility as standard-bearers in the school to model and nurture the awareness of the whole. The Data Team supports the Shared Leadership Team in looking at the whole school and identifying common needs that must be addressed through schoolwide planning (Chapter 7). Teaching Teams drill most deeply into the specific needs of the students in their classrooms and repeatedly instruct, assess, analyze, and intervene. At both levels, it's crucial to remember that data is *not* just test scores but includes a greater array of information and two other audiences for the data: students themselves and the families who entrust them to us.

SEEING FACES OF DIVERSITY AND EQUITY

The importance of disaggregating data to examine the success of groups of students emerged as part of the civil rights movement, long before the No Child Left Behind Act (NCLB). It would continue to be a moral imperative even if the Every Student Succeeds Act (ESSA) didn't continue to require it. How to display, discuss, and plan from this data requires both accuracy and sensitivity. It must be represented in ways that make awareness of the truth unavoidable but handled carefully so that it is not misused. Figures 5.1

Figure 5.1   Symbolic Display of Student Demographics by Race

Whom Do We Serve?

Asian 1.7%   Latino 15.3%   Caucasian 67.7%   African-American 15.0%   Native American 0.4%

through 5.4 present a set of images that made the reality of achievement gaps very clear in a district that was predominately white and middle class. The figures create a symbolic display of how the percentages at the bottom would look if a single classroom of twenty represented the district's general demographics. If this "typical" classroom was represented racially (Figure 5.1), there would be three African American students and three Hispanic students. Asian and Native American proportions are so low that they would not be represented in this particular display and that is intentionally addressed in the discussion. The first round of discussion would focus on predictions and observations. For example, before showing Figure 5.1, ask, "When you think about all the students we serve, what do you predict the distribution is by race?" Then explain the symbolism of the figures and allow time for reflection or "elbow" discussion of what they notice and how it compares to their predictions—and why they might have been more or less accurate. Figure 5.2 shows the "typical" classroom when disaggregated by socioeconomic status (SES). The image of a single dollar is used to represent each of the seven of twenty students who would qualify to receive free or reduced-price meals. Similar predictions and observations would be elicited and the participants might be asked, "If this is the typical classroom, what would 'equitable success' in high school look like?" (The group should identify that equitable success would assure

Figure 5.2 Symbolic Display of Student Demographics by Socioeconomic Status

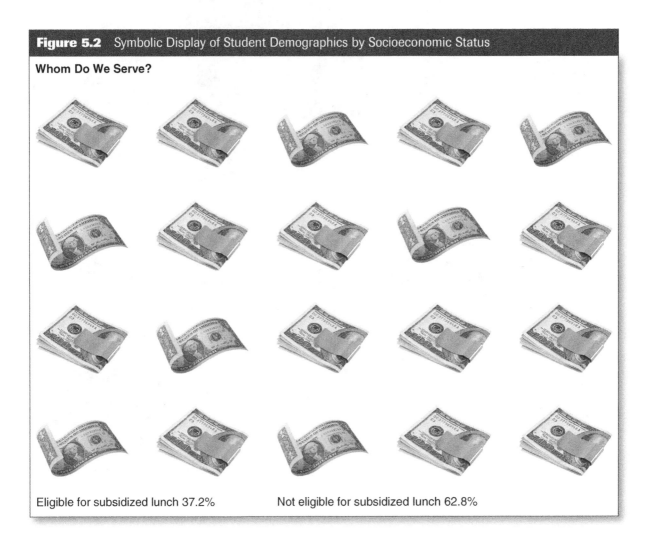

Whom Do We Serve?

Eligible for subsidized lunch 37.2%   Not eligible for subsidized lunch 62.8%

Figure 5.3   Symbolic Display of Student Success by Race

How Are They Doing?

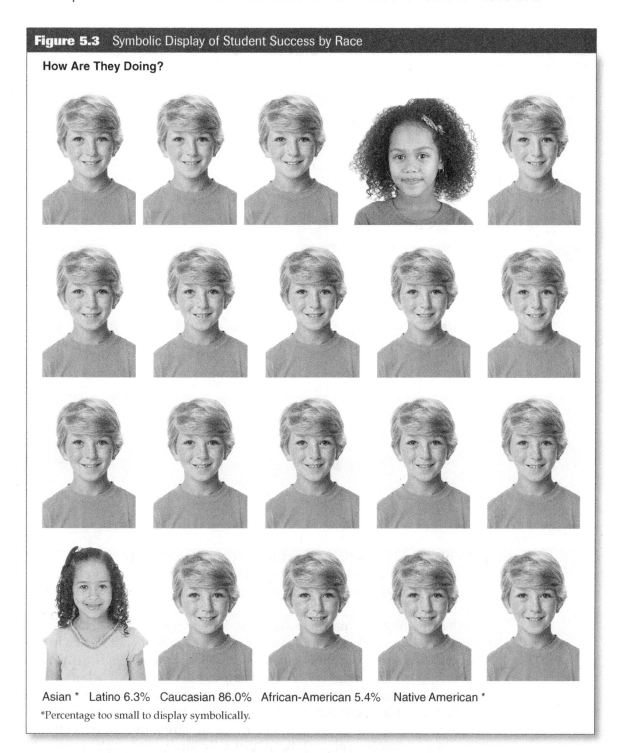

Asian *   Latino 6.3%   Caucasian 86.0%   African-American 5.4%   Native American *

*Percentage too small to display symbolically.

similar distributions of students reaching proficiency and graduation.) Figures 5.3 and 5.4 represent the "success rate" of the district through symbolism of the faces of those who reach proficiency on the high school test. When asked to compare, participants will note that there were *six* students of color and now there are only *two*. In comparison with *seven* students eligible for subsidized lunch in the overall population, there are only *three* in the symbolic display of proficient high school students. As team member representatives from across a district discussed this type of data, there were comments and questions like "So that's what disproportionality

Figure 5.4   Symbolic Display of Student Success by Socioeconomic Status

How Are They Doing?

Eligible for subsidized lunch 15.6%   Not eligible for subsidized lunch 84.4%

looks like" and "What happened to the poor and minority students?" and "My school doesn't look like that, so some schools in the district must have even more minority and low-income students. No wonder they need more support staff."

After the obvious messages from the four figures were discussed, the small percentage of Asian and Native American students not shown in the faces was addressed with this question: "Looking back at Figure 5.1, who are our 'invisible' students?" This prompted awareness of where these students were enrolled and what support they received. For example, two schools had larger percentages of Asian students and some specific programs in place, but the Native American students were scattered throughout schools and had been virtually unnoticed—which had to change. (This reality became more prevalent during the NCLB years when accountability measures were not applied unless the school had a certain minimum number of students per disaggregated group. In one way, this was more fair to schools, but the consequence is that individual students still present in their classrooms may have become even more "invisible.")

Another way of looking at disaggregated data visually is shown in Figure 5.5. A school using results from a national test separated scores of "all" by SES using the traditional measure of qualification for free or reduced lunch. This data display provides context for the data at the top,

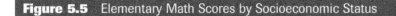

Figure 5.5 Elementary Math Scores by Socioeconomic Status

All students in Grades 2–5 take the standardized test every October. These are the results for this year's students in each grade. Qualification for free or reduced- price lunches is used to identify students as having lower socioeconomic status (SES). The percentile rank indicates that our students scored higher than such a percentage of students taking the test nationwide.

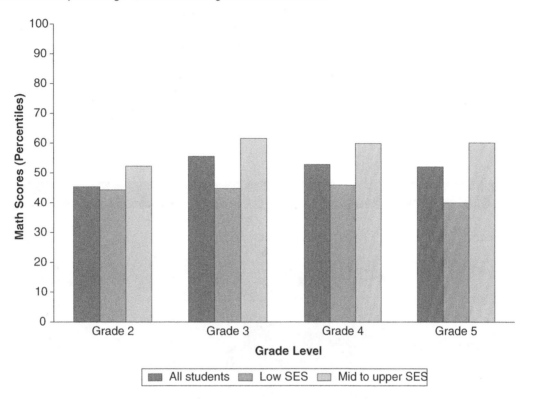

Strengths:
1. The means of math scores for all students in Grades 3, 4, and 5 are above the 50th percentile.
2. The mean math scores for middle and upper SES students are above the 50th percentile at all grade levels.

Concerns:
1. The mean for all second-grade students is below the 50th percentile.
2. At all grade levels, lower SES students score below middle and upper SES students. The discrepancy ranges from 7 percentiles on the second-grade test to 20 percentiles on the fifth-grade test.
3. It appears from this data that lower SES students fall further behind in math as they progress through the grades.

and a synthesis of findings from their analysis at the bottom. What they realized was that they had been fairly comfortable with the overall success of the school because scores were above the 50th percentile, or in their conversations "above average." What they had been missing was the "income gap" and that it was wider at each subsequent grade level. This new knowledge shifted the focus of the school improvement plan and shaped professional development offerings.

The teacher who was quoted at the beginning of the chapter didn't want to lump kids into categories. She was trying to assure that viewers would avoid making assumptions about students based on the groups they might be counted in. Disaggregated data can create a tendency for schools to make decisions and plans based on assumptions and generalizations around identifiable groups of students, without checking those assumptions. Figure 5.6 shows a pie chart of reading scores with a distribution of 20 percent advanced, 31 percent proficient, 31 percent scoring at basic, and 18 percent below basic. This was an urban school with a diverse population, and teachers viewing this distribution were moving quickly to an assumption that they needed to learn about instructional strategies and remediation programs that work best with African American males. They were surprised when the "Below Basic" segment of the pie was sliced three more times—breaking out the struggling readers by gender, income, and race/ethnicity. They were surprised to note that the low readers were not overwhelmingly male as expected. They were primarily—though not exclusively—of lower SES. In fact, the struggling reader group actually represented a racial distribution almost identical to the overall student

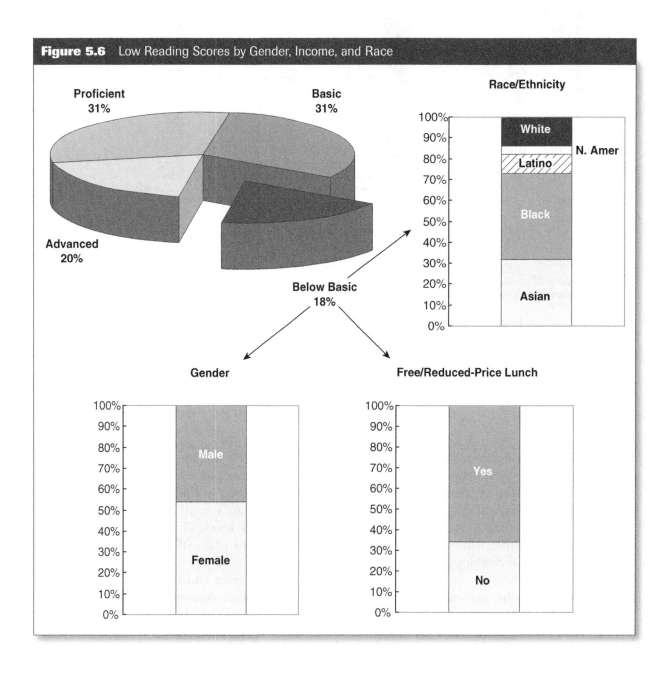

Figure 5.6 Low Reading Scores by Gender, Income, and Race

population of the district. Should staff know about and provide specific help for African American males? Of course. Should every African American male be *presumed to need* it? No.

WATCHING FACES OVER TIME

The educators who were anxious to know more about teaching reading to African American males had a positive intent. They were willing to learn and try new things. They were attempting to become more culturally responsive in their instruction. But they needed to dig for more detail in their data. In the same way, it's important to assure that one-time data is balanced with a look at the faces over time to accurately identify trends like the widening gap from grade to grade revealed in Figure 5.5. Chapter 1 noted that "monitoring rates of progress over time—student and cohort" is one of the uses of data associated with high-performing schools. The data in Figure 5.7 is from four years of sixth-grade students, so each bar does represent a different set of students but with no major changes in demographics in the student population. Increases in the percentage of students reaching or surpassing the proficiency score would be primarily due to the learning opportunities created in the school and could be used to celebrate progress over time.

Figure 5.8 illustrates another approach to identifying trends over time—through middle school and into high school. These graphs compare four different cohorts of students, using the percentage of students meeting standard in fifth grade with scores of the same student cohort three years later as they finished eighth grade—and the scores of exiting eighth graders compared to their scores on the high school test in eleventh grade. Middle school teachers were chagrined to notice that, except for writing, their students were not making gains. As discussion continued, it was finally noted that one new teacher in eighth grade had been much more demanding in the quantity of writing assigned to students. That information validated the need for more stress on writing at all grade levels.

Longitudinal data is also needed for individual students in order to "drill down for student- and skill-specific data" and "plan forward as students rise—to respond to individual skill gaps" as noted in critical uses of data in Chapter 1. So many school-level reports are generated by the state and testing companies that student-specific data is sometimes found only in the reports to parents. I've seen some schools literally retrieve and photocopy the parent summaries before they are sent home. Data warehousing systems now simplify the next steps needed, which are to move the data forward from the test last spring to the teachers who now serve the students in the fall. Only in this way can schools plan forward and target remediation and support programs for maximum effect. When the school year starts, teachers should have access to a spreadsheet for each class. For example, Figure 5.9 provides a profile of a class of fourth graders and describes their language status, gender, as well as whether they are served in Title I, resource special education, or gifted and talented programs. Their test scores from the past two years are compared in reading and overall language. The comparison of these two years of performance data

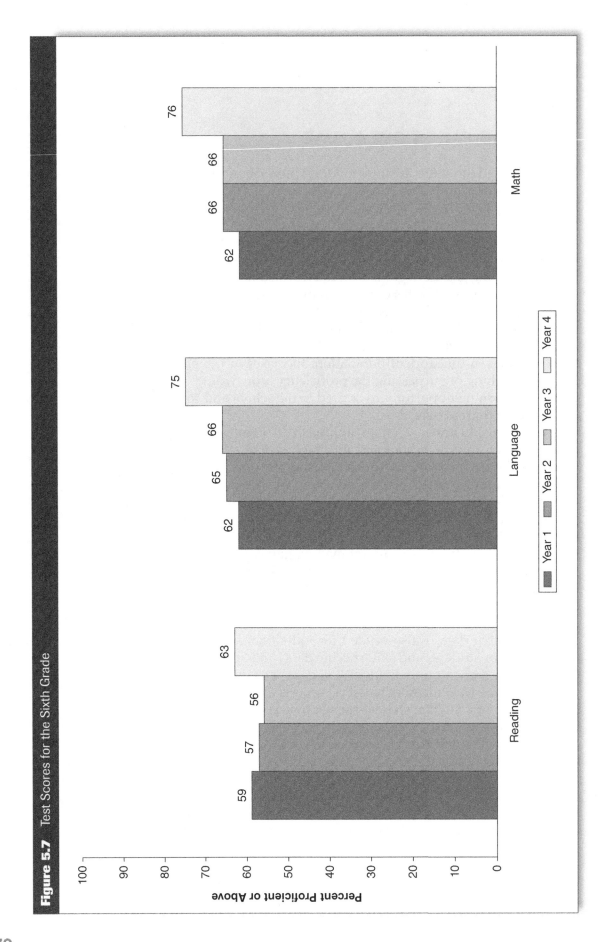

Figure 5.7 Test Scores for the Sixth Grade

Figure 5.8 Three-Year Changes for Grade-Level Cohorts

Percent Meeting Standard 2010–2011 to 2013–2014

	Reading			Math			Writing		
	2010–2011	2013–2014	Difference	2010–2011	2013–2014	Difference	2010–2011	2013–2014	Difference
Grade 5 to 8 Cohort	64.2	56.5	– 7.7	44.8	39.2	– 5.6	39.8	61.8	+ 22.0
Grade 8 to 11 Cohort	55.3	64.7	+ 9.4	36.5	45.3	+ 8.8	45.9	61.3	+ 15.4

Percent Meeting Standard 2009–2010 to 2012–2013

	Reading			Math			Writing		
	2009–2010	2012–2013	Difference	2009–2010	2012–2013	Difference	2009–2010	2012–2013	Difference
Grade 5 to 8 Cohort	64.2	52.2	– 12.0	40.4	39.3	– 1.1	48.4	54.2	+ 5.8
Grade 8 to 11 Cohort	50.6	72.7	+ 22.1	33.0	51.0	+ 18.0	35.6	54.8	+ 20.2

Figure 5.9 Fourth-Grade Class Profile

4th Grade Class Profile

ELL = English Language Learner   EO = English Only   RD = redesignated *Fluent English Proficient*

Student	ELL Level	Gender	Title I Y = yes	RSP Y = yes	GATE Y = yes	SAT9 NCE Rdg 2010	2011	+/-	SAT9 NCE Lang 2010	2011	+/-
1	FEP	M				41	41	0	29	31	+2
2	ELL	F				52	54	+2	64	48	−16
3	ELL	M	Y			29	35	+6	29	31	+3
4	RD	F				37	54	+17	47	45	−2
5	EO	M			Y	65	67	+2	67	50	−17
6	ELL	F				40	36	−4	29	35	+6
7	EO	F				46	35	−9	45	40	−5
8	ELL	F	Y	Y		19	13	−6	20	29	+9
9	FEP	M				21	32	+9	13	39	+23
10	EO	F				35	35	0	44	52	+8
11	ELL	F				38	44	+6	51	48	−3
12	EO	M				33	48	+15	43	50	+7
13	FEP	M	Y	Y		20	1	−19	13	18	+5
14	ELL	M	Y			36	47	+11	44	45	+1
15	RD	M				45	39	−6	64	46	−18
16	RD	M				39	41	+3	48	48	0
17	RD	F				44	41	−3	49	52	+3
18	ELL	F	Y			32	37	+5	32	37	+5
19	FEP	F	Y			29	35	+6	43	31	−12
20	FEP	M				42	28	−14	23	20	−3
21	RD	F				47	45	−2	38	45	+7
22	FEP	F	Y			30	37	+7	41	42	+1
23	RD	F			Y	65	49	−16	54	48	−6
24	EO	F			Y	65	70	+5	54	62	+8
25	ELL	F	Y			35	32	−3	38	39	+1
26	EO	M			Y	58	73	+15	47	56	+9
27	EO	F	Y	Y		21	15	−6	25	10	−15
28	FEP	M	Y			29	39	+10	38	50	+12
29	RD	M	Y			32	42	+10	32	48	+16

Data Analysis

Demographics
24% EO
27% ELL
24% RD
24% FEP
37% Title I
10% RSP
13% GATE

Reading
37% dropped
78% = RD/FEP/EO
66% = female

Language
34% dropped
80% = RD/EO/FEP
70% = female

allow the teacher to see which students may need most support within the classroom. This profile also alerts the classroom teacher about further information that will be needed and collaboration that should occur with specialists on staff so that everyone's work with the student will be aligned and optimally effective.

The district or the school Data Team should make sure these spreadsheets are placed directly into the hands of teachers, especially the new or less experienced. Implementation of a new data warehousing system may provide instant access and capacity for teachers to produce this data set themselves, but technical capability does not automatically translate into human capacity and motivation. Once teachers learn how to use this information and find that it is valuable and useful, they become interested in how they can generate it themselves and what other analysis they can do from their desktops.

Student-specific information is needed at the start of the year to convey expectations about instruction and to utilize resources effectively. It's an expectation that teachers personalize and differentiate instruction, which requires specific knowledge of what students do (and don't) need. When this information is not readily available, two bad things may happen. Days and weeks of instructional time can be devoted to "pretests," which yield information already generated somewhere else and delay the introduction of new content. Or the course syllabus simply rolls right along, with no knowledge of students' previous learning until the first midterm exam yields winners and losers on the grading curve. The specific information by skill for each individual student must be made readily available to teachers. The expectation that this data is used to allocate instructional time, differentiate instruction, and guide flexible grouping must be clearly articulated.

In addition to the "entry data" provided at the start of the year, every teacher also needs a spreadsheet that lists student names on the left and critical skills (e.g., standards, critical learning targets, grade-level expectations) for the grade or course across the top. Annotations in the cells on this spreadsheet will represent mastery as well as specific skill gaps for specific students. Chapter 6 includes the story of how staff at Panther Lake Elementary School created their own data system in order to have ongoing, detailed information available about every student.

FEATURES ON THE FACES ARE MORE THAN SCORES

The educator who stated that "students aren't just numbers" was admirably reminding us of our responsibility to see students as individuals and to look at more information about them than just their academic results. Throughout the NCLB era, the Association for Supervision and Curriculum Development (ASCD) maintained an initiative focused on the "whole child." A welcome change brought by ESSA is inclusion of at least one indicator of student success or school support in addition to the dashboard of results from the state test. Examples might be access to advanced coursework, fine arts, and regular physical education; data on school climate and safety; or support provisions such as bullying prevention or availability of counselors or nurses. These measures become part of the data monitored and used in school planning. ESSA also specifies that districts allocate 20 percent of Title IV funds to programs that support a "well-rounded" education, such as counseling, music and arts, accelerated learning, foreign languages, history, and environmental education. Another 20 percent of Title IV must be directed to programs that support safe and healthy students, which could include mental health services, nutrition, and physical education.

Previous sections have stressed the need for both whole-school and classroom level data related to race/ethnicity, gender, economic status, and identification for special programs and services. But to really know our students collectively and individually, we need to examine other aspects of their school experience. Among these are attendance, behavior, and engagement. Students' own observations and opinions can also provide valuable input for planning school improvement and are discussed further in the chapter.

Attendance

Overall attendance rates are typically tracked and discussed in schools, often with the admonition that "they can't learn if they're not even here." A more fine-grained example of use at the school level is the attendance data provided in Figure 5.10. At this school, the issue of whether to continue open or closed campus had been batted about for months. Arguments raged about rights of students versus risks of driving, nutritious lunch menus versus drive-through junk food, and supervision versus duty-free noons. When the team had heard enough of these complaints, they began to ask themselves whether there was any information that could shed light on this issue. That's when attendance data became meaningful—not as an aggregated percentage of all students for the whole year but analyzed by period of the day. Based on this analysis, staff voted for closed campus. They also noted the increased absences during last hour and began to explore possible explanations including scheduling of study halls and implications of student employment.

Tschannen-Moran (2014) wrote that students' identification with school has demonstrated strong relationships to students' trust in teachers and to the students' achievement. Students' identification with the school includes whether they value the purposes of school and whether they feel a sense of belonging or fitting in. Both of these relate, in turn, to their feelings of safety and their attendance. Who would want to spend time in a place that feels unsafe and with no one to trust?

A high school principal surfaced this connection when he posted a large chart of student names at a staff meeting. He simply asked teachers to cruise by the list as they entered the meeting and put their initials next to the name of any student with whom they had a relationship. Later in the meeting, he stood by the chart on which initials were sparse and explained that these students were their chronic absentees and asked them to use the think-pair-share protocol to reflect on this data. After the meeting, he moved the chart to the teachers' lounge. Within a few days, there were initials by every name.

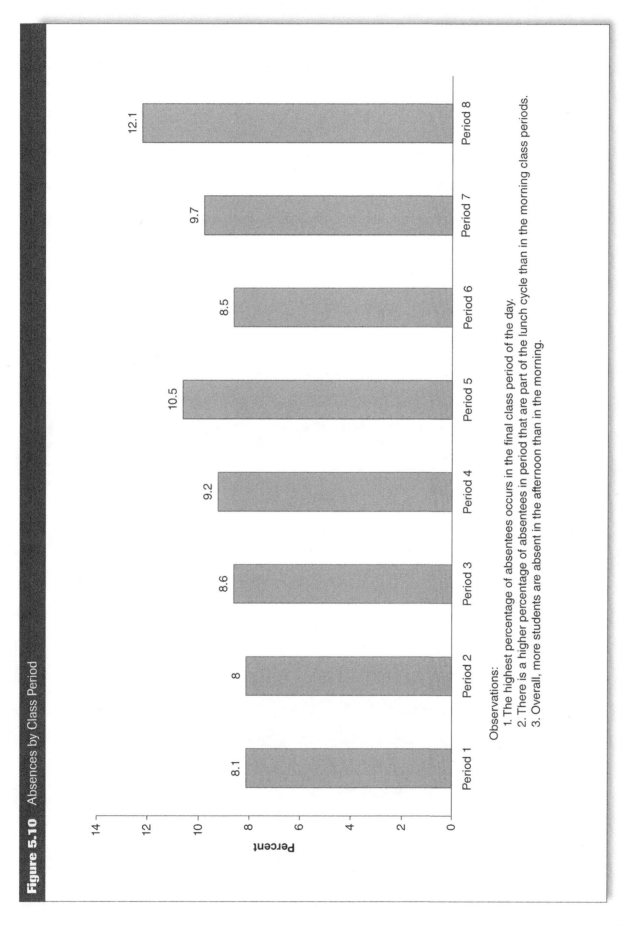

Figure 5.10 Absences by Class Period

Observations:
1. The highest percentage of absentees occurs in the final class period of the day.
2. There is a higher percentage of absentees in period that are part of the lunch cycle than in the morning class periods.
3. Overall, more students are absent in the afternoon than in the morning.

Discipline

States require districts to report numbers of suspensions and expulsions, and that is important data to consider at the local level as well. However, the local data will include more types of disciplinary actions and more detail about who, what, when, and where. For example, staff members at one school were concerned about the number of students sent to the office for disciplinary reasons. They wondered whether student behavior was getting worse, whether the offenses actually merited the principal's attention, and what relationship there might be to the new discipline policy that had been developed the summer before. They analyzed the reasons for referral stated on the "pink slips" that students carried to the office and created the Pareto chart, which lists causes in descending order (see Figure 5.11). First, they noticed that the greatest number of discipline referrals was related to violating school rules outlined in their new policy. This discovery led them to reconsider the consequences in the policy and build in more responsibility at the classroom level before sending students out of the room. They also acknowledged that they could have been more conscientious about teaching the new rules to students and communicating them to parents. As they talked about the second highest occurrence as classroom disruption, they began to consider the need for professional

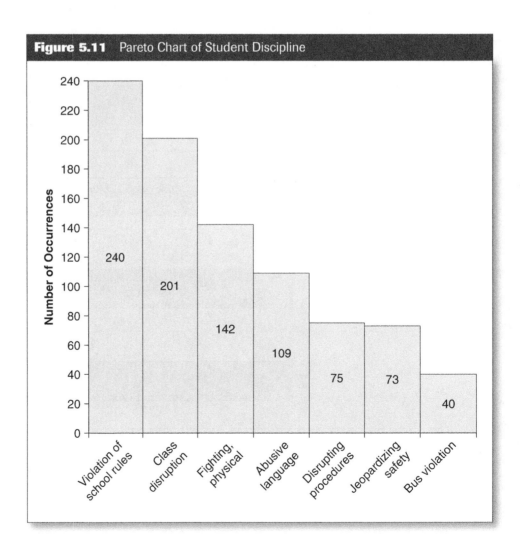

Figure 5.11   Pareto Chart of Student Discipline

development related to proactive strategies to manage student behavior. About this time, they noticed that the cause they were most worried about (physical violence) was not the most frequent problem, and when they compared it with previous years, fighting had not increased at all. Of the 880 discipline occurrences they analyzed, about half fell into the first two categories and could be addressed with different strategies on the part of the adults, rather than tougher consequences on the kids.

A middle school principal (Brennan, 2015) came to a realization that the students who were failing classes and state assessments were the same ones who were often out of class for discipline referrals, suspensions, or just absent. She knew that teachers cared about the students but also realized that the cultural differences between staff and students might be preventing students from interpreting the caring messages accurately. Each teacher was assigned to be in the hallway between periods and interact positively with students—commenting on activities or just greeting them by name. Teachers were taught how to help students use specific skills for interaction in a group and were encouraged to arrange student seating in groups rather than rows and add more opportunities for participation. At the same time, school practices related to behavior were being reviewed. Changes included more focus on celebrations and positives, and institution of a Principal's Advisory Council composed of twenty students from each level who were chosen because other students followed them—for either good or ill. The principal met with these students and talked about school pride and behavior expectations—and asked for their input on activities the school should offer as options for students. In a third endeavor, staff began to track which students had problems in which classes and realized the need to focus on sixth graders who had come with a history from their elementary schools. The school counselor focused extra effort on these students. Both of these last two examples illustrate how data analysis can increase the focus on the personal faces of students and their needs.

The issue of trust between teachers and students is also connected to how schools handle student behavior. Tschannen-Moran (2014) described the impact of low trust: "Not only is there insufficient safety to support the kinds of risk taking necessary to learn new skills . . . teachers may resort to more rigid forms of discipline and control as well as the use of extrinsic rewards . . . [to get the reward] students may go through the motions of a practice, but those motions may prove to be insufficient to produce an experience of valuing the practice [learning] for its own sake" (p. 163).

Student Engagement

Homework completion is often viewed as an indicator of student learning, and some teachers will advocate strenuously that it should be included in students' grades. Others will acknowledge that it might not be a true measure of learning but that it's part of character and good work habits for school and the future and "proves" engagement. As such, it should be stressed and the data monitored and consequences applied. In the middle school just described, teachers realized that homework expectations could create strain in already tense home situations and revised the building policy to refer to it as "home practice" that was often not even recorded. By implementing practices that addressed both academic instruction and student behavior, the school's test scores remained higher than those of other schools with lower percentages of students living in poverty.

Leithwood, Harris, and Strauss (2010) pointed out that leaders of turnaround schools "not only took into account the academic needs of their students but also viewed students' emotional needs as critical factors in the school's improvement efforts" (p. 159). That view is also held by Tschannen-Moran (2014), who stressed that educators must start with "the underlying assumption that as social beings, children do not need to be coerced into wanting to be in positive relationships with their teachers and peers—they are hardwired to need these relationships. Some students, however, need assistance in finding appropriate and effective strategies for establishing and maintaining these connections" (p. 174).

Participation in extracurriculars is a source of data that can reveal a level of attachment students feel toward the school. Datnow and Park (2015) told about a principal who created a list of students who were not enrolled in any extracurricular activities. Teachers were asked to reach out to them and help get them more involved in the school.

In another approach, Sterrett (2012) described intentional creation of a sense of community within classrooms during the day. Morning meetings that include a greeting time, group activity, and a morning message build community and also maximize learning time. They provide students a safe structure to engage with each other and the teacher and an opportunity for teachers to know their interests and connect to them during instruction. The importance of students' emotional connections to school has also prompted a resurgence of conversation about how to use advisory periods in meaningful and intentional ways. Morning meetings and advisories also provide opportunities for teachers to share small details about their own lives outside of school, further building relationships.

HEARING THE VOICES FROM THE FACES

One of the twenty ways high-performing schools work with data (Chapter 1) is to use both objective and subjective data appropriately. Chapter 1 included reminders about *in*appropriate use of assessment data, and the need to confirm our interpretations with more detailed analysis or comparison to other sources has been stressed. Perceptual data—from surveys, interviews, focus groups, and the like—also needs to be analyzed carefully and used appropriately. It can be especially valuable in two ways. It adds to the knowledge base about the school, and it points the way to possible solutions. Perceptual data is needed to answer our questions about whether students feel connected, whether teachers collaborate, and whether parents and community members have confidence in their local schools. It's a challenge to display and summarize this data from surveys, interviews, and focus groups. For example, if the survey is lengthy, don't report the data by listing all the survey items and all the responses with a number or percentage next to them. (If the raw data goes on page after page, the survey was probably too long to start with!) Data Teams have recently found Google Forms to be their most useful tool in designing simple surveys and creating visual summaries of the results. As the Data Team reviews all the data, they can provide a synopsis of which items had the highest and lowest levels of agreement and satisfaction. What items received the most positive responses? The least positive responses? When a survey has been given to more than one group—different grade levels, staff and students, students and parents—ask, In what areas was there highest agreement among the respondents? On what items was the greatest discrepancy?

Interviews and focus groups rely on open-ended questions, and surveys often conclude with an opportunity for comments. All comments should be available for review if a participant has the time and interest, but data discussions can be expedited if the Data Team identifies the major themes and most frequent comments.

Hearing From Students

Students are intimately involved with and aware of the school's needs and successes; at the same time, they are still rarely integrated into analysis, decision-making, and planning processes to meet those needs. Their voices should be directly elicited so they can provide input into those school actions. Figure 5.12 is a Pareto chart that shows the percentage of students in an elementary school who answered yes to a short yes-or-no survey of 17 items. "Grown-ups at school care about me" received the highest affirmation, and items about the playground and lunchtime received the least. This arrangement makes it visually simple to identify cause for celebration as well as topics for further study.

By middle and high school, students should be guided through conversations with adults, self-assessment, and group activities to develop an understanding of their learning styles and what they need to provide for themselves—or ask from their teachers—as they take increased responsibility for their learning. They also become an excellent source of data on prevalent teaching practices, as sought with the survey in Figure 5.13.

An alternative to formal surveys are short, informal queries that may be general in nature or may be developed to gain more detail about a specific topic. These five questions can provide fascinating information when used with students in focus groups, interviews, or advisory periods. If time is limited, just ask one or two.

- When you are in class and you are really learning, what is happening?
- When you are in class and having trouble, what is happening?
- What is the one thing that would really help you learn?
- If you could change one thing about our school, what would it be?
- What is one thing the teachers should know about you?

Hearing From Staff

Chapter 4 provided a protocol for assuring that regular feedback loops were established and provided a channel for every staff member's voice to

Figure 5.12 Results of Student Survey

Percentage Agreement

Grown-ups at school care about me.	95
Teachers use different ways to help me learn.	93
My teachers tell me when I do good work.	88
School is a friendly place.	88
I like subjects I learn about.	85
Classroom rules are fair.	85
School rules are fair.	83
I feel safe at school.	83
There are fun things to do for indoor recess.	80
Playground rules are fair.	80
I like to come to school.	80
My school is nice and clean.	78
Lunchroom rules are fair.	77
My classroom is big enough.	75
Bus rules are fair.	67
The playground has enough to do.	64
I have time to eat lunch.	59

Figure 5.13   Student Learning Survey

Please take a few minutes to complete the following student learning survey. This information will help us better understand our strengths as well as identify areas where we might be able to improve our work in the classroom.

For the period just concluding, did the teacher share the learning goals for the class with you? ___yes ___no

For the period just concluding, was there a summary of ideas at the end of the period? ___yes ___no

For the period just concluding, rate the class from 1 (*low*) to 10 (*high*) on the following goal: "Classes at BHS will engage students and lead to deep understanding about significant ideas."

1   2   3   4   5   6   7   8   9   10

For the period just concluding, use the categories below and approximate the amount of time you spent during the class period engaged in the following types of learning activities. Respond to as many as apply for <u>the preceding period only</u>. Your <u>total for all items should be 100 minutes</u>. If a certain type of teaching or learning did not occur this period, you should circle the "0."

I listened to the teacher talk/lecture and took notes.

100   90   80   70   60   50   40   30   20   10   0

I worked independently on a short- or long-term research-based project.

100   90   80   70   60   50   40   30   20   10   0

I answered questions on a worksheet or from a textbook.

100   90   80   70   60   50   40   30   20   10   0

I participated in a class discussion.

100   90   80   70   60   50   40   30   20   10   0

I worked on an assignment with a small group of students.

100   90   80   70   60   50   40   30   20   10   0

I worked independently on a daily assignment.

100   90   80   70   60   50   40   30   20   10   0

I watched another student or small group give a performance or participated in one myself.

100   90   80   70   60   50   40   30   20   10   0

I did lab work or learned by experimenting with an idea.

100   90   80   70   60   50   40   30   20   10   0

I was given free time.

100   90   80   70   60   50   40   30   20   10   0

I was off task and not doing what the teacher expected me to do.

100   90   80   70   60   50   40   30   20   10   0

Please give your opinion about which teaching and learning strategies are most effective? Why?

be heard by the Shared Leadership Team in its deliberations. Staff members should also be included in surveys or focus groups on specific topics that arise and need more quantifiable data. Open-ended questions can also guide professional development planning. A district in Washington State used these questions for teachers struggling with implementation of a new approach to teaching math:

- From your perspective, what is the biggest difference between [the new program] and the way you have taught math in the past?
- What aspects of implementing [the math program] are going well or best for you?
- What do you observe about your students' experiences and reactions with math this year?
- In general, what are your biggest concerns about using [the math materials] right now?
- What specific aspects of implementation are problematic for you at this time?
- What kinds of help do you need to continue to be more effective in your use of [the math program]? What would specific support look like for you personally?

It was interesting to discover that concerns and needs varied from grade level to grade level, but at each grade level, the concerns and needs were similar across all schools. From this data, it was possible to plan grade-specific, differentiated support that matched the teachers' needs. Teachers' own responses to the third question—students' experiences and reactions—included increased enthusiasm and more conceptual talk about what they were doing. This data helped keep the focus on students and motivated the teachers to continue their own learning of the strategies.

Hearing From Stakeholders

A good practice is to periodically conduct a general climate survey or locally focused survey of multiple stakeholder groups—for example, students, staff, and families. Figure 5.14 illustrates a way to display perceptual data from various role groups. In this example, a survey of twenty-five items included five items that related to each of five categories: Feelings of Safety, Focus on Teaching and Learning, Individual Help for Students, Fair Rules Consistently Enforced, and Home-School Communication. The detail of responses by item would be available for those interested in an in-depth look. What the data display can capture is a sense of which group is most pleased with which aspect of the school and where there is highest and lowest agreement between the responding groups.

Checking for Understanding

Another important aspect of using subjective data *appropriately* is to avoid assumptions and clarify perceptual data that raises concerns so it can provide helpful insights about how to move forward. Respondents are sharing their reality, and it must be accepted as *real* to them, even if it may be factually inaccurate. Rather than arguing with the data,

Figure 5.14 Survey Responses From Teachers, Students, and Parents

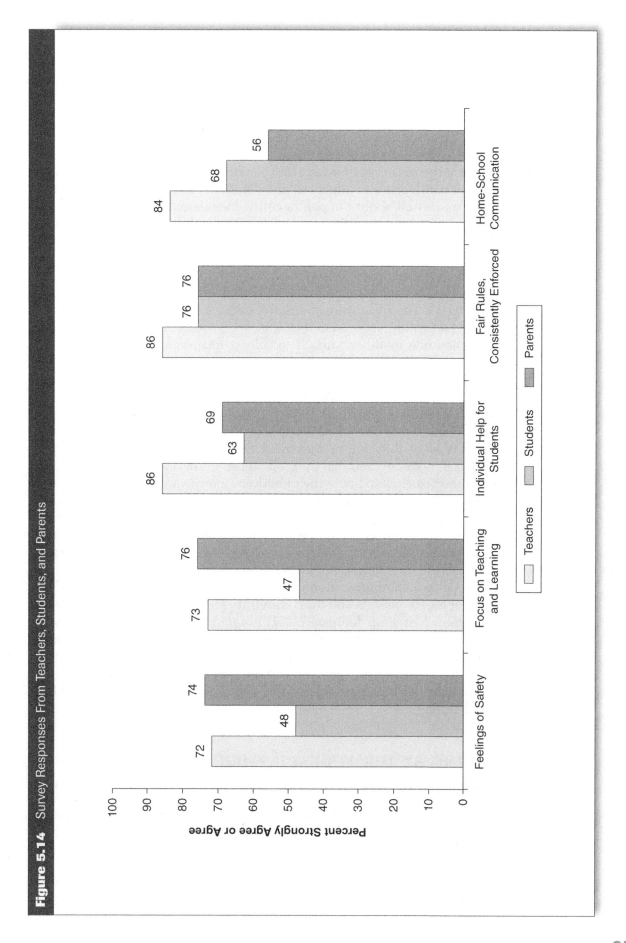

teams must seek to understand. It may be helpful to redirect discussion with prompts like "We know differently . . . but what might have caused them to believe this? What have we not communicated or modeled well?"

For example, a school leadership team had administered a formal survey, based on school effectiveness research, developed by a highly respected consultant group. Most of the responses made sense. There were no surprises except for negative parent responses regarding the format of parent-teacher conferences and "student recognition." They were not too concerned about the parent conference item. Teachers had talked for some time about how they needed to make different arrangements for these important communication opportunities. But they *were* quite distressed about the student recognition item, and they began to list all the ways in which students were recognized for doing good work, demonstrating good behavior, helping others, and so forth. They wondered what more they could do and were about to propose a subcommittee to explore ways to get funding from local businesses to provide more student incentives, when one member said, "I wonder what *parents* thought student recognition means."

After a few moments of silent confusion, a first-year teacher timidly suggested, "Maybe we should ask them." It sounded like a pretty logical next move, and the principal helped identify parents for a focus group, who were invited to come and discuss the items on the parent survey and what they were thinking as they read them. Through the focus group, school leaders discovered that the student recognition that parents wanted was for the principal to know their children's names and for all teachers to get to know even the students who were not in their classes and to address them by name—or at least with more respect than "Hey, kid." The face-to-face communication of a focus group shifted the attention of staff from initiating more extrinsic reward systems to looking at the culture of the school and the interactions between staff and students.

Face-to-face communication is especially needed in schools where the demographics of parents and the community are in sharp contrast with the characteristics of staff. Johnson (2002) pointed out that "those in power often silence the dialogue when those who share the culture of poverty and children of color disagree with proposed solutions" (p. 74). Adults who share the same culture with the students must be engaged in the search for promising practices and program changes to assist their children's learning.

HELPING STUDENTS FACE THEIR LEARNING

Earlier in this chapter, we discussed a spreadsheet on which the teacher would have each student's name and columns for each of the most critical learning goals for the course or grade. Students benefit from having the same information. If we want to change the focus from what I *did* today to what I'm *learning*, students must know what the targets are. Describing student roles in the more specific context of a large-scale literacy initiative in Ontario, Fullan (2009) included these things that students need to be involved in:

- Knowing and understanding what they are expected to learn
- Identifying their own strengths, needs, and interests
- Reflecting on their progress and setting goals
- Taking steps to improve their literacy learning
- Writing nonfiction with ease and coherence
- Advocating for themselves

To fulfill these roles, students would need to know more than the learning targets they are expected to reach. They would also need opportunities to identify their strengths and styles as learners through discussions, strengths inventories, and collections of their accomplishments—both in school and out of school—in success portfolios. They would need a way to track their progress—even the youngest using a simple bar graph of the number of right responses, words recognized, and so on. They would need to know what steps or strategies improve their learning and what the criteria are for writing coherent nonfiction. And they would need to be taught appropriate ways to describe their needs and propose alternatives.

For these purposes, formative assessment is infinitely more appropriate and useful than benchmark/interim or summative tests. Tomlinson (2014) pointed out that students need to understand the role of formative assessment and how it is different from other tests—particularly that errors are expected and that their efforts do not result in a final grade. They need to receive specific feedback from which they can set an immediate next step for practice—whether the feedback is from the teacher or from peers who learn how to help each other.

FACE-TO-FACE WITH FAMILIES

Parents and guardians also need to understand students' learning targets, progress, and various assessment results. Written reports—paper, electronic, and online—are essential and legally required but are completely inadequate to build the trusting partnerships needed to support learners. Chapter 1 referred to this work as "using data in conversations with parents about student performance and programming." Leithwood and colleagues (2010) found that schools making dramatic gains used assessment data as a key factor in raising achievement: "Students and parents now use an e-portal to access individual performance and progress data, and clear information is readily available about using the data to support learning in the home. There is a simple system that everyone understands and uses in the school. Departments use their own data to plan ahead, and these data are shared with students. The system is transparent and clear and used to regularly check progress and identify where interventions and support are needed" (p. 225).

However, Tschannen-Moran (2014) cautioned that these technologies are "more likely to engender trust if their use is preceded by face-to-face communication, telephone communication, or both that establishes rapport with parents, communicates shared goals for student success in both short-term and long-term contexts, and identifies goals for the parent-teacher relationship itself in terms of partnership" (pp. 196–197). This author devoted an entire chapter of *Trust Matters* to the topic of

"Building Bridges of Trust with Families." She explained why trust is so important:

> Research on trust between families and schools has found trust to be positively related to a family's commitment to the school, the school's outreach to parents, and the collective sense of responsibility shared by families and the school . . . when a school community welcomes parents into the school, fosters caring and trusting relationships with parents, honors their participation, and connects with parents through a focus on the children and their learning, parents are then more likely to be involved in the school, with consequent benefits for the students. (Tschannen-Moran, 2014, pp. 203, 207)

She explained that trust is endangered if educators don't follow through on promises or fail to communicate with parents about steps that are being taken. On the other hand, trust is built when parents see that teachers care about their children as individuals, when teachers are "real" and share small bits of information about themselves, and when parents can see that students are making progress. In fact, "whether parents perceive that they have a voice and influence school decisions and whether their children feel a sense of belonging at school both influence parents' trust in a school to a much greater extent than contextual conditions, such as a school's poverty status, size, diverse ethnic composition, and grade level" (Tschannen-Moran, 2014, p. 209). To build these bridges, schools must show some flexibility in working around family schedules and child care issues so that face-to-face communication can occur. And teachers need support to overcome their lack of confidence in their own ability to build these bridges. Many are reassured to know that increasing rapport can be as simple as the tone that intentionally conveys hope and helpfulness, rather than criticism and pessimism.

The work of Bryk and Schneider (2003) on trust in schools bears out the needs for positivity and sensitivity in communicating with parents—especially about data. They cautioned that "because of the class and race differences between school professionals and parents in most urban areas, conditions can be ripe for misunderstanding and distrust. Effective urban schools need teachers who not only know their students well but also have an empathetic understanding of their parents' situations and the interpersonal skills needed to engage adults effectively" (Bryk & Schneider, 2003, p. 45).

Teachers need specific support on how to share data with families. A first step is to promote trusting connections with the families as noted. It is also important to demonstrate how data are handled in safe ways—that student and family privacy is protected, particularly when encouraging them to use electronic systems. A computer lab with staff available to assist will increase the comfort level of parents and guardians trying to access data—and computer(s) must remain available if the school expects families of poverty to access information in this way. In one district, a series of meetings for parents were scheduled at a variety of times and places and provided basic information, such as the meaning of letter grades and course credits and what assessments students would be taking during the year. After the group session, parent advocates (some bilingual) were available to answer questions. They also gathered information about families' preferred communication method—for example, hard copies, e-mail, telephone calls, and their comfort level and access to the electronic system that was demonstrated.

Settings for individual family data discussions must be quiet and private to assure confidentiality. Teachers should let families know all the kinds of data that are available and how to access them but focus the face-to-face discussion on one or two of the most relevant, crucial pieces of data, then invite (and allow time for) family members to raise their questions. Anticipate what their questions may be, and be prepared with short answers free of jargon. Answer all the questions they ask, but don't overload them with more than they ask. Keep the door open for more questions and details as they become more comfortable and curious. Data discussions should always include an exchange of next steps—first what the school will do and how follow-up communication will occur and then what would be helpful as family support. At times when new data is about to be released and discussed, the Data Team or Shared Leadership Team can support teachers by creating a simple protocol to help teachers practice how to focus and share the data in parent-friendly terms.

This chapter has focused on how important it is to "see the faces" in data, hear the voices represented by those faces, and engage in face-to-face conversations about data. All of those exchanges will be easier when data is easy to get and see.

Chapter 6

You Get More Excited About Data When . . . It's Easy to Get

"I'm not sure how to make sense of all these graphs," stated one member of a group discussing conditions that contribute to reluctance to use data. In Chapter 5, the importance of being able to discuss data among staff and with parents was emphasized. While Chapters 2, 3, and 4 focused on culture and structures to support the culture, the focus of this chapter is on some technical points that Data Teams and others must consider as they do preliminary data analysis and prepare it for broader discussion. The phrase "easy to get" in the chapter title has a double meaning. The first part of the chapter promotes ability to understand the data as in "I get it, I understand" or "I don't get what I'm supposed to get out of this." The second part of the chapter addresses accessibility, as in "I can get my hands on the data I need." As Rankin (2015) pointed out, "The design of data reports makes the difference between insight and irritation as teachers review data" (p. 1).

In addition to teachers, families and a broader range of constituents need to be regularly informed and have access to understandable data about student performance, the realities of school needs, and services that are provided. Communication is a two-way street, and communicating about data is like a traffic pattern of multiple streets, some of which are two-way, some one-way, and some limited to specific kinds of vehicles or special purposes like bikes, buses, and car pools. Plans for communicating information about student performance must identify multiple audiences, the specific purpose for communication with each audience, and then the appropriate communicators and channels for each audience and purpose. Audiences for communication about data include the media, community groups such as employers and taxpayers' organizations, teachers, students, and parents. The question of who is the appropriate communicator relates to credibility and trust of the audience. Any member of the public can access data on state websites and read reports based on data released to the media. But the communicator they trust more is their local district and school. For the forty-sixth time, the PDK/Gallup Poll of the Public's Attitudes Toward the Public Schools (Phi Delta Kappa, 2015) asked how respondents rate schools. As usual, the nation's schools are a concern, with only 21 percent giving them an A or B. Getting closer to home, 51 percent gave their community's schools an A or B. But over 70 percent gave an A or B to the school their own child attends. One of the best ways to counter media communications is to provide clear communication locally. This raises another issue of the vocabulary and background knowledge of each audience. Decisions are further complicated by privacy issues related to confidentiality of student information. Making visuals easy to grasp and keeping text short and simple are essential.

TYPES OF DATA DISPLAYS

Data can be displayed in a variety of ways, so a first consideration is the kind of display that can best paint the picture that users need to understand. It's a little like what realtors call curb appeal, referring to the first impression clients have as they approach and drive by a property. A house might have a beautiful interior and an attractive price, but if it's not visually appealing on first impression, the sale will be difficult. In the same sense, if the data isn't visually appealing, the task of engaging people in discussion of the data and its implications for planning and decision-making will be that much more difficult. Data systems, software, and apps are available that can create multiple kinds of data displays. The professional element is the choice of what to use.

Histograms

Histograms include a variety of bar charts that capture and compare information. For example, Figure 2.4 (p. 29) displayed scores on state math assessments in a series of *stacked* bar graphs. Each "stack" shows the percentage of students falling within a set range of scores, making it visually easy to compare differences in the distribution of scores for all students and the scores of students with individualized education programs (IEPs). There are three sets of side-by-side stacks capturing three grade levels.

Figure 5.7 (p. 72) is a vertical bar graph in which each bar represents a different year, so the viewer immediately sees the upward trend within each subject area and the comparison of three different subject areas. Figure 5.10 (p. 77) uses bars to represent the percentage of students absent at each period of the school day. By using three different patterns on the bars, Figure 5.14 (p. 85) communicated the differences in responses from three groups of survey respondents. It's easy to spot the three areas in which students are clearly not as satisfied as either group of adults—teachers or parents.

Pareto Charts

A Pareto chart is a specialized form of bar chart that's useful for breaking down a major problem into more specific causes. This provides a range of options to consider, and groups can more readily identify where to start. (Its name comes from Italian economist Vilfredo Pareto, who posited the Pareto principle that a minority of causes contribute to a majority of the results. This also gave rise to the popular "80/20" principle.) By displaying the bars in descending order, a Pareto chart highlights the factors that hold the greatest share of the data. For example, Figure 5.11 (p. 78) showed that the two highest kinds of discipline referrals are violations of school rules and class disruptions. Figure 5.12 (p. 82) was arranged in reverse, with the most *positive* data (highest agreement) first, so areas to address would be on the right-hand side. This sequence makes the causes for celebration more visible.

Run Charts

A run chart, also known as a line graph, shows data from monitoring a situation or process over time to identify changes. For example, Figure 11.8 (p. 195) shows how reading scores have improved over time for all socioeconomic groups, but a gap still remains. Figure 5.7 (p. 72) showed change over time in a histogram, but the same data could be represented on a run chart with a line for each of the three subject areas and four points on the line for the four years. In this case, because the numbers are so similar in each subject, the lines might be very close together. These are the kinds of considerations that influence choice of data display.

Pie Charts

A pie chart is particularly useful for showing how a set of data or a zero sum resource is distributed. For example, classroom observations could yield data for a pie chart of how much class time is spent in various ways. Figure 5.6 (p. 70) used a pie chart to show distribution of reading scores by proficiency level. One slice of the pie—the lowest performing—was then further broken down using stacked bar graphs.

Grid or Matrix

Sometimes the simplest way to visualize data really *is* in rows and boxes—but as summary data, not all the rows and columns of raw data. Figure 2.3 (p. 27) presented a clear picture in a simple 2x2 grid of scores above and below proficiency and time in district at or less than two years. Figure 5.8 (p. 73) displayed scores from two nonconsecutive years (so a run chart wouldn't be appropriate). The matrix format allowed a column to be inserted to provide the calculated difference so this would not have to be a mental step taken by the viewer.

Symbolic Displays

Symbolic displays are helpful when the precision of the numbers is not as critical as the visual message being presented. Figures 5.1 through 5.4 (pp. 65–68) used faces and money as symbols to represent race and income levels. Figure 6.1 uses arrows as symbols to display a complex set of data—two years of test scores for three different grades in four different subjects. In a district that had been focused for two years on increasing the quantity and quality of student writing, the cause for celebration that writing scores went up at all grade levels jumped out immediately! Of course, these simple ways of presenting data symbolically are summaries. They must be followed by more detailed analysis and discussion, but they help to focus and prioritize that work. Discussion points might include the following:

- Listening scores are down at all grade levels. How much do we value this test? Do we have other evidence of students' listening skills?
- Scores for tenth graders slipped in reading, math, and listening. How much? Is this a significant concern?

As the discussion continues, the interest and need for the numbers will emerge, and the complex array of score reports can be tackled in small increments. And, of course, all the details of all the data would always be made available to those with the interest and time to study them further.

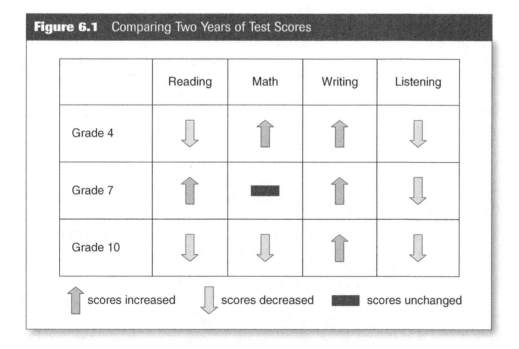

Figure 6.1 Comparing Two Years of Test Scores

	Reading	Math	Writing	Listening
Grade 4	⬇	⬆	⬆	⬇
Grade 7	⬆	▬	⬆	⬇
Grade 10	⬇	⬇	⬆	⬇

⬆ scores increased   ⬇ scores decreased   ▬ scores unchanged

KEY FEATURES OF DATA DISPLAYS

The graph of math scores in Figure 5.5 (p. 69) illustrated three main parts of a data display: introduction, clearly labelled data, and key findings.

Text

The title and introductory comments must be clear enough to verify whether this is the type of data being sought by the viewer. Since this is a generic illustration, the name of a test is not given, but schools should always name the actual test that was administered. The introduction should also spell out terms that may be abbreviated elsewhere in the data display—for example, socioeconomic status (SES).

Sometimes data is shared without discussion—released to the media, posted on a website, sent to families or community members electronically or in backpacks or U.S. mail. In this case, it's important to provide some interpretation of the data, as shown at the bottom of Figure 5.5. Two statements of strength and three statements of concern are provided. In school settings, data displays would often be presented *without* these summary statements so that teams would discuss the data and generate the statements themselves. It's often interesting to compare the summary statements when several tables or teams have reviewed the same data. For future uses of the data, the best, most accurate summary statements would be chosen and included. These statements must be factual observations, not evaluative judgments. For example, Figure 5.5 stated that the mean for all second-grade students is below the 50th percentile. It does not say that the second graders have the poorest performance or that the second-grade math program should be changed. This would be a rush to judgment on what the school's response should be, eliminating the drill down of the data, the study of best practice, and the analysis of current practice that are described in Chapters 7, 8, and 9.

Labeling

On the data display, each axis or component should be clearly labeled. If percentile scores may be in use, then the percent sign (%) should *not* be used. Percentiles should be shown as simply the number, with the full word *percentile* in the heading. Or the "-ile" suffix should be added with the number and percent sign. In this way, the 79th %ile is clearly different from 79 percent. This is an important distinction, because many readers may confuse the more familiar "79 percent of students answered correctly" or "my child got 79 percent of the answers right" instead of "my/ our child(ren) performed better than 79 percent of all test-takers." This embarrassing error occurred in a community forum of School Board candidates when a candidate stated, "The district's test scores are in the 70s, and when I was in school, 70s meant a D. Our schools are only performing at the D level." Most districts would actually be proud of scores at the 79th percentile nationally.

Rankin (2015) recommended that additional text be added in a footer if there are predictable errors often made with such data. For example, a cautionary statement might point out that each grade level of an assessment has a different level of difficulty so grade levels should not be compared directly but should be referenced to national averages. She also cautioned against the use of keys or legends that ask a user to look away, find the code, and look back to apply it to the graph. Every additional step is a risk for misunderstanding or frustration. Whenever possible, place any needed content directly into the chart's title, introduction, or labels.

Comparisons and Calculations

Rankin (2015) also pointed out that most data have no meaning without a comparison. The comparison in the previous paragraph is to a national average. Politically driven changes in state assessments have necessitated comparison to an "equating table" in order to look at consecutive years on different tests. An equity perspective requires comparisons between different groups within the overall student population. It's also important to alleviate viewers' need to do mental math when looking at data. If the percentage of students "proficient and above" is an important factor, provide both percentages *and* the total in both categories. Figure 5.8 (p. 73) provided the calculated difference between the two years of results being compared.

Color

During the era of No Child Left Behind (NCLB), many state assessments moved away from norm-referenced tests reporting in percentiles to standards-based tests reporting proficiency levels. This greatly facilitates the use of color to represent the four typical levels, regardless of the specific names given to them in different states. In Figure 6.2, blue represents the highest level, often called "advanced" proficiency or above the 75th percentile on norm-referenced tests. (Blue is associated with "blue ribbon" awards in many settings.) The traffic light colors are then used: green—good to go—for proficient or 50th to 74th percentile; yellow—caution—for basic or 25th to 49th percentile; red—stop and pay attention—for below basic or below the 25th percentile. At a glance, it's clear that there are many more students in the red zone in math than in reading. Yet there are also more students in the advanced level in math than reading. This is an intriguing pattern that may precipitate soul-searching about the range of sections and courses of math and which students receive what kind of instruction.

A few cautions are important to bear in mind with use of color. Color printers are much more frequently available than in the past, but district and school publications are sometimes (like this book) only available in black and white. Graphs using color need to be sure to include adequate labeling and text information so that accuracy will not be lost if they end up in a black-and-white format. The second caution has a more cultural than technical implication. It's convenient to talk about students in the red zone, but it's a slippery slope toward referring to students by color and creating generalities that are inaccurate and inappropriate. For example, alarm bells should go off in your minds if you hear statements like "Our red kids have IEPs but we need to figure out what program to buy for our yellow kids." Students who score within a performance band are all different. Low-performing students are struggling with different specific skills and for different reasons. Discussions of color-coded data must be handled with sensitivity and the details searched to "find the faces" as described in Chapter 5.

The acid test of your data displays is this: How many places does the viewer have to look to be able to interpret the data? How long will it take to "get it"—to grasp the reality portrayed?

Figure 6.2   Percentage of Students in Proficiency Levels

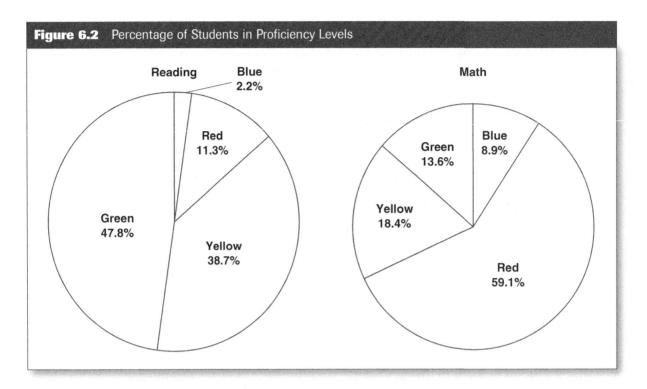

ACCESS TO DATA

Data displays are built from raw data that is received and stored in a variety of ways. Just this year, I have seen a team going through the process of photocopying the hard copy student reports that a test company provided for parents in order to access detailed, individual data they needed. More and more assessment data is provided in electronic format direct to the school or district. In some cases, the data is on a state website that must be accessed each time a data question arises. Vendors promise integrated systems that will house "everything" and make it easily retrievable and offer dozens of different kinds of graphs and reports. The Association for Supervision and Curriculum Development (ASCD) (2015c) "Research Alert" on a recent study by the Gates Foundation reported that 93 percent of the 4,600 teachers surveyed used some form of digital tool to gather data and guide instruction. Sixty-one percent said that data and digital tools made them better teachers, helping them gain insight into each student's strengths, weaknesses, and passions so they can personalize and differentiate instruction. However, 67 percent of these users are less than satisfied with the data and tools they can access. They complain that these tools are overwhelming, containing too much information from too many disparate sources to readily sort out what they are looking for. Too often, there are multiple systems in place, incompatible with one another, requiring them to manually combine related data. Further, access is often too slow to provide information in time to meaningfully modify instruction.

The dilemma of access versus confidentiality also creates problems. I have been involved in lengthy, sometimes contentious, meetings about what job roles should have what levels of access through how many firewalls in the data warehouse. (Data security is discussed further in Chapter 12.)

A secondary language arts teacher (ASCD, 2015d) stated that "the most serious obstacles I face pertain to the data being housed in various web hosts, making it either too time-consuming to find and gather or inaccessible to me as a teacher" (p. 90). A vice-principal spoke to particular challenges at the high school level:

> As students transition out of elementary school, we have fewer useful tools to track student mastery. At the same time, there is more specialization of content, significantly widening the net of skills and knowledge to assess. To clear this hurdle, many middle and high school teachers develop their own formative assessments. However, the next obstacle becomes struggling through the data-collection process, poring over student work, tallying trends in student responses, and entering data into spreadsheets to facilitate further analysis. The momentum for data-based inquiry is often lost in this process. (ASCD, 2015d, p. 92)

An effective data dashboard may be part of the solution. Rothman (2015) reported that state-level dashboards are relatively new but that education systems in other countries have used them for some time—and more districts are creating their own. His recommendations included choosing the right indicators (not only test scores) in a handful of categories, such as those discussed in Chapter 1. He then stressed a need to focus on a few of those as the most crucial indicators that would have priority for development and access. For each of these, targets should be set and a color-coding system can be developed to highlight where targets have been met. The district's role providing and securing data is explored further in Chapter 12. In Kent, Washington, one school didn't wait—they created their own.

DOING IT OURSELVES: A SCHOOL CREATES ITS OWN DATA SYSTEM

Panther Lake Elementary School serves a diverse student population of more than 600 students in kindergarten through sixth grade. They support the learning needs of their students through a variety of federal and state funding streams: Title, Learning Assistance Program (LAP), English language learners (ELL). Dollars always come with strings attached, so Principal Beth Wallen and her staff have always needed to keep track of data for external accountability reporting purposes. Their internal mission has been to make best use of all available resources to directly support individual students, not just meet program requirements. Looking back over thirteen years, Beth recalls that student progress data was kept in a lot of different ways and teachers would turn in paper reports. They started saying, "Have you heard of doing this electronically?" So they began to create and use a few spreadsheets to enter scores and separate groups of students and do their reports. Around the same time, Panther Lake was formalizing its Response to Intervention (RTI) model and needed a system that would meet both a cultural and technical need: create a culture of "all our kids" by being accessible for widespread use among staff and have the capacity to track student learning over time. They needed to be able to enter data around the definitions of Advanced (A), Basic (B), Strategic (S), and Intensive (I). The Strategic category would include students one year below standard, with Intensive representing two or more years below standard. Teachers wanted to be able to monitor student progress every thirty days and talk about each student, asking, "What changes are we seeing?" But frustration mounted as they were crunching numbers by hand and calculator. Two more design needs were identified: How can we all be in a tool at the same time? And how can we get the tool to do the calculations of change from one score to the next?

Two of Panther Lake's National Board Certified teachers joined Principal Wallen to tell me more about the spreadsheet system that's been developed over time to meet these needs. Cara Haney is an instructional coach and Emily Coleman is a kindergarten teacher with extra pay for time associated with the special assignment of maintaining the data system. They described how teacher leaders started pursuing spreadsheet capabilities and constructing the system so that all staff could enter data at the same time and the tool would calculate differences in the students' scores and levels (A, B, S, or I). Some other data tools were already available, but Panther Lake's passion wasn't about pulling and crunching numbers. Their action orientation was about being able to *use* data in their team discussions. Their goal was for precious team time to be focused in a definite ratio: only 25 percent of their time spent figuring out the data and 75 percent figuring out what to *do* about it. Wallen realized there was a lot of technical expertise among the staff and turned them loose to create. The result is Panther Lake's "Schoolwide Data Gathering Tool."

Features of the Tool

A key feature of the system is the grade-level profile seen in Figure 6.3. Every student in the grade is listed in one spreadsheet, which helps create a more collective sense of responsibility and collaboration than each screen being a separate teacher's individual classroom. Not shown in Figure 6.3 is the first column of the spreadsheet, which would be students' names. For each student, the spreadsheet provides teacher name, continuous enrollment, gender, ethnicity, special education status, ELL status and level, and score levels from progress monitoring every thirty days.

Another spreadsheet records the actual assessment score information. On Figure 6.4, each set of four rows captures one student's scores on the benchmark or interim assessments given three times a year. Scores are moved forward from the spring of last year (LY), and this year's scores are entered in the fall, winter, and spring. Not visible here are the color codes used to highlight scores that are at or above standard in green, approaching standard in yellow, and below standard in red. To support the goal of focusing team discussion on action, Figure 6.5 aggregates data in summary form every thirty days. The first grid illustrates how the tool enables teachers to quickly see the number and percentage of their students at each level— Advanced, Basic, Strategic, Intensive. Directly below it is the at-a-glance picture of which students are struggling broken out by special education status, ELL, and ethnicity. But Panther Lake teachers are not just

Figure 6.3 Panther Lake Grade-Level Profile

Teacher	Continuously Enrolled	Gender	Ethnicity	Special Ed	ELL	Hispanic	ELL Level	30 Day	60 Day	90 Day	120 Day	150 Day	180 Day	Reading Year's Growth Y/N
Avolio	Y	M	H			YES	4	B	B	B	B			
Avolio	Y	M	M		yes		3	-	-	-	-			
Glover	Y	M	M					B	B	B	B			
Avolio	Y	M	A					A	A	A	A			
Ackerman	Y	F	H			YES		-	S	B	B			
Avolio	Y	F	A					S	S	B	B			
Avolio	Y	F	A					B	B	B	B			
Avolio	Y	F	W					B	B	B	B			
W/D	N													
Ackerman	Y	F	H			YES	4	S	S	B	B			
Avolio	Y	F	H			YES		B	A	A	A			
Avolio	Y	M	H			YES		S	S	S	S			
Glover	Y	F	W	yes				B	B	B	B			
Ackerman	Y	M	A		yes		3	-	S	-	-			
Ackerman	Y	F	B					S	S	S	S			
Avolio	Y	F	M		yes		3	S	S	S	S			
Glover	Y	F	B					S	S	-	-			
Ackerman	Y	F	H		yes	YES	3	S	S	B	B			
Thomas	Y	F	P	yes	yes		2	-	-	-	-			
W/D	N													
Avolio	Y	M	A			YES	4	S	S	S	S			
Avolio	Y	M	H		yes	YES	3	-	-	-	-			
Ackerman	Y	M	B					S	S	B	B			
Glover	Y	F	A					S	B	B	B			
Avolio	Y	M	A		yes		1	-	-	-	-			
Glover	Y	F	W					A	A	A	A			
Thomas	Y	M	B	yes				-	-	-	-			
Avolio	Y	F	A					A	A	A	A			

Figure 6.4   Panther Lake Assessment Scores

Testing Seasons	DIBELS Fluency (WPM)	DIBELS Accuracy	DIBELS Daze Score (Adjusted)	DIBELS Composite Score	SBA ELA Level/Score 2014-2015	i Ready	IRLA	"IRI" Reading Passage Grade Level	"IRI" Reading Passage Word Recognition	"IRI" Reading Passage comprehensio	Gender	Ethnicity	Special Ed	ELL
SpringLY	149	99%	30	441	2424	546	0	5	99	80	M	A	0	0
Fall						582	0	4	100	90				
Winter						559	0	4	100	90				
Spring						0	0	0	0	0				
SpringLY	147	98%	23	457	2577	624	0	8	98	70	F	W	0	0
Fall						633	0	0	0	0				
Winter						647	0	8	98	100				
Spring						0	0	0	0	0				
SpringLY	167	100%	40	581	2567	619	0	7	99	90	F	B	0	0
Fall						620	0	6	98	70				
Winter						630	0	7	100	100				
Spring						0	0	0	0	0				
SpringLY	120	99%	22	464	2490	540	0	5	99	100	M	W	0	0
Fall						521	0	4	99	90				
Winter						541	0	4	99	100				
Spring						0	0	0	0	0				
SpringLY	124	100%	20	418	2516	570	0	5	95	90	M	H	0	0
Fall						542	0	5	95	100				
Winter						595	0	6	97	90				
Spring						0	0	0	0	0				
SpringLY	121	99%	22	373	2489	547	0	5	99	100	M	H	0	0
Fall						546	0	4	99	70				
Winter						569	0	5	99	90				
Spring						0	0	0	0	0				
SpringLY	64	89%	20	216	2430	518	0	5	97	100	M	A	yes	0
Fall						531	0	4	95	70				
Winter						545	0	4	98	90				
Spring						0	0	0	0	0				

focused on struggling students. They also want to make sure that students at and above standard are making progress and not allowed to "slide." So the tool creates the grid at the right showing movement of students from the previous thirty days. All nine Advanced students remained high. Nine students moved up from Strategic to Basic (S to B). While four students dropped from Strategic to Intensive (S to I), four others moved up from Intensive to Strategic (I to S).

Using the Tool

At the beginning of the year, teachers decide what assessments will be used at each of the thirty-day benchmarks, and the system is calibrated to

Figure 6.5 Panther Lake Levels and Changes

90 Days		
Reading	Number	Percent
A	9	11%
B	26	32%
S	21	26%
I	25	31%

90 Days			
Reading	Special Ed	ELL	Hispanic
S	0	6	8
	0%	29%	38%
I	6	13	5
	26%	52%	20%

90 Days		
Writing	Number	Percent
A	9	11%

Reading	
A to A	9
A to B	0
A to S	0
A to I	0
B to A	0
B to B	17
B to S	0
B to I	0
S to A	0
S to B	9
S to S	17
S to I	4
I to A	0
I to B	0
I to S	4
I to I	20

A = Advanced, B = Basic, S = Strategic, I = Intensive

be ready to produce these displays. Data from some of the larger assessments is imported into the system to provide "one-stop data-shopping."

During the year, time is provided for all teams to work with their data. The district provides four principal-directed professional development days. At Panther Lake, these are converted into a bank of thirty hours used for a range of data activities. At team meetings, the screens are displayed on the SMART board and comments are heard in the spirit of "Oh, look at these kids! Who are they? What are we doing for them?" Teachers refer to the data to set up intervention groups, plan how they will deploy paraeducators to support students, and focus on priorities and strategies in the regular core instruction.

The Schoolwide Data Gathering Tool also facilitates parent conversations. For example, weekly Family Support Team meetings have data readily available to reference in work with parents on plans to help students be more successful with academic concerns or other challenges. Teachers also use the information in conversations with parents about classroom placement, interventions provided to support the child, and other topics.

In recent years, the Schoolwide Data Gathering Tool has also helped teachers with data on their own performance. State requirements for teacher evaluation have required staff to demonstrate student growth. At Panther Lake, teachers have not needed to do extra work to provide this evidence—it's already there in the data tool. One segment of the instructional framework used for teacher evaluation is Professional Communication and Collaboration. Using data from the tool with colleagues and parents provides evidence for these criteria as well, again without the stress of compiling extra information just to defend one's performance.

Advantages of Creating Their Own

The biggest advantage stated for Panther Lake's homegrown tool is that it enables teams to "see everything in one place. It's the most user-friendly tool we have. There were so many other data sources—you almost need a recipe book for all of them and that's not the best use of our time."

Panther Lake staff also realize that when you own a tool, you can change it whenever you want to. They talk about "making constant tweaks." Every year, the tool has improved and become more comprehensive. "It's always evolving. Every year we learn something new and we can change it. Having it in-house means being able to do those changes so it's continuous and ongoing. Everybody understands and appreciates it."

Teacher leaders described Wallen's vision for Panther Lake as "for all kids and to do the best we can for kids. So when mandates come down, it's 'what can we do to make this manageable for teachers so it comes right back to helping kids.' It's become our culture." The principal's comment was "I just try to create conditions—they are the superstars. It's their great ideas that have evolved this process so much. They are problem-solvers— such a high-functioning staff. The focus on teaching and learning is always happening, and now we have information at our fingertips. It's hard work, but it's good work. It helps us keep a pulse on our kids and the progress we're making and they're making."

Chapter 7

You Get More Excited About Data When . . . It Fits a Bigger Picture

One of the reasons people may be reluctant to use data is that they can't see where it all fits, which is another way of expressing the need to make it actionable: Where will this data work go? This concern is natural and is common. From his international perspective, Michael Fullan (2004) observed that "the most perennial complaint that locals have is that they don't understand the big picture" (p. 90). This chapter will describe two "big pictures" or processes in which data work becomes a meaningful, sustainable way of doing business continuously. First we look at the school level and review the components and connections to data in the school improvement process led by the Shared Leadership Team. This representative team deals with practices that shape the overall school culture and designs and monitors schoolwide structures like the Multi-Tiered System of Support (MTSS) for students. Then we move closer to the classroom level and outline the cyclical work of curriculum, instruction, and assessment conducted in Teaching Teams, as well as an open-ended inquiry process.

A CONTRAST OF CASES

Consider the comments of the principals in these two brief interviews. Focus less on the specific change they discussed, and zero in on how they did—or didn't—use data. Also consider ways in which the leadership team in each school painted a bigger picture of the context for the change—the rationale of why and how this change would be beneficial and how it would look when it was in place.

School A

Author: Hi, I see from the conference program that you're doing block scheduling at your school. How long have you been at it?

Principal A: Well, it's about a year and a half now. We're into our second year of it.

Author: Why did you make that kind of a change?

Principal A: Well, I'm sure you've heard of our school. Our district is known as one of the most progressive in the state, and our Board likes to be sure we're on the cutting edge. The superintendent called me in one day and said that the School Board members were getting on his case because the elementary schools were doing multiage and looping and stuff like that, and the middle schools had these new "houses," whatever they are, and they wanted to know what we're going to do for restructuring at the high school. So we did some checking around and went to a national conference, and block scheduling seemed to be the thing that's hot, so we came back and started to work on it.

Author: Did you run into any resistance? How did you go about implementing such a change?

Principal A: Well, there were already enough schools doing it that I could call around and find out what the problems seemed to be. A couple things they all mentioned were the hassles of getting the master schedule put together and trying to explain the whole thing to parents who just had images of the way high school was back when they went to school. So we decided we'd head off the resistance by just dealing with those right off the bat. I took my department heads to my cabin for a retreat for a couple days right after school got out, and we worked out the master schedule. That way it would be all in place for teachers when they came back in August, and we wouldn't have to spend weeks' worth of meetings trying to iron it out. We did the best we could to make people happy, but we knew there's just no way to please them all. And for the parents, I've got a good friend with kids in the school who runs a public relations firm. He volunteered the time to make up a brochure that we could send to all the parents in early August and give them fair warning so they could get used to the idea. It's a good thing I work year-round, because there sure were a lot of people calling in to ask me about it.

Author: Is it working for you? How do you know?

Principal A: Well, like I said, we're in our second year. We had a lot of glitches, and some people didn't like it at first—but we just stuck to it and we made it through. The Board was real supportive that we wouldn't just give up after one year. And it must be good for the kids. Last week, my assistant principal was getting ready to throw out some old referral slips, and he noticed there were only about half as many hallway disciplines as the year before. So obviously we're doing something right.

School B

Author: Hi, I see from the conference program that you're doing block scheduling at your school. How long have you been at it?

Principal B: Well, I guess there's two ways I could answer that. If you mean how long we've been using it, I'd say two-and-a-half years. This is our third year. But if you mean how long we've been *working* at it, I'd say three-and-a-half years because I'd count the year we spent making up our minds and getting ready for it.

Author: Why did you make that kind of a change?

Principal B: Well, now you're in for a longer answer if you have time. It seemed simple at first. We were getting ready for the accreditation people to do a site visit, and we were checking off stuff they look for—like a mission statement, for example. We remembered we had one from the last time around, and we got it out to review. We actually liked it and decided to keep it, but as we were talking about it, we sort of wondered if it was for real or not. We had things like critical thinking and problem-solving and having a caring, personal community in there—but we really hadn't been thinking about whether they were true. So we decided to make those three things a real priority in the next couple years. Then we had to get data together—you know they want a school profile. And we got to wondering if maybe we could find out about critical thinking and problem-solving and caring community from stuff in there. Well, we did and we didn't like it. On test score measures of problem solving, we weren't very good. When we had teacher focus groups, people were complaining about the poor quality of written work and the shallow answers in class discussions. When we looked at survey data from the students and parents, we were disappointed at how many didn't agree that they had two or three adults to turn to with problems or didn't agree that the school treats each student as an individual, and so on. We started asking why not and eventually decided that it's pretty hard to teach to high levels of Bloom's taxonomy and get quality work, etc., in forty-two-minute periods—and pretty hard to know kids as individuals with 170 different faces in front of you every day. That's when we realized that our own structure was keeping us from meeting our goals, and we decided to change it.

Author: Did you run into any resistance? How did you go about implementing such a change?

Principal B: That's a long story, too. We knew we could never make everyone happy, but we wanted to be sure that everyone got to be heard. So we decided to devote two months for study of the various problems and put everyone on a study group. And we weren't just random about it either. My leadership team and I looked over the staff list and thought about each person and what might trouble them—like the math teachers are going to worry about continuity and the PE teachers are going to worry about sports, etc. So we put them on the group that would deal with their issue and made sure each group also had some people who were real excited and optimistic. We gradually worked through the issues, until we got a schedule that everyone agreed was the best we could do—not best for them personally but overall best. And while the teachers were working, we also had a couple groups of parents and community members raising their questions and getting ideas and reactions from the people they knew, etc. It helped us decide about communication strategies and gave us some advocates out in the town. Anyway, when school got out for the summer, we had all the plans in place and we had structured our August staff development days as a preparation. We had three days where experts gave us content in the morning, and then we met as departments in the afternoon and they helped teachers restructure their instructional units for September with a variety of teaching strategies. That way, they were ready to go and knew how to modify their lessons as the year went on.

Author: Is it working for you? How do you know?

Principal B: Well, for one thing, we have some new documents in the curriculum office that show how we changed our course syllabi and some sample lesson plans. That's been really helpful for new teachers coming in and proves we really did follow through on the changes in instruction. And then last spring we did the same surveys as three years ago. The students and parents sure gave us better ratings for personalization and caring. And our test scores are up across the board—so I guess our emphasis on higher-level thinking and sticking to our standards for quality work has really paid off. I think you'd have a real tough time getting this crowd to go back to the old schedule.

Data Use in School A and School B

Uses of data in School A *may* have included the number of inquiry phone calls from parents and *perhaps* the reduction in hallway discipline referrals—although that was certainly an unintended positive consequence. Uses of data in School B resembled many of the data uses in high-performing schools described in Chapter 1 (see Figure 1.4 on p. 13). Connections were made between their mission and their data. They used actual student work as a source of data, not just test scores. They looked at existing practices and the impact on meeting students' needs. They used information about teacher needs to think about the communication and professional development that would be needed to move forward with the change. They monitored the change and reviewed data to determine its impact on students.

A theme throughout this book—a goal in writing it—is to help schools move from a compliance perspective to a real spirit of commitment to their students and each other. School A was clearly stuck in compliance mode—"the Board made us do something." School B *started* from a compliance perspective—how do we keep our accreditation—but used its own internal beliefs and data to generate commitment. School B is an example of the Leadership for Learning characteristic of high-performing data use reported in Chapter 1—"using data to move beyond problem identification to problem-solving; gathering additional data to better understand the causes or factors related to the problems in question." Through their process, they strengthened the culture of collective responsibility (Chapters 2 and 3) and utilized a variety of working structures (Chapter 4).

COMPONENTS OF THE SCHOOL'S BIG PICTURE

Through more than two decades, practitioners have expressed appreciation for the simplicity of Figure 7.1—the "big picture" of the school improvement process coordinated by the Shared Leadership Team, supported by the Data Team, and engaging all staff and stakeholders at key points. Keeping it simple has a few downsides. It doesn't look like an ongoing cycle—unless you print it and wrap the paper around into a cylinder. It looks too linear—and true change is too complex to be viewed as a set of straightforward steps. But a truer picture of how the data work in any component can take a team back to revisit something previous would have arrows going everywhere. Starting on the left, the way we read, implies that must be the first thing to work on. But many of these components have been "in place" or "on paper" for years now. The discussion should not be "Okay, let's start with our Mission . . . AGAIN" but rather "What do we have in place that we are all actually using? Does it matter? Does it affect how we do things? Are we connecting all of these pieces into a meaningful whole?" The author has to write about these components in some sequence. The reader's responsibility is to determine your own starting point. Jump in "somewhere." Above all, don't undo or redo anything that's working—just test for evidence that it really *is*.

Figure 7.2 builds on the basic components of the school improvement picture by adding the word *DATA* to represent the various types

Figure 7.1   The Big Picture of School Improvement

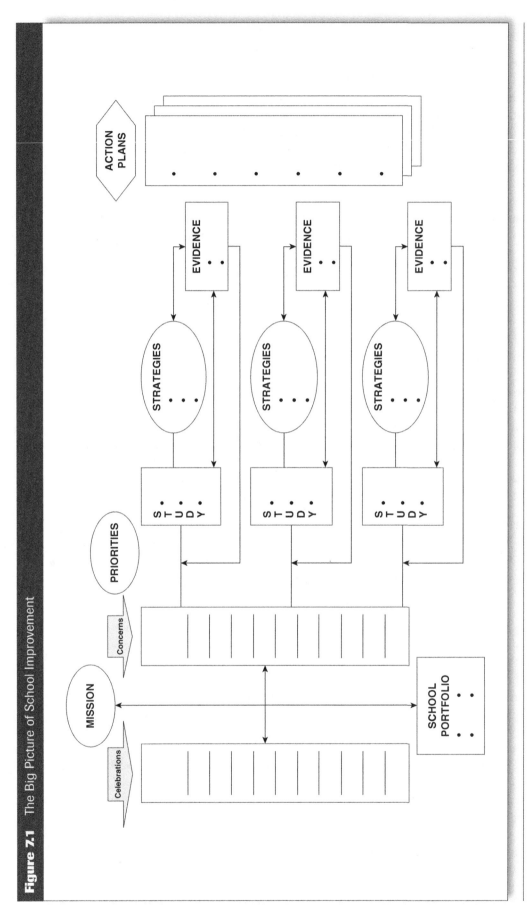

of data work that come into play. It also includes a new set of diagonal arrows, aiming back to the *School Portfolio*. This illustrates how the additional data gathered and analyzed at each step feeds back into the ever-expanding portfolio of data available for future understanding and planning. Along with more detailed explanation of each component shown in Figures 7.1 and 7.2, the following sections will highlight critical data questions to be addressed and the actions that will be guided by the results.

Mission

Chapter 2 explored connections between individual and shared beliefs about students and about assessment and data. To review, this author does not parse out the various distinctions between mission statements, vision statements, values, collective commitments, and the like. I use the single word *mission* to capture the reality that everyone needs to contribute to a set of statements that all will embrace and that will be ubiquitous visually and verbally and used deliberately to question assumptions, statements, and plans. Language has power and should be used in powerful and positive ways. A vision can also be a hallucination. Something we value can be kept in a vault and never seen, whereas the word *mission* indicates action with a very specific goal and skilled, practiced roles and evidence of success. In a rescue mission, for example, there is a specific objective, there is a sense of urgency, and everyone involved knows just what they must do to make the collective effort successful. That is the degree of passion and the high stakes that should be associated with statements that schools create together—for some students, the stakes may literally be a matter of life and death.

Figure 7.2 shows no word *DATA* in the Mission oval, and that is not an oversight. Our mission should be driven by our ethics and determination, regardless of the challenges that might emerge from the data. Moving ourselves from compliance to commitment means asking, "What is it that *we* want to be? Why are *we* here? What work do *we* know we need to do—and want to do—regardless of mandates? Why did *we* set out to work with young people in the first place?" Courageous professionals leave school every June exhausted and somehow regroup and rejuvenate themselves, and return in August—their motivation *must* be for some greater cause than fulfilling state and federal laws. The action we must take is to test ourselves against that mission. This was the "aha" moment for School B—the reality that the mission was not being carried out. The two-way vertical arrow between Mission and the School Portfolio demonstrates the need to provide evidence that the mission is being fulfilled, as described in Chapter 2. Our sense of mission tells us *what* and *why*. The data give us clues to figure out *how*.

School Portfolio

The term *School Portfolio* is used here to describe the collection of data that relates to the specific school. I use the term *portfolio* because it seems analogous to the body of work that a student or an artist gathers as his or her portfolio of student work. Their portfolios are intended to demonstrate

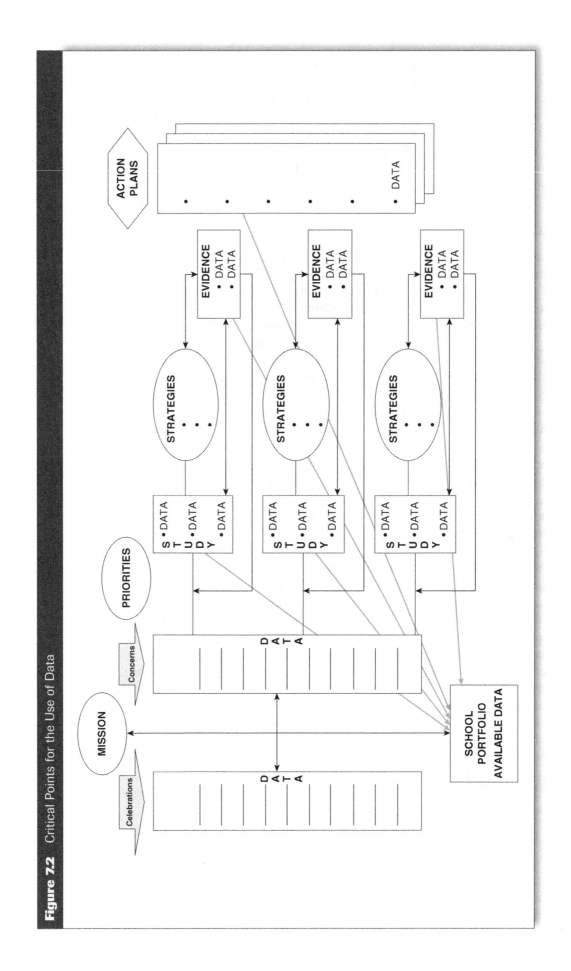

Figure 7.2 Critical Points for the Use of Data

three aspects of the work: the range of skills, the very best final products, and artifacts that provide evidence of progress and learning. A school also needs to present the wide variety of needs it addresses, examples of success to celebrate, and evidence of improvement occurring where needed. School B was creating its portfolio as they looked at test scores and student work and survey data.

Figure 1.2 (p. 11) summarized many sources of data available in most schools and suggested ways of organizing the findings into categories. For example, on Figure 7.1 there are four bullet points in the School Portfolio box, and they stand for specific kinds of data: Academic Student Data, Nonacademic Student Data, Staff Data, and Parent/Community Data. Chapter 5 emphasized the need for the last three categories—especially the nonacademic student data referred to as "faces" or "whole child indicators." Mountains of raw data from these various sources are housed in various formats throughout the district. They may or may not be integrated into a commercial data warehouse or a spreadsheet tool like Panther Lake Elementary School developed (Chapter 6). But over time they can be tapped to answer questions the school encounters in its search for underlying causes and points of leverage.

Celebrations and Concerns

Figures 7.1 and 7.2 show two columns for listing Celebrations and Concerns, with a two-way arrow connecting them. These headings were presented in Chapter 4 in the Data Discussion Chart. It is vitally important to celebrate successes for the energy and optimism they provide, as well as to assure that successful practices are sustained and not lost during initiation of new efforts. The listing of concerns also has a twofold purpose. One purpose certainly is to heighten awareness of continuing needs for growth. But they are intentionally not listed as weaknesses. They are intended to help identify multiple opportunities to make a difference—not as a to-do list to tackle all but as a first step toward finding the entry points that will most powerfully leverage other factors and lead to greater learning for staff, then students.

The sentence stems provided in Chapter 4 help jump-start the development of statements of findings from the multiple sources of data. These statements can be summarized in lists, as these two columns represent. If the school has had lots of data but didn't participate in collaborative analysis and summarize findings, this overall picture of Celebrations and Concerns may be thin at the beginning. Be assured that it is a baseline for continued growth in collaborative data use. It is a continuous work in process. It will be updated at least once a year as another round of test scores is received and another state report is submitted.

Concerns to Priorities

The boxes that hold Celebrations and Concerns on Figure 7.1 include many lines to represent many entries. But the next component, labeled Priorities at the top, has only three lines—intentionally reminding us of the advice from Fullan, Reeves, Schmoker, and others that we must focus on a few. Two copies of Figure 7.1 would allow for six goals and strands of work and that should be an absolute maximum, while also allowing for a mix of academic learning goals with other, nonacademic factors that need attention.

By openly listing all the concerns, educators have the opportunity to consider many possible entry points and find connections and interrelationships. This will help them zero in on a few areas where initial efforts can be leveraged toward more widespread gains.

Sometimes there are many possible starting points and strong allegiances to preferred initiatives, which can raise conflict about *what* to work on. This consumes time and energy before productive effort can even get underway. The next section provides a protocol in which the entire staff can engage to identify the limited set of priorities from which goals will be developed.

Goal-Setting Matrix

This prioritizing process is a combination of the traditional nominal group process and a decision matrix, which has been effective in many settings. It is grounded in the baseline data of the School Portfolio and brings both objective and subjective data to the table. The steps include the following:

- Review of the data
- Individual reflection
- Round-robin listing
- Individual rating on three criteria
- Adding individual ratings
- Individual ranking of five priorities
- Group ranking of five priorities
- Discussion
- Repetition of individual ratings and rankings

Please note the number of steps that occur *before discussion*. This sequence provides an equitable opportunity for participants to share all concerns, engage in personal reflection, and observe how their perceptions compare to the rest of the group before participating verbally.

Review of the Data

As a result of the Celebrations and Concerns discussion, a summary of findings from multiple data sources is available. An alternative is the Carousel Data Analysis activity described in Chapter 10, which raises this question: What needs for school improvement might arise from these data? Those responses may also form the kickoff for this data review. Copies of the School Portfolio Data Summary need to be visually available to all participants as hard copy, posted charts, or electronic documents.

Individual Reflection

After participants have a chance to review the concerns previously identified, stimulate further reflection with this question: What are all the things that anyone might say could be improved about our school? As the question is displayed, underline the word *all*, and emphasize that this is the participants' opportunity to create a comprehensive list for consideration. They should be candid and jot down any concern they have.

Then call attention to the word *anyone*, and remind them to present not only their own viewpoints but also concerns of others they have discovered in survey data or private discussions. Stress that the word *could* expresses our commitment to continuous improvement and does not imply that "everything is wrong" or that "everything will end up in the plan."

Observe the individual reflection and allow time until most participants seem to be done writing. Emphasize that every one of their concerns will be included and that it will be helpful if they look them over to be sure they are brief, specific, and easily understood. Phrases of three-to-five words without verbs are very useful, as they help prevent premature judgements about what action should be taken. Focus on the "what," not the "how." Mention that a broad concern like student test scores will be more helpful if it is broken down into specifics like "reading informational text" or "multistep problem-solving."

Round-Robin Listing

If the group consists of 25 or fewer participants, serve as recorder and enter the concerns as the first column of Figure 7.3 yourself. (Alter the template so the first column is widest.) Quickly typing on a SMART board and/or in a shared document is convenient. If you are working with a large group, subdivide and have multiple recorders, who will then combine lists during a break.

Round-robin listing means that each person states one concern from his or her list, and this is repeated around the circle. Everyone must listen carefully and cross off items that other people mention to avoid duplication. The recorder should assign a letter to each item as it's listed to facilitate ranking and discussion later.

Individual Rating on Three Criteria

People get more motivated to work toward goals if there is clear evidence of need, an intrinsic sense of their importance, and a feeling that the goals are achievable and within their reach. The three criteria in the next columns represent these characteristics of "goals that get done." The first question—How severe?—provides one more opportunity to connect with the data. Ratings of 5 go to any concerns they feel are severe needs, especially areas of student performance with the lowest test scores or survey items with highest percentages of dissatisfaction. The same rating— whether a 5, 4, 3, 2, or 1—can be used many times. The second question—How crucial?—emphasizes the need to establish goals that are closely linked to the mission of the school and/or are particularly urgent and important. Ignore the ratings from the previous column and rate each item according to this criterion only. The third question—How responsive?—allows participants to acknowledge that some concerns

Figure 7.3 Goal-Setting Matrix

Area of Concern	How Severe? Rate each item 1–5. 5 = greatest dissatisfaction with results (i.e., lowest test scores, worst problem).	How Crucial? Rate each item 1–5. 5 = most important issues; needing most immediate attention; most essential to the mission.	How Responsive? Rate each item 1–5. 5 = most amenable to change; within power of school.	Total of Individual Ratings	Individual Ranking Rank order 5 items only with 5 as highest priority.	Group Ranking
A.						
B.						
C.						
D.						
E.						
F.						
G.						

may be severe and crucial but outside the scope of influence of the school. Use of this column addresses reality and feasibility. Ratings of 5 are given to those concerns that the school can address independently. A rating of 1 indicates that the participant feels the school really can't do anything about the concern.

Adding Individual Ratings

In this column, participants add the numbers from the three ratings they gave to each item. An ideal goal area would have fifteen points, having been acknowledged as severe in the data, crucial to the mission, and completely within the school's influence. Such ratings are rare but very telling. The underlying principle is that the higher the total, the more priority the item deserves.

Individual Ranking of Five Priorities

The action here changes from rating—in which numbers can be used multiple time—to *ranking*, which requires only one use of a 1, 2, 3, 4, and 5. Each individual is given five stick-on notes or index cards with the numbers 1–5 and is asked to put the letters of the items from column one to which they assign those rankings, one per note or card.

Group Ranking of Five Priorities

With the priority cards placed in alphabetical order, the recorder can quickly note all rankings given to the item by letter. It is useful to write down all the numbers that are given (rather than totaling on the fly) so that the pattern or range of responses is noticeable. After rankings are tallied, total the numbers. In most cases, there will be a group of concerns that cluster together with high ranking, and then a drop down to another set or the rest of the list.

Discussion

Set a few ground rules, which may include the expectation that only advocacy statements will be made. This means that people express why they think a concern *is* of great importance and should be a top priority, but do not argue *against* other specific items. Sometimes it's also useful to set a number of times that any individual can advocate—or a time limit on each particular speech.

Repetition of Individual Ratings and Rankings

A second round of rating and ranking is often unnecessary because five or fewer priorities become very clear and the discussion does not indicate strong disagreement with any of them. If there is a wide range of responses, the discussion could include specific requests for "someone who gave this a 5" to tell us more about it. These questions and responses may lead to consensus. However, they sometimes lead to the need for more accurate information and additional reflection time before a final decision is reached. Help the group decide what information is needed, who can provide it, and what time will be needed. Then schedule another brief session to look at the new information before a second of ranking determines the school's priorities.

Priorities as Goal Statements

The wording of the goals is important. As Hord and Sommers (2008) have reminded us,

> Most people have absolute clarity about what they don't want . . . help yourself and others to define what they *do* want . . . clarify the goal . . . shifting the conversation from what people don't want to what they do want is critical to the conversation and to taking effective action . . . Once you move the conversation to what we do want, you will notice a change in energy and language. The language becomes more constructive, creating possibilities about how to get to the desired state, and the energy level of the conversation is higher. (pp. 100–101)

In recovery mode from No Child Left Behind (NCLB) and adequate yearly progress, it is particularly essential to conduct goal setting as an internal, intrinsic activity. Many organizations have adopted the acronym of SMART goals based on the work of O'Neill and Conzemius (2005) and have focused on statements that are strategic and specific, measurable, attainable, results-based, and time-bound. Of those attributes, I sometimes wish the *A* would stand for *aspirational*. I have seen many examples of weak goals that represent little challenge, indicate low commitment to equity or outright avoidance, and simply reinforce low expectations for some groups of students in particular. On the other hand, I recall a group of kindergarten teachers who challenged the School Board of a district that was writing goals for a new strategic plan. The Board had been discussing whether the goal to "lower dropout rate" should be set at 5 percent or something closer to 10 percent. The teachers appeared before the Board with photos of their kindergarten classes and stated, "We can save you time and tell you which of these children are already struggling. Are you giving us permission to stop trying since it will be okay if 8 percent of our kids don't make it?" Their point was that the goal should be "100 percent of students who enter kindergarten will graduate"—arguing passionately that any lower goal might be attainable but lack the vision of equity they sought to instill. Whatever they are called, the following must be considered:

- Goals must be challenging.
- Goals must be limited in number.
- A proportion of the goals must focus direct attention on classroom practice.
- Goals must include the type of evidence that will be gathered to measure progress.

This template captures most elements of a SMART goal:

By _____ (time), _____ (quantity, percentage) of students will _____ (do what) as measured by _____ (evidence, not necessarily test). Using the word *students* right in the goal statement greatly increases the focus on student learning as the measurable outcome—the end—for which all other goals and strategies are the means. The openness of what students "will _____" allows this goal framework to be used for goals based on academic achievement, measured by an assessment, or on any of the whole child indicators measured by attendance, participation, service, etc. The exact wording of goals may not be in final form at this stage of the process. The deeper analysis to come in the STUDY phase will provide further insights and ideas about sources of evidence that may refine the goal itself.

Study

We learn again from Hord, Roussin, and Sommers (2010) that

> the professionals will examine multiple sources of student data to identify areas where students are performing successfully and areas that require teaching attention. When a priority area for attention has been identified, the professionals determine what they will revise or change in their teaching practices that will enable students to learn well. Subsequently, professional learning is specified that will develop the capacity of the professionals to use the new practice in an effective way . . . [this] requires ongoing, substantive, and job-embedded professional development. (p. 7)

In addition, I would simply increase the scope of study to include learning conditions and organizational systems and policies. This draws on the nonacademic, or whole child, sets of data for consideration in planning change.

The three bullet points in the STUDY component represent three kinds of investigation that should occur before Strategies are selected and Action Plans are laid out. For each of the priority areas—let's say reading and math and attendance—the first bullet point represents the necessity for deeper analysis of the data to get specific about the variations in student performance and the characteristics of the struggling learners. One of the uses of data described in Chapter 1 was to "identify and plan for student populations with specific needs." This includes the schoolwide responsibility for systems to support English language learners (ELLs), students with individualized education programs (IEPs), and others. The day-to-day responsibility for these students as individuals rests with the teachers in their Teaching Teams, but expectations and provisions for collaboration between general education teachers and special education teachers need to be set with a schoolwide perspective in mind, including systems for Response to Intervention (RTI) or MTSS.

The second bullet point represents a thorough examination of the research and best practice literature related to that priority area. After being more clear and specific about students' needs, the second inquiry question is "What are the most effective ways to meet these needs?" Here, the word *DATA* is a reminder to carefully sort out opinion blogs from actual evidence of impact on learning. Chapter 8 focuses on this "looking around" use of data—examination of best practice.

The third bullet point in each of the STUDY boxes represents honest analysis of the existing practices within the school related to that goal area. The purpose of the inquiry is to ask, "What are the gaps between best practice and our practices as a school?" Chapter 9 focuses on the "looking within" use of data.

An example of these three study tasks might flow as follows. The concern is reading achievement. The first bullet point would prompt inquiry into the specific skills that many students are missing and who are the specific students who are missing more skills than others. Let's say it turns out that most students are doing well reading some kinds of text but decidedly less successful with informational text. In response to the second bullet prompt, staff would not have time to study everything that works for something as general as "literacy" or even "reading" but would look specifically for powerful strategies for unlocking informational text. Once that search identified effective strategies, the third bullet point would cause teachers to ask, "Who's already doing this in our school? How did they learn about it? Are their kids being more successful than the rest? What and how can they share with the rest of us?"

Ample time must be provided for this STUDY phase. School B spent two months considering the pros and cons and types of scheduling that might remove their instructional time barrier and support their goal related to critical thinking and problem-solving. Chapter 9 describes use of a cause-and-effect diagram that can help focus attention on factors that may be related to the school's goal and provide opportunities for change. Chapter 8 explores the "look around" for best practices, and examples of ways to "look within" at current practice are described in Chapters 9 and 11.

Strategies

The Strategies selected for implementation must be consistent with the school's mission, linked to needs arising from data, and proven effective in other settings. Back in the Study component, there were three bullet points representing three different lines of inquiry. In the Strategies component, three bullet points serve as a reminder that there is no single silver bullet or magic potion or program that can solve a complex problem. If an unmanageable number of possible strategies are being tossed about, the Decision Matrix shown in Figure 7.4 may be useful. Adaptable for many kinds of decisions, the first step is to decide what attributes would be possessed by the "ideal" decision. In this case, an ideal choice of strategy would be consistent with mission, would increase collaboration, could facilitate parent involvement, and would need no new resources. The Shared Leadership Team might be the group gathering proposed solutions and analyzing their potential.

A powerful combination of effective strategies must be created and coordinated. These questions may also help narrow down to the decision

Figure 7.4 Decision Matrix					
Possible Solutions	**Criterion #1**	**Criterion #2**	**Criterion #3**	**Criterion #4**	**Individual Total**
List all items under consideration	Rate each item 1–5, with 5 being ideal. Example: Consistent with mission and beliefs	Rate each item 1–5, with 5 being ideal. Example: Increases staff unity and collaboration	Rate each item 1–5, with 5 being ideal. Example: Includes component for parent involvement	Rate each item 1–5, with 5 being ideal. Example: Needs no new resources	

point: What do we commit to doing collectively to strengthen our practices and elevate them to the same level proven to be effective? Are the strategies we've identified robust enough to accomplish our goals? Are they specific enough for every teacher to understand and implement them? The need for this clarity of roles and descriptions of practice will become more clear as we explore the development of Action Plans further in Chapter 9.

Evidence

In the past, traditional methods of program evaluation and school improvement claimed success by reporting evidence that selected strategies were implemented. Glowing accounts were provided of the number of teachers who attended training and the number of new initiatives begun. Individual teachers kept track of student progress in idiosyncratic ways at the classroom level, but there was little assurance that this data matched schoolwide goals or could be aggregated to show student progress for the school as a whole. As noted in Chapter 1, high-performing schools identify formative assessments they will use to monitor students in a more frequent, more authentic and less threatening way than the large-scale assessments they also administer and analyze. The two bullet points in the *Evidence* component represent the need to verify *implementation* of the selected strategies **and** assure that this effort has an *impact* on student learning. School B mentioned the new schedule, professional development and new curriculum documents—evidence of implementation—as well as improved student achievement data and higher levels of satisfaction on surveys—evidence of impact.

The two-way arrow between Strategies and Evidence reminds us that determining what evidence we need and learning how to gather it will also inform what we need to do as strategies so the evidence we seek will be available. Some of the data needed as evidence will automatically come from the state to the district and on to the school. Other data will be school-specific and must be intentionally collected. The plans for how to collect this data should be explicit and intentional. Figure 7.5 illustrates how one middle school identified all the sources of qualitative and quantitative evidence that would be needed to monitor their progress. This chart guided the work of the Data Team so they could plan ahead and make sure the data were gathered and would be available to monitor progress and celebrate success. Chapter 11 provides specific examples of how other schools have gathered and reported evidence of implementation and impact.

Figure 7.5 Middle School Evidence Plan

Tools	Attendance, Sign-in Sheets	Fliers, Notices, Articles	Meeting Notes, Documents	Assignment Sheets in ISS	Staff Survey	Parent Survey	Student Survey/ Interview	Targeted Methodology	Overall GPA Analysis	Overall Test Score Analysis	% Participation in Extracurricular Activities
Discipline											
Consistent implementation of HLS	X		X					Analysis of infractions by category			
Improving effectiveness of ISS				X				Improvement of grades and decrease of use by ISS users			
Parent Involvement											
P.I.E. nights	X	X						Parents come; grades up and homework up	X	X	
Lighted schoolhouse	X	X					X				
Calendar of events		X					X			X	
Directory of parents to volunteer			Directory X		X	X					
Directory of teachers' pictures and information			Directory X		X	X					
Community action team	To be developed in the future										
Continue PTSA	To be developed in the future										

Tools	Attendance, Sign-in Sheets	Fliers, Notices, Articles	Meeting Notes, Documents	Assignment Sheets in ISS	Staff Survey	Parent Survey	Student Survey/ Interview	Targeted Methodology	Overall GPA Analysis	Overall Test Score Analysis	% Participation in Extracurricular Activities
Teaching and Learning											
Powerful Learning											
Application of Dimensions of Learning			Training participation X		X					Analysis by level	
Schoolwide Enrichment Model							X	Analysis by Friday attendance			
Expanded Learning Support			House plans X		X		X	Pre- and post-test		Analysis by level	
Communications											
Thursday bulletin with staff issues page			X		X						
Staff liaisons, mediation team	X		X		X			# of referrals and resolutions			
Technology for better parent-teacher communications					X	X		Homework completion			
E-mail; dismantle computer lab			X		X						
Team-building activities	X				X						
	Qualitative Measures						**Quantitative Measures**				

Source: Used with permission of Blane McCann, John Bullen Middle School, Kenosha, Wisconsin.

Action Plans

The *Action Plans* blocks on Figure 7.1 are a reminder that more detailed planning is needed to assure implementation of the strategies that were selected and collection of the needed evidence to document success. Specific, concrete Action Plans identify the who, when, where, and with what funding. Chapter 9 provides guidelines and an Action Plan Template, along with an example related to attendance.

Posting the Big Picture

The components of Mission, School Portfolio, Celebrations and Concerns, Priorities, Strategies, and Evidence signal major decisions about what the school's focus will be, what new work the school will initiate, and how the school will determine its effectiveness. This overall plan-at-a-glance can be displayed, publicized, and referred to frequently. Some schools have enlarged Figure 7.1 to poster size and used it as a worksheet to guide their planning discussions.

One school filled a huge bulletin board in its foyer with the components from Figure 7.1. Staff members created a beautiful poster of their Mission statement and displayed it on the top left corner of the bulletin board. In the lower left corner, they posted the executive summary of their conclusions from analysis of the data in their School Portfolio. Goals for the Priorities they set were lettered in calligraphy on sentence strips. Strategies for each goal were connected by colored string, which gave them the ability to connect several strategies to more than one goal area. Criteria they would be monitoring were posted as sources of Evidence. Their combined master plan was illustrated with a series of laminated monthly calendars that highlighted the events from the Action Plans. Any visitor to this school knew what was happening and why. Any new idea or grant opportunity had to pass the acid test of proving where it would fit on that crowded, colorful bulletin board. A "big-picture view" like this helps keep leaders, staff, and stakeholders grounded when multiple efforts seem overwhelming and things may feel like they are starting to spin out of control.

KEY POINTS FOR STAKEHOLDER INVOLVEMENT

Chapter 4 described the composition of the Shared Leadership Team, Data Team, and Teaching Teams. Parent representatives and community members were not included as standing members of those teams—only because direct, ongoing participation on a group that meets for several hours a month is difficult to orchestrate. My own follow-up after training school improvement teams that included community members has verified that very few of these stakeholders remained active once the mission was written and initial goals set. The need for a Shared Leadership Team to discuss the school culture, which may include staff dynamics, and the focus on provisions for struggling learners may raise issues of privacy, confidentiality, trust, and comfort.

The difficulty of maintaining consistent participation of stakeholder representatives is exacerbated by the need to assure that constituents represent the full range of parents and community members who are part of the school's clientele. This is more readily accomplished on an ad hoc basis—adding broad representation for specific purposes at key points in the process. For example, creating the initial School Portfolio should include gathering input and perceptual (usually survey) data from *all* family and community stakeholders. Assisting with the analysis of that data is an excellent opportunity for a focus group—perhaps several focus groups from different groups and neighborhoods. Their purpose would be to help clarify how parents may have interpreted the questions, hear their suggestions for change, and gauge how they might react to various strategies the school is considering.

Chapter 6 described the school leadership team that had administered a formal survey, based on school effectiveness research, developed by a highly respected consultant group. Most of the responses made sense. There were no surprises except for negative parent responses regarding the format of parent-teacher conferences and "student recognition." The task force was cochaired by two members of the school improvement team and included volunteers who agreed to help analyze the survey data. They were not too concerned about the parent conference item. Teachers had talked for some time about how they needed to make different arrangements for these important communication opportunities. But they *were* quite distressed about the student recognition item, and they began to list all the ways in which students were recognized for good work, good behavior, helping others, and so forth. They wondered what more they could do and were about to propose a subcommittee to explore ways to get funding from local businesses to provide more student incentives, when one member said, "I wonder what *parents* thought student recognition means."

After a few moments of silent confusion, a first-year teacher timidly suggested, "Maybe we should ask them." It sounded like a pretty logical next move, and the principal helped identify members of a focus group, who were invited to come and discuss the items on the parent survey and what they were thinking as they read them. Through the focus group, school leaders discovered that the "student recognition" parents wanted was for the principal to know their children's names and for all teachers to get to know even the students who were not in their classes and to address them by name—or at least with more respect than "Hey, kid." The face-to-face communication of a focus group shifted the attention of staff from initiating more extrinsic reward systems to looking at the culture of the school and the interactions between staff and students. Face-to-face communication is especially needed in schools where the demographics of parents and the community are in sharp contrast with the characteristics of staff. Johnson (2002) pointed out that "those in power often silence the dialogue when those who share the culture of poverty and children of color disagree with proposed solutions" (p. 74). Adults who share the culture of the students must be engaged in the search for promising practices and program changes to assist their children's learning.

Specific tasks and defined time commitments can provide opportunities for many more stakeholder participants, can attract those with interest and expertise to apply to just one aspect of the process, and can make it easier to recruit busy people. These ad hoc groups can also be scheduled to meet at times that match their availability—rather than during the school hours when the full Shared Leadership Team may typically meet.

PICTURING THE WORK OF TEACHING TEAMS

Figure 4.1 illustrated the relationship between the Shared Leadership Team and the Teaching Teams its members represent. In its brief on the need for education data, the Alliance for Excellent Education (Slaven, 2015) described differences between the "whole school" focus and the work in Teaching Teams:

Schools use data and learning information to measure students' learning schoolwide and hold teachers, and the school as a whole, accountable for student performance. Principals [and others] monitor student learning information across grade levels and work with teachers to identify those units, subjects, or classes where students are struggling . . . teachers collaborate as grade-level and subject-specific teams to identify learning trends among individual students, classes, or an entire grade level. Armed with accurate and specific data about student learning, teachers can collaborate on teaching approaches and work with . . . specialists to address the learning of individual and groups of students, often flexibly arranging students based on need to provide research-based interventions. (pp. 2–3)

Figure 7.6 illustrates these roles of Teaching Teams. While the work of school improvement planning, shown in Figures 7.1 and 7.2, may represent an annual cycle, this work of Teaching Teams is shorter, more frequent, and focused more closely on the individual faces of students as emphasized in Chapter 5. This cycle represents the ongoing curriculum work and planning of instruction and assessment that must be predictable and relentless in all Teaching Teams. A more open-ended type of inquiry that can also be part of the professional learning of a Teaching Team is presented later in the chapter.

Preplanning the Grade or Course

Summer and semester breaks are two times that teachers have traditionally engaged in the "curriculum work" of examining the content they are responsible to teach. This work is summarized in the upper left-hand corner of Figure 7.6. It begins with *identifying the academic standards* aligned to the grade or course description. These may be standards from a national source, such as the Common Core State Standards, from a state-delineated set of academic standards, or from a professional organization that represents a specific content area, such as the Common Career Technical Core developed by the National Association of State Directors of Career Technical Education. As Reeves, Marzano, and others have pointed out, there are far too many standards and a pervasive need to *prioritize* them. Standards rise from important to essential or critical when they represent all three criteria Ainsworth (2003) referred to as endurance, leverage, and readiness. Standards with endurance, such as understanding cause and effect, have relevance for application in the real world and throughout a lifetime of learning. Standards with leverage have horizontal application—cutting across multiple disciplines and content areas. And standards with readiness implications involve skills that are essential for success in subsequent levels of schooling, sometimes call prerequisites. Each of these critical, or "power," standards must be *analyzed* carefully in order to understand the *level of thinking* that will be required to demonstrate real proficiency, and to identify necessary *vocabulary* that must be preassessed and/or explicitly taught in order to assure that all students can navigate the language of the concepts. Many academic standards span grade levels with increasing levels of complexity, and it's important and reassuring for

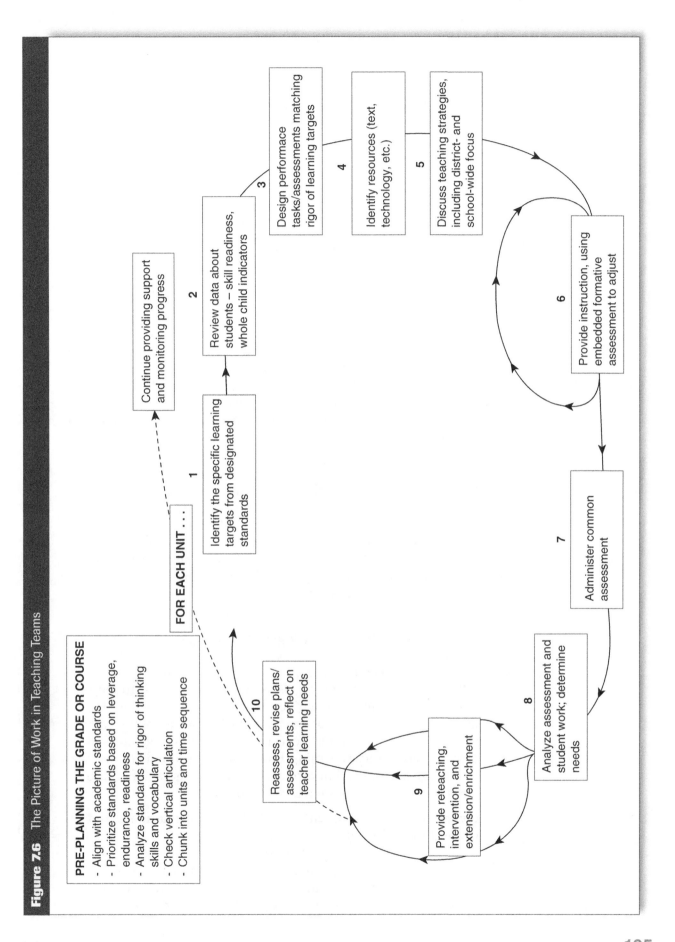

Figure 7.6 The Picture of Work in Teaching Teams

PRE-PLANNING THE GRADE OR COURSE
- Align with academic standards
- Prioritize standards based on leverage, endurance, readiness
- Analyze standards for rigor of thinking skills and vocabulary
- Check vertical articulation
- Chunk into units and time sequence

Continue providing support and monitoring progress

FOR EACH UNIT . . .

1. Identify the specific learning targets from designated standards

2. Review data about students – skill readiness, whole child indicators

3. Design performace tasks/assessments matching rigor of learning targets

4. Identify resources (text, technology, etc.)

5. Discuss teaching strategies, including district- and school-wide focus

6. Provide instruction, using embedded formative assessment to adjust

7. Administer common assessment

8. Analyze assessment and student work; determine needs

9. Provide reteaching, intervention, and extension/enrichment

10. Reassess, revise plans/ assessments, reflect on teacher learning needs

teachers to know how their responsibility fits the learning progression of the overall standard. This necessitates *vertical articulation*—conversations with teachers at one grade (or course) higher and one lower—in order to understand the flow of student learning and avoid duplication or teaching of skills and concepts out of the most logical and student-accessible sequence. Having clarified the demands of the standards they will teach, the year or semester is *"chunked out"* into an approximation of the *sequence and time allocations* that will be assigned to the content. This should not be confused with the lock-step pacing guides that emerged too frequently during the NCLB era, requiring every teacher to be on page x on day z in order to cover all the standards. But it is necessary to have general agreement on time parameters in order to coordinate collaboration on common work during the course of instruction.

Cycling Through a Unit

Figure 7.6 illustrates a cycle that occurs for each unit of that course of instruction. The dominant arrow represents movement through ten types of tasks that occur approximately in sequence and are numbered as steps for convenience. Throughout this cycle, Teaching Teams participate in the high-performing data uses (Chapter 1) of identifying formative assessments to balance large-scale high-stakes tests and using formative assessments at regular intervals throughout the year. During these steps, team members will explore the critical questions introduced by Kamm (2010):

> Which research-based strategies will we use to ensure that each student has mastered the priority skills and concepts? How can we effectively engage students to be active participants or leaders in their own learning? How will we assess that each student has learned the targeted skills and concepts? What interventions will we establish to provide lifelines for students who are not proficient in essential skills and concepts? How will we enrich the learning of students who are already proficient? (p. 169)

1. **Identify the specific learning targets from designated standards.**

    Unlike a standard that may encompass an entire course or grade level or even multiple grade levels, Moss and Brookhart (2012) described learning targets as "what you intend students to learn or accomplish in a given lesson" (p. 9). These are the immediate goals of instruction that the teacher is monitoring during the lesson in order to check for understanding. As used later in Step 3, these learning targets also represent the new knowledge and skills that formative assessments will measure to assure that students are ready to move on.

2. **Review data about students—including skill readiness and whole child indicators.**

    This step does not imply that formal preassessment is necessary for every cycle of teaching and assessment that lasts only a few weeks. As Teaching Teams have accessed data from the previous grades and assessments, they will have prior information already available. This step is a reminder to review what the team knows about students' cultures, life experiences, and learning styles, as well as the other data that reflects their faces as noted in Chapter 5. For example, Brennan (2015) described her reaction to the discovery that students who were failing classes and state assessments were the same ones who were visiting the office for discipline, were suspended, or were often absent. Although staff had discussed relationships, classroom management, and discipline matrices, they realized that they needed to be more explicitly intentional in their use of knowledge about students to build relationships and create the classroom conditions that increase motivation. Consideration of student needs does not change the learning targets—it informs the planning of instruction and assessment so that the learning targets are most effectively and equitably accessible for the students.

3. **Design performance tasks and/or assessments matching the rigor of learning targets.**

    This step highlights a key aspect of the sequence of work in Teaching Teams. The assessment is developed *before* the instruction is planned so that teachers can assure that the tasks and activities used during instruction will allow students to demonstrate—and the teacher to observe—whether the learning targets are being met. The items in the formative assessment must match the cognitive demands of the learning targets identified in Step 1. Teaching Teams should review their previous experience teaching these concepts and skills in order to recall and anticipate common errors and misconceptions that have occurred. Multiple-choice items can be developed in a very intentional way so that incorrect choices identify the kind of error students are making. Teaching Teams also need to agree on the criteria for success that will represent proficiency to both teachers and students. This may entail development of a product such as a scoring guide, answer key, attributes of a complete answer, or a common rubric for multiple uses (e.g., essay writing, mathematical problem-solving). It also requires agreement on what the "cut score" or level will be that represents successful learning.

4. **Identify resources (text, materials, technology, etc.).**

    Steps 4 and 5 go hand in hand. Once teachers have identified the learning targets and described what success will look like, they share ideas about resources available in textbooks, online resources, lab materials, etc. This may be a radical departure if traditional practices have been a chapter-by-chapter walk through a published textbook.

5. **Discuss teaching strategies, including district- and school-wide focus.**

    All team members teach to the same learning targets and apply the same success criteria, but this does not mean that every teacher's lesson plan will be identical. Each classroom has a different composition of different students with different needs; teachers are different, too. But professional learning implies that teachers share what they have found to be effective from their knowledge and experience with this content. They often work together to develop critical or essential questions that will be posed to students. A question that prompts substantive student dialogue and allows the teacher to note students' thinking processes and comprehension is not easily developed on the spur of the moment. Teaching teams may also support each other with ideas for increasing active student engagement. They may review participation strategies such as cold calling, randomization by computer or craft sticks, or ABCD response cards (Wiliam, 2011).

6. **Provide instruction, using embedded formative assessment to adjust.**

On Figure 7.6, a circular arrow is shown cycling around this step in the lower right-hand corner. It represents the need to use observations of student learning (or lack) from each day's lesson to plan and provide instruction the following day. The whole class may need review of a step in a skill, or reteaching of a concept with different examples. A small group or a student may need individual support with a specific need. As Slaven (2015) pointed out,

> Richer, real-time sources of information, known as formative assessment, help teachers understand what content and skill students have not yet mastered and where additional instruction or support is needed. Formative assessment refers to a wide variety of methods—including teacher observations, class discussions, student projects, digital content, and many other options—that teachers use to monitor student comprehension *during a lesson*. Unlike the typical standardized tests that measure a student's knowledge only at the end of a course or at the end of the school year, formative assessment provides a deeper picture about the progress of a student's learning *each day*. (p. 2, italics mine)

In the language of RTI or MTSS, these embedded assessments and the responses provided in the next day's lesson represent Tier 1 in-class adjustments. This is also where differentiation strategies are employed, and personalized learning may eventually develop.

New opportunities include technology clickers, individual whiteboards, or text responses from student cell phones. Exit tickets serve as formative assessment when they are designed to match the success criteria of learning targets—and can engage students in self-assessment of their progress. In other words, every time students participate, it represents a formative assessment opportunity that should be used intentionally.

7. **Administer common assessment.**

The strategies that teachers use to engage students and gather *embedded* formative assessment (Wiliam, 2011) during the instruction will vary from teacher to teacher. The *common* formative assessment that Teaching Teams develop together (Ainsworth & Viegut, 2006) is a more formal exercise that will be used by all teachers of the same grade or course. It would be administered to all students of that same grade or course on an agreed-upon date, with time scheduled promptly for collaborative analysis of the results.

8. **Analyze assessment and student work and determine needs.**

    Figure 7.7 provides a generic protocol for analyzing student work that is particularly useful for Teaching Teams looking at the results of common formative assessments. Part I illustrates how a common formative assessment may have items related to three learning targets that have been addressed in the past two to three weeks. (If a common formative assessment addresses more than three learning targets, it may be an indication that too much time or content has been added since the last teaching-assessing cycle). Part I is completed by each teacher before the team meets. This can be done on one shared document or brought to the meeting on separate documents with copies for all. For students who were not successful, there is a place to note common errors that occurred in their work.

    Part II of the protocol suggests four topics of discussion in the analysis meeting. Students should always be provided with feedback, and this area prompts the need to discuss meaningful feedback on strengths as well as areas to work on. The second topic also encourages teachers to share what worked with their students so that more can benefit in future. As one teacher stated, "If something worked and your children really benefited from it, wouldn't you want as many children as possible to gain from that?" (Tschannen-Moran, 2014, p. 133). Part II also captures notes on plans for reteaching and individual support, which will inform Steps 9 and 10.

    Part III focuses on refining teacher work and determining the learning needs of the educators, which can lead to professional development planning and the kinds of teacher inquiry described in following sections.

9. **Provide reteaching, intervention, and extensions or enrichment.**

    As noted by the circular arrow in Step 6 of Figure 7.6, teachers have already been adjusting instruction from day to day based on formative assessment they gathered. At Step 9, three parallel arrows represent more intense responses based on the data just reviewed. Part II of Figure 7.7 guides teachers in making plans for this additional support and extension. In some cases, the school psychologist, counselor, or other educator with special expertise joins the Teaching Team once a month to discuss needs for follow-up through more robust interventions such as RTI or MTSS. Or teams may provide a range of follow-up by taking a day or two to regroup and redistribute students among the classrooms represented on the team. Figure 7.6 also shows the reteaching arrow continuing on as a dotted line. Even as the teachers move to the next unit, ongoing support and progress monitoring will be needed for some students.

Figure 7.7   Analysis of Student and Teacher Learning

Team:	Date:	Grade/Course:

Student Task/Assessment:

PART I. ANALYSIS

Learning Target 1:

Students not proficient	Students proficient	Students above proficient
Common errors		

Learning Target 2:

Students not proficient	Students proficient	Students above proficient
Common errors		

Learning Target 3:

Students not proficient	Students proficient	Students above proficient
Common errors		

PART II. Responses to Student Needs:

Feedback to provide to students

Strategies used that contributed to success

Plans for reteaching common errors

Plans for individual support

PART III. Notes for Teacher Work and Learning:

Revisions to unit plan

Revisions to assessment

Based on how our students learned, what do *we* need to learn?

10. **Reassess students and continue providing support and monitoring progress. Revise instructional plans and assessments for future, and reflect on teacher learning needs.**

The first sentence of this step is the work focused on student learning and the ongoing support mentioned previously. This support must be provided outside the time that core instruction occurs in the classroom so that the student is not denied access to the general curriculum and the opportunity to learn and demonstrate learning of the designated targets. This dotted arrow would continue around—or weave in and out and braid with—the dominant arrow of subsequent units.

The second sentence of Step 10 prompts reflection on the learning needs of the teachers. As shown in Part III of Figure 7.7, analysis of students' responses on the common formative assessment may point out revisions that are needed to the unit planning stage or to the assessment itself. The bottom line is, based on what *students* still needed, what might *we* need to learn in order to be even more effective as we work with another group in future?

INQUIRY IN TEACHING TEAMS

The cycle of curriculum, instruction, and assessment work conducted in Teaching Teams is essential, routine, and predictable. Another more open-ended way of using data in Teaching Teams is to pursue a question or questions about classroom experiences, issues, or challenges that arise right where teaching and learning occurs. This process has been described in various ways as inquiry or action research. Hord and Sommers (2008) referred to it as collegial learning and described six steps, which include (1) identifying an area or issue that requires staff's change of knowledge and skills, (2) deciding what to learn to gain the new knowledge and skills and how to learn it, (3) engaging in the learning, (4) applying the learning appropriately in classrooms, (5) debriefing with colleagues about how it went and assessing effectiveness, and (6) revising, based on the new learning from experience, and applying again (pp. 144–155).

Sagor (2000) presented a series of seven steps in a similar vein. Step 1 is selecting a focus based on this question: What elements of our practice or what aspect of student learning do we wish to investigate? In other words, action research is a form of professional learning in which educators study the data on their students' learning in relationship to their own teaching. In Step 2, teachers clarify their theories about why students are performing as they do (or not). They generate a research question or hypothesis, such as this: If I use Marzano's process for teaching the academic vocabulary of this standard more explicitly and have students maintain an academic notebook, they will be more successful reading the related informational text. Steps 4, 5, and 6 involve collecting data on their usage and students' performance, analyzing the data and sharing results with colleagues. Step 7 is to take informed action moving forward—continuing the practice that proved to be successful, or refining or trying a different strategy. This approach provides a framework for trying out different approaches and ideas on a small scale, builds a culture of reflection and collaboration, and helps teachers improve student learning.

A new perspective on the short-term inquiry approach blends the informal action research of teacher teams with longer term experimental studies conducted by researchers. An initiative of the Carnegie Foundation for the Advancement of Teaching (Sparks, 2013), "improvement science" allows educators in a wide variety of settings to try out new interventions for periods of ninety days or a semester. School districts coordinate networks of teachers and principals with researchers in cooperation with the National Science Foundation and the Institute of Education Sciences.

Demonstration classrooms focus on a specific problem, such as student attendance. The hope is that by involving K–12 teachers and principals earlier in these studies, it will be possible to more confidently assure that promising new interventions will succeed when taken to scale.

VIEWING TEACHING TEAMS IN ACTION

A picture is worth a thousand words, and a video of a working team can fill in the vision of this practice better than multiple pages. Since 2010, Learning Forward and Corwin have presented the Shirley Hord Teacher Learning Team Award to honor a team of teachers that demonstrates excellence in professional learning. This annual award recognizes a school-based learning team that exhibits evidence of successful implementation of a cycle of continuous improvement that results in increased teaching effectiveness. Like School B, their cycle may have evolved as they looked at their students' needs. Or their process may have been guided by other structures and guidelines than described here. But their work has provided opportunities for increased student and professional learning. Go to www.learningforward.org, and search "Hord Award winners" to view video of award-winning teams involved in painting the big picture of collaborative work and student growth.

Chapter 8

You Get More Excited About Data When . . . It Saves Resources

Chapter 7 included a multipurpose decision matrix (Figure 7.4), which included the issue of resources as one criteria affecting a choice of strategies to implement in service of an established goal. The uses of data described in Chapter 1 address this reality: data is needed to help educators focus on most critical priorities to conserve time, energy, and money. They can't waste money on things that won't work or don't fit their values and context. They must not squander the even-more-precious resources of time, energy, and morale on things that don't have a demonstrated high probability of achieving the results they seek. This includes abandoning practices that aren't currently working or have resulted in weakening the values and culture of the school.

One key to conserving resources is to be clear about the difference between goals and strategies as described in Chapter 7. One of the two high schools contrasted there confused a goal with a strategy when they tackled block scheduling as the goal itself—a change for the sake of change. The other high school had clear goals and chose block scheduling as one of the strategies to accomplish their goals. The rush of time to "get a plan done" can push educators to leap into decisions before giving them adequate consideration, but the cliché "go slow to go fast" is very accurate. A bad choice of strategies not only wastes the time and energy of those diligently attempting to implement it, but also wastes precious time of students. Each year that goes by without effective intervention is a year of possibility that our students lose as they move on and out of our classrooms and schools.

CONSOLIDATING MULTIPLE AND EXISTING PLANS

In a session with staff at a state Department of Education, I shared the frustration practitioners had expressed about how many different plans they had to create and file—and in many cases, forget in the press of confusion, overlap, and duplication. After a few moments of protest, these well-intended leaders began to list plans they knew about and/or required themselves as part of their jobs. On that day, the list was 46. Your school may be affected by and involved in many of those in Figure 8.1 and others. Some have changed names. The various "Titles" have been somewhat reorganized from the No Child Left Behind Act (NCLB) to Every Student Succeeds Act (ESSA), but virtually all remain in substance. Important questions to be asked as you consider ways to save resources are

- How many plans are we into already?
- Where are they?
- What do they require of us?
- Is the school the major focus or is the primary activity and responsibility a function of the district? (See Chapter 12 for more about the district role.)

Plans that clearly fall within the scope of the school context need to be reviewed and aligned in every way possible with the School Improvement Plan described in Chapter 7 and further in Chapter 9. For example, the existence of a reading improvement plan mandated by the state to the

Figure 8.1 Possible Plans Already in Place

- Self-Study Plan for Accreditation
- Crisis Response Plan
- Safety Procedures
- Reading Improvement Plans
- State Technology Grant Plan
- Technology in Literacy Challenge Fund Plan (Grant)
- School-to-Work Plan
- Readiness to Learn Plan
- Comprehensive School Reform Design (Grant) Choice and Plan
- K–2 Professional Development Grant Plan
- 21st Century Community Schools Grant Plan
- District Strategic Plan
- District Assessment Plan
- Transportation Plan
- Facilities Expansion Plan
- Asbestos Management and Education Plan
- Budget Development Plan
- District Staff Development Plans
- School Staff Development Plans
- Individual Staff Development Plans
- Bilingual Education Plan
- Highly Capable/Gifted Plan
- Response to Intervention (RTI) Plan
- Title I Plan
- Title II Plan
- Title IV Plan
- Title VI Plan
- Title IX Plan
- Carl Perkins Plan
- Migrant Education Plan
- Homeless Education Plan
- ADA Accessibility Plan

district indicates that one priority area has already been identified as reading and probably includes some strategies that have already been selected or mandated for implementation. These should be reflected in the school's single-aligned plan rather than being housed in a separate place and creating the probability that the school will add more strategies, with the resulting potential for overload and fragmentation, and poor implementation of any of the promising practices. June Rimmer (2016) wrote of two critical tasks:

> (1) Ensure that every initiative is well aligned to the vision and goals of the school, particularly for struggling students; and (2) make certain that the staff understands how all of the district and school initiatives are integrated, aligned and support the vision and mission of the school. The alignment and integration of school initiatives can be extremely challenging, and when not done, or not done well, can result in fragmentation, poor communication, lack of focus, isolation, mistrust and, quite frankly, a bit of chaos. For this work to be done well, a number of processes must be in place: There must be clarity and agreement on a shared vision and mission grounded in equity and excellence; there must be a widely understood theory of action about ways to address problems of practice at all levels; and there must be clearly articulated measures of success and a school-wide commitment to adopt only those initiatives that are aligned to the vision and that address the defined problems of learning, practice and support. Finally, leaders must ensure there are equity-based systems in place for ongoing assessment of program implementation, performance management, and student and school performance. Accomplishing this degree of clarity, alignment and systems is a significant feat, requiring ongoing reflection and refinement . . . one person cannot do all the work of school leadership, nor should one try. Leadership of a school should be the work of a team of leaders. (pp. 10–11)

TESTING ASSUMPTIONS
BEFORE SEEKING SOLUTIONS

The discussion of putting faces on data in Chapter 5 included an example drawn from data that first illustrated the distribution of student scores in proficiency levels and then disaggregated the scores of students "below basic" according to race, gender, and socioeconomic status (SES). This illustrated the need that one-time data from a large-scale assessment should always be "sliced and diced" in a variety of ways and compared with other measures to avoid rapid leaps to conclusions that are tempting given the press of time. The reality that struggling students represented all populations within the school challenged a well-intended but inaccurate assumption that had been leading to adoption of a plan aimed *only* at one population—black males. This is an example of why it's important to be tightly focused on very few goal areas, because multiple strategies will be necessary to meet the range of needs identified when the data is carefully reviewed.

Chapter 5 included two nonacademic examples of the need to use data to test assumptions before potentially spending money, time, and/or energy on misguided change efforts. Figure 5.10 (p. 77) displayed attendance data that helped to create changes in school policy that required no money at all—but, to be honest, did require some time and energy explaining the rationale for having closed campus. Figure 5.11 (p. 78) illustrated how a Pareto chart helped pinpoint the main sources of school discipline issues and steer the school away from costly items like their interest in more monitors (human and electronic) on the school buses.

Use of data to test assumptions can also contribute to the dynamics between adults in the school culture. Frustration was high at one elementary school because the lunch personnel seemed to take too long to serve the children, and this caused longer lines and reduced the classroom teachers' own lunchtime. The teachers thought the answer was to hire more kitchen staff to serve the children—a costly response—or to create different menus—a proposal that kitchen staff found insulting. Based on the menus, teachers predicted how long it would take to complete serving. The staff then monitored the lunch line for ten days to verify the actual time it took for students to be served. Each teacher recorded arrival time, the time the first student was served, and the time the last child was served. Figure 8.2 shows that the effects were much less than teachers expected. On eight out of ten days, the variation in serving time for the whole school was four minutes or less. On every one of the ten days monitored, the actual serving time was from two to twelve minutes less than predicted.

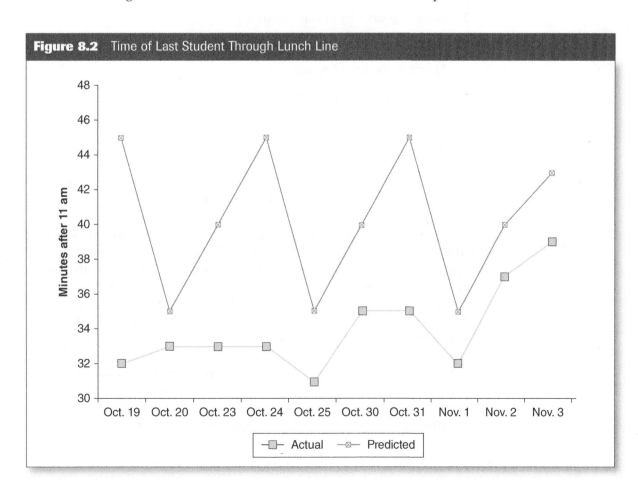

Figure 8.2 Time of Last Student Through Lunch Line

Ruffled feathers were smoothed, and time and energy that might have been expended on a staffing issue could be conserved for other purposes. This type of data, gathered to resolve a specific problem, might be included in the School Portfolio or might simply be compiled and analyzed to better understand a situation, and archived if needed for future reference.

CONFIRMING BEST PRACTICES

One of the biggest and best changes that I have noted since first writing about use of data has been increased access to practitioner-friendly ways of identifying effective strategies. At the time of the first edition, Gordon Cawelti, executive director of the Association for Supervision and Curriculum Development (ASCD), introduced me to the concept of meta-analysis in a conversation on a hotel-airport shuttle bus and shared a chart he had been working on. By the second edition, meta-analyses by Robert Marzano had been published as *Classroom Instruction That Works* (Marzano, Pickering, & Pollock, 2001) and "The Essential Nine," which were summarized in publications by ASCD (Varlas, 2002) and the National Staff Development Council (NSDC) (now Learning Forward). They included the following:

1. Identifying Similarities and Differences

2. Summarizing and Note Taking

3. Reinforcing Effort and Providing Recognition

4. Homework and Practice

5. Nonlinguistic Representations

6. Cooperative Learning

7. Setting Objectives and Providing Feedback

8. Generating and Testing Hypotheses

9. Cues, Questions, and Advance Organizers

These aspects of teacher behavior and their impact on student learning became the focus of many training initiatives and remain important as essential tools in a teacher's repertoire. Marzano's work has continued to expand first into *The Art and Science of Teaching* (Marzano, 2007) and now into an online resource. Subscribers can pay for a year of access to *The Marzano Compendium of Instructional Strategies* (Marzano, 2015), which presents forty-three instructional elements in ten categories, with a total of 332 instructional strategies described.

A less well-known source of information on effective practices is the IRIS Center, headquartered at Vanderbilt University in Nashville, Tennessee, and Claremont Graduate University in Claremont, California. This center is funded by the U.S. Department of Education's Office of Special Education Programs, with a primary objective to create and infuse resources about evidence-based instructional and intervention practices into preservice preparation and professional development programs. Developed in collaboration with nationally recognized researchers and education experts, IRIS resources are designed to address instructional issues like Response to Intervention (RTI), classroom behavior management, and early childhood instruction. A useful summary of organizations providing sound analyses about instructional strategies is provided as *Trustworthy Sources for Current Evidence-Based Practices for Students in Grades K–12* at http://iris.peabody.vanderbilt.edu/module/ebp_01/cresource/q2/p06/list-of-organizations. The site can also be searched for reports and training modules.

Perhaps the most powerful surge in attention to evidence-based practices is the work of John Hattie, captured in *Visible Learning* (Hattie, 2009) and the handbook for teachers (Hattie, 2012) that followed. Hattie (2009) explained his use of the term *visible* as describing those conditions "when teachers SEE learning through the eyes of the student and when students SEE themselves as their own teachers" (p. 238). Hattie did not conduct meta-analyses but took on an even greater challenge to synthesize over 800 meta-analyses already present in the vast literature no practitioner could possibly absorb. His methodology produced a ranking of practices using a metric called effect size. To oversimplify his methodology with apologies to Hattie, the effect size is essentially the difference in standard deviations of the mean performance of student groups that *did versus did not* experience the practice—or the difference in performance of the same student group *before and after* experiencing the practice. Using this metric, Hattie ranked 138 strategies in order of their effect on learning. All but five of those had some degree of positive impact on student learning—but many were limited to only the same degree of influence as just putting a teacher, any teacher doing anything, with a group of students. Hattie (2009) found that "the effect size of 0.40 sets a level where the effects of innovation enhance achievement in such a way that we can notice real-world differences, and this should be a benchmark of such real-world change . . . a guideline to begin discussions about what we can aim for if we want to see students change . . . a 'standard' from which to judge effects" (p. 17). Hattie referred to this effect size of 0.40 as the "hinge point," roughly the equivalent of the average effect we'd expect from a year of schooling. This is not a criterion on which to make decisions but the place to *start* discussion of changes that could truly make a difference rather than potentially expending resources on efforts already demonstrated to be popular but far less powerful. Figure 8.3 provides a simple list of strategies that meet the "hinge point" criteria. The intent of this limited overview is not to do a disservice to Hattie's in-depth and comprehensive work but to provide a teaser to readers of this simple text and extend a challenge to dig into *Visible Learning for Teachers* (Hattie, 2012). Read to be sure *your* definition of the practice is the same as the researchers' focus. The relevance of saving resources of time, money, and energy is this: Why even take time to talk about practices that have little to no prospect of helping you meet your goals? If your favorite solution to every problem isn't on this list, what more do you need to find out to even justify proposing it? If you've been trying something that is high on this list, but it isn't having results, how will you dig for the specifics about effective implementation and refine your efforts?

Figure 8.3	Sixty-Six Influences on Achievement That Rise Above Hattie's Hinge Point	
Rank	**Domain**	**Influence**
1	Student	Self-report grades
2	Student	Piagetian programs
3	Teaching	Providing formative evaluation
4	Teacher	Micro teaching
5	School	Acceleration
6	School	Classroom behavioral
7	Teaching	Comprehensive interventions for learning disabled students
8	Teacher	Teacher clarity
9	Teaching	Reciprocal teaching
10	Teaching	Feedback
11	Teacher	Teacher-student relationships
12	Teaching	Spaced vs. mass practice
13	Teaching	Meta-cognitive strategies
14	Student	Prior achievement
15	Curricula	Vocabulary programs
16	Curricula	Repeated reading programs
17	Curricula	Creativity programs
18	Teaching	Self-verbalization/self-questioning
19	Teacher	Professional development
20	Teaching	Problem-solving teaching
21	Teacher	Not labeling students
22	Curricula	Phonics instruction
23	Teaching	Teaching strategies
24	Teaching	Cooperative vs. individualistic learning
25	Teaching	Study skills
26	Teaching	Direct Instruction
27	Curricula	Tactile stimulation programs
28	Curricula	Comprehension programs
29	Teaching	Mastery learning
30	Teaching	Worked examples
31	Home	Home environment
32	Home	Socioeconomic status
33	Teaching	Concept mapping

Rank	Domain	Influence
34	Teaching	Goals
35	Curricula	Visual-perception programs
36	Teaching	Peer tutoring
37	Teaching	Cooperative vs. competitive learning
38	Student	Pre-term birth weight
39	School	Classroom cohesion
40	Teaching	Keller's PIS
41	School	Peer influences
42	School	Classroom management
43	Curricula	Outdoor/adventure programs
44	Teaching	Interactive video methods
45	Home	Parental involvement
46	Curricula	Play programs
47	Curricula	Second/third chance programs
48	School	Small group learning
49	Student	Concentration/persistence/engagement
50	School	School effects
51	Student	Motivation
52	Student	Early intervention
53	Teaching	Questioning
54	Curricula	Mathematics
55	Student	Preschool programs
56	Teacher	Quality of teaching
57	Curricula	Writing programs
58	Teacher	Expectations
59	School	School size
60	Student	Self-concept
61	Teaching	Behavioral organizers/adjunct questions
62	Teaching	Matching style of learning
63	Teaching	Cooperative learning
64	Curricula	Science
65	Curricula	Social skills programs
66	Student	Reducing anxiety

Source: Hattie (2009, pp. 297–300).

Another way in which to consider "saving resources" is to compare strategies that have similar levels of success but huge differences in cost. For example, some make a strong intuitive case that smaller class sizes will help students. The costs are huge and the gains in meta-analyses of previous class size reduction studies have only demonstrated an effect size of 0.21. In contrast, consider that reciprocal teaching has an effect size of 0.74—and costs nothing at all except the professional learning needed by staff.

When new strategies are considered and eventually selected by the Shared Leadership Team or Teaching Teams, it's important to be transparent about the process that was followed, the evidence that was used, and create general awareness even before more detailed professional learning may be provided. Some study groups have tried to raise awareness of promising practices by selecting excellent articles and placing copies in everyone's mailbox—and have been disappointed at the lack of reaction to them. Other groups have told me about two strategies that seem to work better. Rather than reproducing a whole article, they prepare a summary on a 3 × 5 card that they distribute. They mention that the full article is posted in several key places in the school and invite anyone interested to talk to one of them about it or meet with them for breakfast on an appointed day. Of course, in most cases the full article can also be accessed by providing a URL. The advantage of referring teachers to a posted example is the greater possibility that they may see each other looking, may be scanning it at the same time, and may be more strongly prompted to engage in collaborative discussion and reflection.

Staff from another school told me that they post an article on a large piece of bulletin board paper in the lounge. They highlight the main points so it can be rapidly skimmed and hang markers beside it. Casual readers leave "graffiti" comments about the article, which prompt others to read and react as well. The informal interaction energizes the thinking of the staff and sometimes generates ideas for consideration that are brought to the leadership team and then shared with the whole faculty.

LEARNING FROM BEST-IN-CLASS SCHOOLS

The first three chapters of this book reviewed uses of data throughout the era of NCLB and described the demoralizing effects on teacher efficacy. The importance of moving discussions forward from legal compliance to local commitment has been a theme throughout. The urgency of attending to achievement gaps is underscored once again. But there *is* always a "but . . ." and some are legitimate. It's not admirable to say, "But you don't understand the kind of kids we have to deal with," but it *is* understandable to say, "We looked at the schools with the best test scores in the state and their demographics are totally different from ours." Magazines love to sell issues that describe the best high schools in the United States, for example, and rarely do they represent a random sample of school populations. Two kinds of comparisons are useful in a School Portfolio. One is comparison of the school's own performance over time. The other would be a comparison to schools that are similar in nature and achieve desired results. This is *benchmarking*, as the term is used in the business sector. A business asks, "Who's in the same kind of business we are with the same kind of product trying to reach the same market—and doing it best?" A school might ask, "Who works with a similar student population in a similar context and has high achievement?"

Balancing equity with empathy, I still feel it's important to include this section that allows a focus on "schools like us." Inspiration comes from what's been accomplished in "schools like ours." When I supervised high-poverty schools, it was thrilling for staff to discover that "wow, we may be lowest in our district, but we're in the top five in the state when you look at the same free and reduced lunch count!" Books and articles abound that provide success stories from highly challenged schools. Websites of the various state departments of education have become much easier to search and find schools that are "best in class." For example, the State Report Card section on the website of the Washington State Office of Superintendent of Public Instruction includes a function called Compare My School. A criteria such as percentage of poverty, mobility, or English language acquisition can be entered, and schools are identified that match those criteria. Their performance can then be compared and contact can be made with those performing at exemplary levels, or making significant progress.

On the other hand, an affluent school resting on its reputation may feel successful because "our scores mirror the state's." They may experience a rude awakening and urgent call to action when faced with an awareness of what the outliers in their group are accomplishing. And complacent adults who attribute low achievement to the characteristics of their learners may be enlightened to discover that the same types of students perform much better in other school settings. These comparisons help identify models for further study and can lead to networking with other schools.

Schools function as true learning communities when they actually observe other schools in action—hearing the voices, feeling the energy, sensing the passion, and seeing the evidence. Face-to-face contact and interaction are still the most powerful forms of communication and collaboration, although electronic exchanges and telephone and videoconferencing increase accessibility. Schools that are serious about studying their practices—and have the courage to compare themselves to "peak performers"—should get acquainted with high-achieving schools "like us" and with "gap-closing" schools. Few learning experiences are as stimulating as one-to-one opportunities to ask, "What do you do? Why do you do it? How did you make it happen?" and to hear the answers directly from those who overcame the obstacles. With regard to saving money, time, and energy, another important question is this: "What did you consider and decide *not* to do? Why? What lessons learned would you pass on to us?"

VETTING NEW PROGRAMS

The uses of data in high-performing schools included identifying and planning for student populations with specific needs. This often leads to discussion of "programs to adopt" that require schoolwide action versus the earlier discussion of practices that can be incorporated by individual teachers or groups of teachers in Teaching Teams. Careful work to sustain momentum doesn't mean that a three-year plan will look exactly the same in Year 2 and Year 3 as it did when it left the drawing board. Better ideas may come along. The strategies that were selected and implemented may not be achieving the desired results. We need to be scanning the horizon all the time to be informed about new developments. But we need to be cautious consumers. The following questions can provide a helpful guide in discussion of whether something new can and should be synthesized with the ongoing efforts of the school or district.

What Are the New Program's Underlying Values and Beliefs? Do Those Values and Beliefs Match Ours?

A lot of programs are packaged with materials and activities that look attractive and appeal to our instincts and intuition. But do they articulate their philosophy? Do they describe the theoretical foundation on which they are based? Is it consistent with the discussions about mission and priorities that have occurred in our school and district? Or, even if it's a good solution for some, will it simply dilute the mixture of energy and effort already under way *here*?

What Results Does This Program Promise? Are They the Same Results That We Want to Achieve Through Our Goals?

"This is really great for kids" is a claim heard so often especially in the exhibit halls at conventions. Because we care about children, we feel guilty if we don't listen. But how *carefully* do we listen? In what *way* is it great for students? *Which* students?

What Evidence Is There That This Program Has Achieved Those Results in Other Schools?

When we are trying so hard to produce proof of our effectiveness with students, why do we let consultants and companies off the hook so easily? "It sounds like something kids would like" is an inadequate reason to adopt a new model. "Teachers really like all these resources" is good but also not adequate. Where's *their* data?

What Steps Are Required to Implement This New Program? Are There Other Processes in Place in Which We Do That?

In the past decade, new labels been placed on existing practices. Covers saying "standards-based" have been slapped onto old workbooks and test-prep materials. Who cares if what we call our effort sounds "old school" if the practices continue to be endorsed as evidence-based, regardless of what they are called? Pendulums swing back and forth. Certain program names become popular or unpopular. Something like Direct Instruction gets a bad name because of a specific product or situation, when the practices embedded within it have generated a Hattie-style effect size of 0.59. Throwing something out that's working is just as detrimental as keeping something that *isn't* working.

What Resources Are Needed to Implement This Program? Can We Afford It?

The reality of resources is that they are not just money but the time and energy of the human resources of the district. Just as individuals can burn themselves out doing good works and end up being unable to help themselves or anyone else, schools and district can, with all good intents and purposes, exceed their organizational capacity and end up in worse shape than they started. The question of "affording" it is not just a budget question; it's also an issue of commitment, credibility, and constancy of purpose.

SAYING "NO, THANK YOU"

The visual reality of Figure 7.1 (p. 108) is that there's literally "only room" for three priorities (also stated as goals). Schools that stay on course identify no more than three to five priority areas—academic and affective—and select a combination of strategies for each that represent a challenging but doable change agenda. If a new approach can't answer any of the previously stated questions to your satisfaction, the proper answer is "no, thank you." This can also be true for money. There are times when the best answer to a possible grant is also "no, thank you." If it doesn't match something that's already in your plan and if the time to generate the application and administer the grant and write the necessary evaluation at the end exceeds the benefits it will bring the school or district, you can get along without it just fine. An administrator once described a rejected grant opportunity this way: "I was up at 4:00 a.m. trying to write this proposal when I realized that by the time the proposal was done, I would have put about $10,000 worth of time and energy into the needs assessment for it, and the planning, and all this work—in order to get a $5,000 grant. I threw the stuff away and went back to bed."

Speaking to Wisconsin educators in 2016, Doug Reeves addressed this need to maintain focus and conserve resources by mimicking a familiar children's ditty with his version of "here a grant, there a grant, everywhere a grant, grant." He acknowledged that it was logical for a principal to ask him, "How can I walk away and leave good money on the table?" Reeves' answer was succinct: "If it will distract you from the focus of what you have built commitment to do, it's not good money. And don't walk—run."

Chapter 9

You Get More Excited About Data When . . . You Can Do Something About It

The era of No Child Left Behind (NCLB) was stressful and demoralizing for many teachers—especially for those serving the most needy student populations, threatened with punishment for not meeting legislated goals. Some wonderful teachers (including my own goddaughter) left the profession feeling overwhelmed and unsupported. The work of looking at data and turning the analysis into *action* is just one more burden if educators feel they have no control over the outcomes, no hope of succeeding. Tschannen-Moran (2014) wrote,

> The sense of collective efficacy of the faculty, that is, the shared belief among a school's teachers that they have the capability to facilitate successful outcomes for all of their students, influences the effort that teachers invest in preparing for and delivering instruction as well as the extent to which they persist in finding new instructional strategies for students who are struggling . . . Collective teacher efficacy beliefs have repeatedly been found to be related to student achievement even when school SES, minority composition, and past achievement were held constant. (pp. 158–159)

This chapter addresses uses of data that include planning backward to find gaps in the instructional program and looking within to analyze curriculum and instructional strategies. It also focuses attention on factors that increase educators' sense that they *can* do something about the concerns that arise from their data.

STICK TO YOUR OWN SPHERE

One behavior that undermines a collective sense of self-efficacy is a hyperfocus on student needs that are real, that do impact their learning in school, but that are not directly within the teachers' sphere of influence. While many educators are driven by passion and are highly engaged in volunteer work and activism about hunger, homelessness, and other social issues outside the school day, there is truth in statements that "we can't change the family structure" and "we can't fix all society's ills." If that's the end of the discussion, it's whining. If the discussion continues with "But we *are* in charge of seven hours a day and this is *our house* and we will make sure what *we do here* is the best that's possible for their needs," then it's empowering.

That is why I find "CEL's Stance on the Achievement Gap" (Center for Educational Leadership [CEL], 2016b) to be so compelling. (Access at https://www.k-12leadership.org/about-us.) It states,

> The elimination of the achievement gap is at the core of our mission here at the Center for Educational Leadership. This is the gap that for decades has represented disparate learning outcomes for many students of color, students living in poverty, students whose first language is not English, and students with special needs when compared with their counterparts. We believe that these gaps can be eliminated when all students have:
>
> - Full access to quality learning experiences and powerful instruction daily
> - Grade-level instruction on curriculum that is aligned to high academic standards
> - Engagement with rigorous content and intellectual work
> - Learning experiences that build on their culture, their personal experiences, and their learning and performance styles
> - Engagement with authentic learning that builds their capacity to think critically, to use knowledge to create new knowledge and to apply learning to real-world problem solving.
>
> The research is clear and conclusive. The teacher is the most influential factor on student learning, and students must experience quality teaching consistently from year to year and from classroom to classroom to attain and sustain high levels of achievement.

Quality learning experiences, grade-level instruction, student engagement, culturally responsive practices, and higher-level thinking are surely within the sphere of influence of the school and district. They are factors that we *can do something about and **must**.*

A starting point is to analyze all factors contributing to a situation locally and select the points of entry and leverage that match the goal and the capacity of the school. A tool or protocol like the cause-and-effect diagram is one helpful way to reach that conclusion. Shown in Figure 9.1, the cause-and-effect diagram is a visual representation of the relationship between contributing factors and an issue or problem. Because the product branches out like the skeleton of a fish, it has become known as a "fishbone."

The question, "What factors contribute to . . . ?" is stated across the top, and the "head" of the fish represents the need or issue being analyzed. A horizontal line represents the spine of the fish. Some formal group process handbooks emphasize that causal factors fall into categories and that the categories should be identified first and the first "fishbones" should represent these categories, such as procedures, people, policies, and plant. I leave the process less structured because it is essential that participants feel safe, even honored, by identifying every possible contributing factor, whether they agree with it or not, or whether it fits a predesignated category. Similar to brainstorming, every idea is captured and no judgments are made. Encourage participants to think of what "other voices" or "those not in the room" might add. Probe with questions like "And what might that be connected to?" "Is something else underlying that?" "Why might that be happening?" In some settings, I've improvised and added dotted lines across or around the fishbone when people notice new interrelationships. Sometimes I've switched colors of markers to illustrate new connections.

After the diagram is drawn and all ideas are included, guide the group to think about the factors they identified. Acknowledge factors over which the school or organization has no control and check them off (as in Figure 9.1) or X them out. But be sure the entire group agrees they are outside the sphere of influence. Sometimes team members challenge

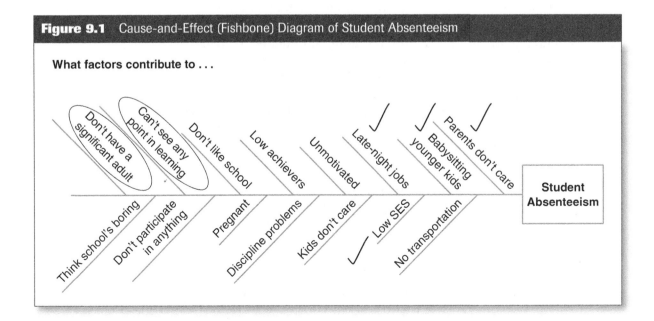

Figure 9.1   Cause-and-Effect (Fishbone) Diagram of Student Absenteeism

each other in very powerful ways before rejecting a possible focus of action. Next, zoom in on the factors that most closely match their perceptions of their own situation and that they are able to influence and willing to address. Circle or star these "entry points" that will guide their selection of strategies or interventions.

The example used in Figure 9.1 comes from one of the most powerful "midcourse" transformations I have observed. It not only demonstrates how to do the activity but it also answers this question: *Won't all this emphasis on data make us less humane and forget about students' feelings?*

Ten school leadership teams had been selected to participate in a three-day workshop that would guide them through the process of developing a school improvement plan. They had been asked to bring student data and draft versions of any work they had already done on mission statements, goals, or Action Plans. It was fascinating to observe their approach to the day.

One table looked like a display at a newsstand, except that every now and then a hand would reach out and feel around for a coffee cup, which would then disappear behind the newspaper—more specifically, the sports section.

At another table, a group of early arrivals were poring over a stack of computer printouts. Heads together and unaware of the caterer's late delivery of the pastries, the participants were engrossed in a discussion of which subtests from a recent assessment matched their curriculum and mission closely enough to merit major attention as they set their improvement targets.

Another group entered carrying the lid of a copy paper box with waves of green-and-white-striped computer paper spilling haphazardly over the edge. Locating the table with the school's name on it, the carrier dropped the box onto the floor—*thud!*—and kicked it under the table with the side of his foot—*thwack!* Having thus dispatched the dreaded data, this group attacked the coffee and doughnuts table with much greater zeal.

I was beginning to have qualms about the day when another member of that group approached me and began a speech. "In all fairness, I really ought to let you know that there's no reason for us to be wasting three days at this workshop. We already have our school improvement plan done." Swallowing hard, I asked him what they had planned for the coming year. "Well, we got our biggest problem figured out. It's kids not coming to school. And we've got two plans for working on it. First, we got a business partner that's going to donate us some equipment so we can program it to call those kids and get them going in the morning. Second, we got a committee all lined up to work on our attendance policy so these kids can't get by with skipping. And we'd rather spend our time working on that than sitting in here."

I managed to thank him for his honesty and ask him to stick around for this first day, listen carefully, and think about his school's plan. At the end of the day, we'd talk again and see what could be worked out to honor his group's time. "Well, I guess we might as well. We're already here and, besides, it's raining."

During the first part of the morning, I engaged the teams in a review of research on school effectiveness and provided an overview of the activities we would be doing over the three-day period. I gave each group some time to talk about whatever data they had available and share the concerns that emerged from this discussion or others that had taken place at their school. During the report out, members of this group repeated that their attendance data showed a need for improvement.

Lunch was provided in the room right next door—and it was still raining—so the reluctant team continued into the afternoon. That's when we began to discuss the importance of understanding the problem we're addressing and some of the causes or related factors so we know where to begin changing it.

The group began its fishbone of student absenteeism with "Parents don't care" and went right on to list items like "No transportation," "Babysitting younger kids," "Pretty low socioeconomic," and "Stay up too late at their night jobs." The other groups were getting along well, so I tried to coach this team a little. "You seem to have a pretty good handle on the students' family situation. Got any thoughts about the kids themselves?"

The next phase began with "Kids don't care either," "Unmotivated" (when they take care of siblings and hold down night jobs?) and went on to "Discipline problems," "Low achievers," and "A couple of them are pregnant." About this time, I noticed one person digging around under the table, but the table had a skirt around it and I didn't want to get too nosy, so I ignored him.

The work on the fishbone was bogging down again. I tried to build rapport. "It's really too bad some kids are like that, but I'm glad to see you're aware of them. Could there be any other source of factors that relate to whether kids come to school or not?" A soft voice from the other end of the table said, "Well, they don't like school when they do come." Several people just stared at her, so I reached over with my own marker and wrote, "Don't like school" on a new fishbone. A few others added things like "Don't participate in anything," "Can't see the point of learning," and "Don't seem connected to anyone."

Just then, a head popped up with the copy paper box in his hand and a dazzling grin on his face. "Wait a minute. I've just been digging through here, and it looks to me like there's no more than 20 kids in the whole school that are causing our attendance rate to look so bad." My challenger responded immediately. "Oh, yeah? So, who?"

As the analyst mentioned a name or two, other members of the group began to comment on individuals. "Well, if Joey can just make it from the bus to the door without a fight, he does pretty well in class." "Sam doesn't have any trouble getting here, but he's so interested in messing around the art room he doesn't follow his schedule." "If Suzy wasn't so worried about her weight, she might have time to think about her work."

Because of the data, the participants suddenly began to talk about students as individuals. As they did, one brave soul said, "You know, if they are so low income, do you think they'll have phones to call?" Another drew courage and said, "If they really don't care about school, what good will it do to suspend them for skipping?" My challenger shrugged and said, "Well, maybe our plan isn't quite right, but look at that fishy thing. We can't do anything about that stuff."

I delightedly agreed. "You're right. There are a lot of things that are beyond our control. Let's mark them off and see what we have left that we could tackle." Check marks on Figure 9.1 show the items they eliminated. But they didn't check off very many because some members of the group began to argue that maybe the system *could* make some kind of provision for transportation and that they had heard of some schools that provided in-school child care. As the last step with their fishbone, they circled the items that could be entry points for a new Action Plan.

The next morning this group got there first. By the end of the day, the group had developed a plan that would provide each of the chronic absentees with an adult in the school (teacher, custodian, volunteer) who would check in with him or her each morning before school and follow up at the end of the day to see if the student was taking work home. The mentoring plan the group created is included here as Figure 9.10 (pp. 168–169). A year later, I met an administrator from that district at a conference and asked how things were doing. He told me that this particular school had made the most progress with its school improvement plan and that it was easy to sense a dramatic difference in the culture of the school. Their data helped them identify a concern, the cause-and-effect analysis increased their sense of efficacy and generated use of more specific data, and their actions engaged staff and students—they were energized by work they *could* do something about. The use of data humanized their attitudes when they began to see the "faces" in it.

ANALYZE THE OFFERED CURRICULUM

Many authors have used the terms *written* curriculum and "taught" curriculum to contrast what's contained in instructional documents and what is actually used by teachers. Robert Marzano (2003) described the need for a "guaranteed and viable curriculum" as a path of learning that is assured to every student and that can be provided within available school time— capturing both equity and efficacy in one phrase. In previous editions, I advised "analyzing the taught curriculum" and certainly feel that is still a critical step. But I've chosen the adjective *offered* for this section to highlight how one of the issues in achievement gaps is that some students don't even have the opportunity or *chance* to engage in the high-quality learning experiences needed for future success.

Chapter 7 described the work of Teaching Teams in planning the curriculum for their course or grade based on high academic standards. The need to prioritize and focus on power standards that are most critical for leverage, endurance, and readiness was emphasized. Those processes might be summarized with these four essential questions:

- Which skills do we consider most critical for long-term success in school and beyond?
- Where do these appear in the curriculum?
- When are they taught? How often? For how long? With what materials?
- Who teaches this exceptionally well so we can learn together?

Even when the *written* curriculum is guaranteed and viable at a high level and even when it's actually *taught* in classrooms, equity and closing achievement gaps will drive a fifth critical question:

> Who is *in* the classrooms where and when this guaranteed, viable, high-level, standards-based curriculum is being provided? In other words, to *whom* is the curriculum *offered*?

This question relates to students with individualized education programs (IEPs) as well as to other groups of students in the school. If the IEP goals represent grade-level standards, then the student must be served *in*—not pulled away *from*—an environment where he or she is exposed to the regular curriculum.

The work of Ruth Johnson (2002) contains an extensive collection of references and resources about "gap-closing" schools that have succeeded in eliminating or dramatically reducing discrepancies between the achievement of white students and students of color. She pointed out that when schools and communities face reality and attempt to change their worlds, more examples of success are noted and correlated with specific actions. Teachers who had low expectations for student performance become "warm demanders" and insist on conscientious effort. Changed beliefs and attitudes that result in a learning environment of caring and higher expectations nurture students with greater self-efficacy and persistence.

Cultural responsiveness is another aspect of gap-closing schools. Adults acknowledge the legitimacy of the cultural heritage of every child and learn enough about it to build bridges of meaningfulness. Use of a wide variety of instructional strategies increases success at connecting with the diverse needs and styles of the learners. Students are actively taught to know and praise their own and each others' cultures, and multicultural information is incorporated across the subjects taught in the school—not just in Social Studies and on ethnic holidays.

Gap-closing schools increase students' opportunity to learn by extending learning time through before- and after-school programs, summer school, and sometimes even Saturday sessions and acceleration opportunities during other breaks in the school year calendar. Every moment is considered an opportunity to learn, from social instruction on the playground to "books on the bus" that makes productive use of time en route. Every child is exposed to a rigorous curriculum, including the scope and sequence of mathematics courses that is needed to keep the "gate" to college open for all who wish to pursue it. Programs are varied and enriched with learning experiences that challenge and stimulate learning beyond the basics.

Closing the achievement gap requires adherence to core learning principles and coherence in systems. The taught curriculum must be tightly aligned with essential skills and standards for high-quality intellectual performance, with support provided to assure students can and do learn. Given the challenge of time and the urgency to accelerate learning to close the gap, teachers do not have the luxury of spending time on topics and activities *they* enjoy—but must *find joy* in effectively teaching what the students most need. The instructional program is planned to provide a balance of basic and advanced skills, assuring the foundation but also stretching students to higher-level thinking. As one middle school teacher pointed out to her team, "Just because they can't read the text, doesn't mean they can't *think* about the concepts."

Johnson (2002) devoted an entire section to the powerful role of high school guidance counselors as gatekeepers. Through conscious or subconscious assumptions about who will "be able to handle" particular courses, far-reaching decisions are made that close windows of opportunity for students. For example, educators need to rethink the gatekeeping practices that consistently prevent students with previous low scores from any opportunity to even attempt the essential skills and concepts of algebra. Johnson includes examples of data gathering to examine the practices of the counseling office at the same time that teachers are analyzing their classroom practices.

The moral imperative must be to prepare all students for the college option rather than using bureaucratic policies and prerequisites to certify who is or who isn't "college material." It is all about transforming the expectations and behaviors currently present in many schools and systems so that there are high-level options for all students.

Response to Intervention (RTI) approaches have added a further dimension to the question of access and opportunity. In some situations, interventions have focused on additional practice of previously taught (and failed) skills but not explicit instruction to accelerate student learning and thereby impact the achievement gap. If these support programs are provided in pull-out models during the school day, they must be analyzed in terms of what classroom activities students are missing—compared to what they are being provided in their support program. If, for example, they are missing a stimulating discussion that involved higher-level thinking facilitated by a certificated teacher in order to have a rote memory practice session with a volunteer, we are replacing one learning experience with another that has less to offer. This practice may actually result in the student having a weaker, rather than stronger, instructional program—thus increasing rather than decreasing the distance from meeting standard. Other issues involve the scheduling of double-dose programs for critical subjects like algebra—which can have good results for mathematics but prevent the student from accessing elective courses. It may be an elective course that interests the student to come to school in the first place—so be very careful, intentional, and individual when making decisions about what students will be sacrificing in order to receive needed and well-intended support.

FILL CURRICULUM GAPS

Chapter 5 addressed the need to keep longitudinal data on each student, and make sure that data is used to "plan forward" (Figure 1.5 [p. 17]) and keep track of skills that will continue to need support as well as strengths and styles of the student that will help future teachers. The use of data to "plan backward" is not about the students but about the curriculum and instruction. While cohorts of students move forward and skill information moves with them, other students are following them along the same instructional pathway. If spreadsheets of student skills show "empty cells" downward an entire column (i.e., a common lack of proficiency for almost all students), it is likely to be the taught or untaught curriculum that is at fault, not the learners. Drilling down the skill-specific data means looking at item analysis reports that provide a breakdown of skills or subtests, in addition to reviewing how students have performed on formative assessments. The analysis is to check for areas where students have experienced the same struggles, over multiple years, even when it's different kids each year and different tests or assessment types. These discussions often occur in the curriculum review of Teaching Teams and in the cycle of teaching and analyzing student work shown in Figure 7.6 (p. 125).

CRITIQUE THE CULTURE

Just as students have individual patterns of skill development and classrooms have idiosyncratic practices, every school has a "feel" of its own. Experienced practitioners who visit many schools sense the culture within seconds. It may be happy or stressed. It may be casual or purposeful. It may be civil or rude. Those who live in the culture may be too immersed in survival to be aware of how it differs from other schools, or how it affects those entering it for the first time. During the STUDY phase (Figure 7.1 [p. 108]), it's important to gather data on schoolwide phenomena as well as teaching practice and student performance.

Somewhere between the "prison" and the "social club" would be a school culture that's intentionally academic, purposeful about learning for both adults and students. The equity considerations presented in this chapter by CEL and Ruth Johnson's work extend from curriculum and instruction into the learning environment. Figure 9.2 consists of four pages, providing a powerful tool for assessing the degree to which the schools' culture fosters high achievement.

Findings from an instrument like this will lead to discussions about the culture of the school as experienced by students, as well as the expectations that are conveyed by staff. It will often lead to review of the school's mission, vision, values, and norms—to see if they are consistent with the characteristics of a school with academic expectations and focus. It may also lead to further discussion of how adults influence the school culture by the way they behave toward each other.

COMPARE BEST PRACTICE
AND TYPICAL PRACTICE

Chapter 8 focused on selecting effective practices in order to marshal resources of money, time, and energy toward strategies with the greatest degree of potential to meet goals and enhance teachers' sense of efficacy. Sometimes the results of that phase of STUDY (Figure 7.1) are met with "But we already do that" or "I tried that once and it didn't work." This creates a need to be very specific in articulating what the powerful practice looks and sounds like in use and verify how that compares with the actuality of typical practice in the school. The next sections present a series of questions that model the deep introspection needed when "looking within" (Figure 1.5 [p. 17]) at schoolwide practices. Take, for example, the need to understand what it means to be standards-based.

Figure 9.2 Assessing Institutional Reforms in the Academic Culture of Schools

Name (optional): _____   School: _____
Position: _____   Date: _____

(Fill in for postassessment *only*.)
Filled out instrument in 200 —?   Yes —   No —

Directions: Please fill in the circle under the number that you believe best represents your school. One (1) is the lowest rating and five (5) is the highest.

Area	Underachievement	Rating					Higher Achievement
Leadership/ Planning/ Decision Making	* Little or no collaboration between administrators and teachers about strategies to raise student achievement.	1 -O-	2 -O-	3 -O-	4 -O-	5 -O-	* Frequent and regular collaboration and joint problem solving to design and evaluate strategies to raise student achievement with a focus on access and equity.
	* Mostly top-down style of leadership; leadership teams function in isolation from colleagues; roles and commitment unclear.	1 -O-	2 -O-	3 -O-	4 -O-	5 -O-	* Frequent collaboration with administrative leaders; teams skillfully engage with each other and planning and decision-making involves all major stakeholders.
	* No use of data.	1 -O-	2 -O-	3 -O-	4 -O-	5 -O-	* Regular planning and use of data for inquiry; disaggregation of data.
	* No vision or strategic planning; add-on fragmented programs; no inclusion of stakeholders.	1 -O-	2 -O-	3 -O-	4 -O-	5 -O-	* Consensus on shared vision for school; focus on systemic issues that reform institutional policies and practices.
	* Meetings focus solely on operations, adult agenda.	1 -O-	2 -O-	3 -O-	4 -O-	5 -O-	* Meetings and activities have a clear focus on instruction.

What evidence supports your assessment? _____

Area	Underachievement	Rating					Higher Achievement
Professionalism/ Responsibility	* Low achievement and poor school functioning blamed on others.	1 -O-	2 -O-	3 -O-	4 -O-	5 -O-	* Staff views improved achievement and school functioning as its responsibility; analyzes institutional practices; highly committed staff; includes the entire school community.
	* 20% or more teachers lack credential.	1 -O-	2 -O-	3 -O-	4 -O-	5 -O-	* 90–100% of the teachers are fully credentialed.
	* Few teachers, counselors, and administrators are engaged in continuous meaningful professional development that will result in improved academic achievement.	1 -O-	2 -O-	3 -O-	4 -O-	5 -O-	* All professionals are continuously developing their professional skills.
	* Most professionals are not up-to-date in fields.	1 -O-	2 -O-	3 -O-	4 -O-	5 -O-	* Staff experiments; keeps up-to-date in fields; experiments with new strategies; evaluates progress and regularly uses data; teacher is a researcher; visitations to other sites with successful practices.
	* Nonrelevant, isolated, sporadic, or nonexistent staff development; in-service is the only form of staff development.	1 -O-	2 -O-	3 -O-	4 -O-	5 -O-	* Systematic, comprehensive, and tied to staff needs—up-to-date strategies, peer teaching, coaching, collegiality.

What evidence supports your assessment? _____

(Continued)

Figure 9.2 (Continued)

Area	Underachievement	Rating					Higher Achievement
Standards/ Curriculum	* Curriculum and courses are not aligned with state/national standards.	1 -O-	2 -O-	3 -O-	4 -O-	5 -O-	* Curriculum and courses are aligned with state/ national standards.
	* Few students are engaged in standards-based tasks.	1 -O-	2 -O-	3 -O-	4 -O-	5 -O-	* All students are engaged in rigorous standards-based tasks; 90–100% of students score at levels demonstrating mastery.
	* Little or no agreement on consistent process to measure and report student performance.	1 -O-	2 -O-	3 -O-	4 -O-	5 -O-	* Consensus and commitment to ensuring standards-based rigor in curriculum and course work for all students; consistent framework for measuring student progress and providing feedback.
	* Curriculum actually taught is thin, fragmented.	1 -O-	2 -O-	3 -O-	4 -O-	5 -O-	* Students are taught a rigorous, balanced curriculum, rich in concepts, ideas, and problem solving.
	* Remedial instruction is isolated to low-level skills based on discrete facts.	1 -O-	2 -O-	3 -O-	4 -O-	5 -O-	* All students are taught a curriculum that is at or above grade level; students pushed toward higher-order thinking.
	* No technology included in the curriculum.	1 -O-	2 -O-	3 -O-	4 -O-	5 -O-	* Students have technology integrated into curriculum.

What evidence supports your assessment? _____

Area	Underachievement	Rating					Higher Achievement
Instruction	* Mostly lecture format; students passive, emphasis on low-level skills.	1 -O-	2 -O-	3 -O-	4 -O-	5 -O-	* A variety of successful, challenging, and interactive instructional strategies are used, such as cooperative learning, directed lessons, extended engagement time for learners; use of high-quality technology and software programs.
	* Multicultural issues and concepts are not integrated into standards-based instruction. No use of students' authentic learning outside of school to connect what is being taught in school.	1 -O-	2 -O-	3 -O-	4 -O-	5 -O-	* Multicultural issues and concepts are integrated into standards-based instruction. Use of students' authentic learning outside of school to connect what is being taught in school.
	* Repetitive low-level drills, heavy use of workbooks.	1 -O-	2 -O-	3 -O-	4 -O-	5 -O-	* Higher-level skills taught; progress assessed frequently; production rather than reproduction of knowledge is encouraged.
	* Lots of pullout programs isolated from regular classroom instruction; emphasis on remedial instruction.	1 -O-	2 -O-	3 -O-	4 -O-	5 -O-	* Students taught all subjects that lead to college entrance; addresses needs of diverse student populations.
	* Student abilities and achievement assessed solely on standardized skill-based tests.	1 -O-	2 -O-	3 -O-	4 -O-	5 -O-	* A variety of indicators are used to measure student performance.
	* No use of standards-based assessments.	1 -O-	2 -O-	3 -O-	4 -O-	5 -O-	* Appropriate and frequent use of standards-based assessments.

What evidence supports your assessment? _____

Area	Underachievement	Rating					Higher Achievement
Expectations	* Academic goals are unfocused; no attention to access and equity.	1 -O-	2 -O-	3 -O-	4 -O-	5 -O-	* Goals are clearly focused on student achievement, access, and equity.
	* Students from low-income and certain ethnic backgrounds are viewed as not having the potential to gain high-level knowledge and skills.	1 -O-	2 -O-	3 -O-	4 -O-	5 -O-	* All students viewed as potential high achievers—staff believes all students are capable of mastering the high-level knowledge and skills.
	* Students considered not capable of taking required courses for 4-year postsecondary institutions.	1 -O-	2 -O-	3 -O-	4 -O-	5 -O-	* Students have access, are supported and prepared for 4-year postsecondary institutions.
	* Staff conversation reflects much negativity about children; staff assumes no responsibility for low levels of achievement.	1 -O-	2 -O-	3 -O-	4 -O-	5 -O-	* Staff constructively focuses on institutional and instructional practices that need changing and engages in discussions about ways to help students learn at high levels.
	* Students are informally and formally labeled in negative ways, e.g., slow, remedial, dropouts.	1 -O-	2 -O-	3 -O-	4 -O-	5 -O-	* Students are not negatively labeled.

What evidence supports your assessment? _____

Area	Underachievement	Rating					Higher Achievement
Learning Opportunities/ Grouping/Tracking/ Labeling	* Students separated by perceived ability into rigid homogeneous groups.	1 -O-	2 -O-	3 -O-	4 -O-	5 -O-	* Flexible grouping for short periods of time; most/all instruction in heterogeneous groups.
	* Lower-level and remedial groups get least-prepared teachers, watered-down curriculum.	1 -O-	2 -O-	3 -O-	4 -O-	5 -O-	* All students have opportunities to be taught by best-prepared teachers.
	* Only high-achieving students taught advanced-level information/ skills/technology.	1 -O-	2 -O-	3 -O-	4 -O-	5 -O-	* All students get same rigorous core curriculum—variety of strategies including technology are used.
	* Few options for low-achieving students.	1 -O-	2 -O-	3 -O-	4 -O-	5 -O-	* Students form study groups; extended days are provided, other student supports are introduced and implemented; practices are altered when necessary to better serve students.
	* Levels that students function at are seen as unalterable.	1 -O-	2 -O-	3 -O-	4 -O-	5 -O-	* All students viewed as having the capacity to achieve at higher levels.

What evidence supports your assessment? _____

(Continued)

Figure 9.2   (Continued)

Area	Underachievement	Rating					Higher Achievement
Parent Involvement	* Parents are considered indifferent toward child's achievement.	1 -O-	2 -O-	3 -O-	4 -O-	5 -O-	* Staff, parents, and leaders use a variety of strategies to motivate and accommodate parents as partners in their children's education. Families learn to become effective advocates for their students.
	* Education viewed as a domain of professionals; little or no collaboration between staff and parents.	1 -O-	2 -O-	3 -O-	4 -O-	5 -O-	* Collaborative process where staff and parents assume joint responsibility for student performance, homework, communication.
	* Parent involvement limited to a few persons; insensitivity to cultural differences hinders participation.	1 -O-	2 -O-	3 -O-	4 -O-	5 -O-	* Parents, leaders, and staff use effective strategies to achieve broad participation and representation of all ethnic groups in activities.
	* Parents, students, and other community members are not aware of and rarely provided information about preparing students for higher education.	1 -O-	2 -O-	3 -O-	4 -O-	5 -O-	* Parents, students, and community partners actively participate in planning and implementing of programs.
	* Information rarely translated into the parents' dominant languages; communications seldom relate to achievement.	1 -O-	2 -O-	3 -O-	4 -O-	5 -O-	* Translation to parents' dominant languages consistently provides for effective school communication (oral and written) focused on student achievement.

What evidence supports your assessment? _____

Area	Underachievement	Rating					Higher Achievement
Support Services for Students	* Few or no tutoring services, tutoring usually in the form of a homework club; limited numbers of students utilize services.	1 -O-	2 -O-	3 -O-	4 -O-	5 -O-	* Ample support services closely integrated with instructional program; variety of tutoring programs offered with a flexible schedule; coordinated with core curriculum; regular participation of students who need assistance.
	* Little coordination among special programs; no mechanism to catch students "falling through the cracks."	1 -O-	2 -O-	3 -O-	4 -O-	5 -O-	* Special programs integrated into regular instruction; counseling programs aligned.
	* No agreed-upon plan for handling attendance, discipline, vandalism problems, uncaring environment; no review of implications on academic achievement.	1 -O-	2 -O-	3 -O-	4 -O-	5 -O-	* Agreed-on procedures for handling attendance and discipline problems, reduced referrals, suspensions, caring environment; monitoring impact on academic achievement.

What evidence supports your assessment? _____

Are We *Really* Standards-Based?

The development of academic standards during the 1990s (and multiple iterations since) resulted in a keener awareness and common understanding of what should be taught. But far too often being standards-based has been mainly perceived as being sure to "cover" all the standards. The attributes listed in Figure 9.3 (p. 160) were compiled to provide a more complete understanding of standards-based teaching and learning. In addition to conveying expectations for school and classroom practice, these characteristics were used as a diagnostic instrument. School leadership teams considered each item, and rated their progress from 1 (aware, but no action) to 4 (implemented consistently in all classrooms). Participants in one principals' workshop noted that they all had the same items ranked lowest—numbers 9, 13, 14, and 15. This prompted the realization that major new work was needed in the whole area of classroom-based assessment and that input was provided to the staff development coordinators. Just as students need clear expectations and models of what their work should look like, staff members need a clear picture of what it means to be standards-based.

Are We *Really* Providing a Balanced Reading Block?

A popular term in the vocabulary these days is *balanced*—for example, balanced assessment, balanced literacy, balanced reading block (see Figure 9.4). One district discovered that this meant many different things in practice, and created a diagnostic tool in the form of a *discussion guide*. Note that only the school and grade level are identified at the top so individual teachers are not identified. This kind of tool should *not* be used as a reporting form given to each individual teacher to "fill out and turn in." Rather, grade-level teams would use it to reflect on the past month of instruction, review plans they have made, think about activities and materials that were assigned to students, and analyze how each of these components are taught and how much time is devoted to them.

In the same way, schoolwide reading programs and interventions should be analyzed to identify whether all components are provided, including explicit instruction. Some school leaders have been dismayed to note that funds for improving student achievement have supported numerous strategies—all of which could be used to provide various formats for independent practice and none of which provided explicit instruction for new skill acquisition.

Are We *Really* Implementing the Strategies We Agreed On?

Another way of checking typical practice is to see what's really going on in classrooms. The past few years have seen an interest in methods referred to as learning walks, classroom walk-throughs, instructional rounds, and other terms. Chapter 11 explores these practices in more depth as one of the ways in which to gather data as evidence of implementation of the Action Plan. The following example provides a simple data-gathering tool that can be used for initial diagnosis of common practice. It was used at a high school where teachers and administrators had first worked together to identify a set of practices they all would employ regularly in their classrooms (see Figure 9.5).

Assistant principals and some department heads decided to aim for brief informal visits to ten classrooms a day, three days a week—just using a simple note-taking form and reporting back on the frequency of the strategies

Figure 9.3   Indicators of Standards-Based Teaching and Learning

1. The district develops clear statements of what students should know and be able to do.

2. Standards apply to all students with high expectations for their success.

3. The teacher knows how each lesson relates to district and state academic standards.

4. Students know what they are learning, what standards are related to it, and why they are learning it.

5. Standards are constant; instructional strategies and time are the variables.

6. Planning begins with standards rather than materials.

7. Practice activities are clearly aligned to standard(s) with the student as worker and the teacher as coach.

8. Students know how the teacher expects them to show what they've learned.

9. Students frequently evaluate their own work before the teacher does, using the same criteria.

10. Feedback to students is related to performance levels on standards, not based on comparison with other students.

11. Student performance data is used to revise curriculum and instruction.

12. The assessment system includes a balance of external tests for program evaluation and classroom assessments for individual student diagnosis and instruction.

13. Students have multiple opportunities to demonstrate achievement of standards.

14. Assessment of student achievement is consistent across teachers and schools, using common performance indicators.

15. Teachers work with colleagues to share and compare scoring of classroom-based assessments.

Figure 9.4	Balancing the Reading Block

School _____   Grade _____

Essential Reading Components	Strategies/ Techniques	Materials	Approx. # of Minutes/Week
Explicit instruction in phonemic awareness			
Explicit instruction in phonics			
Explicit instruction in vocabulary			
Explicit instruction in fluency			
Explicit instruction in comprehension skills and strategies			
Explicit instruction in thinking skills			
Opportunities to respond in a variety of ways			
Whole group instruction			
Small group instruction			
Individual instruction			
Reading aloud to students daily			
Shared reading daily			
Guided reading daily			
Independent reading practice daily			
Experiences with fiction			
Experiences with nonfiction			
Experiences with other forms (e.g., lists, directions)			
High expectations and clear standards for all students			
Continuous evaluation			

observed. Some initial concern was raised that the form included the room number, but teachers were assured it was just to avoid making multiple stops in some rooms and completely missing some others (see Figure 9.6).

The goal of ten classrooms each on three days each week would have resulted in 360 walk-through visits in a month—a goal not reached—but it did spur observers to prioritize time for this activity. After one month, 240 short visits had occurred, and the results—just totals with no names or room numbers—were posted at the staff meeting (see Figure 9.7). For example, observers saw 158 examples they identified as clear expectations, so that was observable in 66 percent of the drop-ins.

One staff member observed that "I think the ones with lower percentages so far are harder to do. Like you only saw frequent assessment in 20% of the walk-through visits. In college, I was taught a lot about how to teach, but not much about stuff like formative assessment. Maybe we need to have some professional development on that." After another two months, the use of the agreed-upon practice had increased significantly, but use of formative assessment remained the least common practice (see Figure 9.8).

This data—a simple but focused look at typical classroom practice—provided further input to shape professional development planning.

These schools that challenged themselves with the questions about what they "really" do provided courageous examples of comparing best practice and typical practice. Richard Elmore (2002a) pointed out the importance of this analysis:

Figure 9.5   Five Elements of Powerful Teaching

❖ High Expectations

  ▪ Clearly stated

  ▪ Consistently enforced

❖ Important Curricular/Content

  ▪ Standards-based

  ▪ Summarized regularly

❖ Student Centered Lessons

  ▪ Active participation

  ▪ Options available

❖ Challenging Material

  ▪ High on Bloom's taxonomy

  ▪ Supported with help

❖ Frequent Assessment and Feedback

  ▪ Teacher, peer, and self-assessment

  ▪ Knowledge of progress

Figure 9.6 Walk-Through Form for Five Elements of Powerful Teaching

Date of walk-throughs: _____

Room No.	High Expectations— clearly stated, consistently enforced	Important Content— references to standards, summarized	Student Centered— active participation, options	Challenging Material— high Bloom's, help available	Frequent Assessment— feedback from self, peers, teacher; progress noted

Figure 9.7	Walk-Through Data—One Month				
No. Visits	High Expectations— clearly stated objective, consistently enforced	Important Content— references to standards, summarized	Student Centered— active participation, options	Challenging Material— high Bloom's, help available	Frequent Assessment— feedback from self, peers, teacher; progress noted
240	158 66%	120 50%	96 40%	72 30%	48 20%

Figure 9.8	Walk-Through Data—Three Months				
No. Visits	High Expectations— clearly stated objective, consistently enforced	Important Content— references to standards, summarized	Student Centered— active participation, options	Challenging Material— high Bloom's, help available	Frequent Assessment— feedback from self, peers, teacher; progress noted
240	158 66%	120 50%	96 40%	72 30%	48 20%
260	178 68%	156 60%	125 48%	89 34%	57 22%
225	175 78%	167 74%	140 62%	101 45%	81 36%

School improvement doesn't happen by getting everyone to come to the auditorium and testify to their belief that all children learn—not if it means sending everyone back into the classroom to do what they've always done. Only a change in practice produces a genuine change in norms and values. Or, to put it more crudely, "grab people by their practice and their hearts and minds will follow." (p. 3)

DETERMINE WHAT TO TRY—AND WHAT TO STOP

Chapter 8 described the work of identifying practices that have been demonstrated to produce desired results and match the goals of the school. This work led to creation of questions about current practice, in order to determine whether or which of those evidence-based strategies were used consistently. The work described in this chapter—comparing best practice with typical practice—can raise two directions of action. One is the obvious—what do we need to do *more* of? In the previous case, more frequent assessment and feedback to students was needed. The other question is less obvious but absolutely essential—what will we do *less* of or stop altogether?

An example of a reason to reconsider a practice is whether its effects have been those that were intended (hopefully, yes) *as well as* whether those efforts have created any unintended consequences that conflict with the underlying goal. Writing this third edition provides me with a chance to provide an example and illustrate my own reconsideration of a strategy that once seemed sound. The second edition included a section titled "Ramping Up the Roster" in which I described a strategy I had learned from an esteemed source that provided a starting point for teachers and schools overwhelmed by the increasing demands of NCLB. I wrote the following:

> As soon as they [teachers] become familiar with students and their current level of development, they list their students in order of performance on standards, from most advanced to those most challenged. Then they draw a line across the list at a point that roughly separates those who are already "over the bar" and those below it. They begin by focusing interventions and individual help on the three students closest to the standard, knowing that their grouping strategies will also address the needs of other students at the same time. As these students move closer to and above the line that represents [proficiency], teachers move down the list and focus intensely on the next set of students. The results . . . have been demonstrated in improved test scores and annual performance indicators for the last three years." In my work with schools since then, I have found this to be a strategy that did indeed generate short-term gains on state test results – but I have also seen unintended negative consequences that disturbed me. The *unintended (I'm sure)* consequences that concerned me were the prevailing use of a term "bubble kids" (e.g., Goodwin, 2015) and a sequence of comments like "let's concentrate on the kids that actually have the potential to be proficient – those other kids will never make it anyway."

Please follow instead the example of Laurel Street Elementary School (Bromberg, 2013) where the principal states, "Rather than focusing only on the 'bubble kids' who are on the cusp of proficiency, Laurel Street educators set a goal for each student based on his or her incoming level of achievement . . . the goals are always ambitious, typically set within the proficient or advanced range." Second, always review current and proposed strategies in terms of *both* their proven ability to raise achievement *and* their match with an equity focus and a sense of collective responsibility for *all* students.

DEVELOP ACTION PLANS

Figure 7.1 (p. 108) provided the big picture of school improvement, led by the Shared Leadership Team and the ongoing work of Teaching Teams. Chapters 5 and 6 focused on kinds of data to gather and analyze. Chapters 8 and 9 have provided concepts and tools for the STUDY phase of digging deeper into the data, identifying best practices, and analyzing current practice. This study leads to the selection of strategies that will be added—and some that may need to be abandoned. Once those strategies are identified—probably two or three for each priority goal—they need to be viewed in their entirety with these two questions in mind:

- Will the combination of this set of strategies raise achievement for all students?
- Will the combined set of strategies also directly address disparate learning needs and narrow achievement gaps?

When the answer is yes, Action Plans can be developed to capture the steps of implementation, as well as the evidence that will be gathered to show progress (Chapter 11). The right-hand side of Figure 7.1 illustrated a set of Action Plans that back up the overall School Improvement Plan by providing the details of "what, who, when, where, and how will we know."

A common characteristic of "school improvement plans that never happen" is that they identify strategies they will use (cooperative learning, a self-esteem program, block scheduling) without analyzing what implementation of those strategies will entail. Any one of the strategies mentioned represents many substeps needed to provide training and support for implementation. When schools select popular options like learning styles and block scheduling, their plans often involve training in the content knowledge without sufficient consideration of changes that need to be made in the school itself to reflect and reinforce those concepts. Although plans will surely be adjusted during implementation, they must be sufficiently developed to clearly represent the magnitude of change they require and the demands they place on people, time, and budgets.

Because an Action Plan needs to identify specific steps, timelines, and resources, it is important to involve people who have access to information about school calendar, budget, and a "big picture" perspective of all that is occurring in the organization. School teams often find it helpful to include a central office support person in the action-planning stage. If a major innovation such as multi-age classrooms is being implemented, it is advisable to invite a consultant or a team member from another school that is already using the approach. These resource people can provide advice on how they approached the change and even more valuable insights about problems they didn't anticipate and what they might have done to avoid them.

The detail required in action planning often brings the realization that the strategy or approach to be used is a much more complex change than was anticipated. In some situations, it is helpful to identify major subtasks and assign a small group to develop that part of the Action Plan. For example, a major change like multi-age classrooms would need a component of parent education and communication. Involvement of parents in this planning subgroup would be essential.

School improvement plans come in many formats. Some are developed in chart form. Others are written in narrative. Some work well. Some look nice and accomplish nothing. The common elements of those I find useful are shown in Figure 9.9:

- Steps to be taken and activities that will occur
- Persons who will be responsible to guide, coordinate, and monitor the activity
- Additional persons who will be involved
- Resources needed (money and materials)
- Time required and schedule
- Indicators that will be monitored and used to evaluate effectiveness

A simple way to begin is to use these elements as column headings on a large bulletin board or wall. The sequence of planning is "work all the way down, then work across for each activity." In other words, first list all the steps that need to be taken. Repeatedly ask, "And what else will that involve?" This

Figure 9.9 Action Plan Form

Activities: Steps to Be Taken	Persons Responsible	Persons Involved	Resources Needed	Timeline	Monitoring, Evaluation

Figure 9.10 Action Plan for Mentor Program

School: Any Town Middle School

Improvement Objective: To improve student attendance

Members of Team or Task Force:

M. Black	M. Green
J. White	J. Jackson
B. Brown	

Strategy: Develop 1:1 student-adult mentor relationships for chronic absentees

Rationale: Research findings indicate that student engagement and personal bonding with adults in the school are related to attendance and achievement.

Activities: Steps to Be Taken	Persons Responsible	Persons Involved	Resources Needed	Timeline	Monitoring, Evaluation
Develop criteria to identify the chronic absentees	Counselors	SIT subcommittee	Part of June workshop time	During June workshop	Criteria approved by SIT at August meeting
List the students who need to be involved	Counselor on SIT	Homeroom teachers	—	During June workshop	Presented and approved by SIT at August meeting
Set expectations for students who participate	Counselor on SIT	Homeroom teachers	—	During June workshop	Presented and approved by SIT at August meeting
Notify parents and get permission to contact students	Counselor	Counseling secretary	—	Before registration in August	Parent permissions returned
Set expectations for adult mentors	SIT subcommittee chair	SIT subcommittee	—	During June workshop	Approval by SIT at August meeting
Develop training for mentors	Assistant principal/ staff development coordinator	SIT subcommittee/ homeroom teachers	Food for picnic	July	Approval by SIT at August meeting

Activities: Steps to Be Taken	Persons Responsible	Persons Involved	Resources Needed	Timeline	Monitoring, Evaluation
Recruit and select mentors	Assistant principal	Homeroom teachers	—	July and August	List of mentors
Match students to mentors	Assistant principal	Counselors	—	July and August	List of possible matches
Hold mentor training and gain commitment	Assistant principal/ staff development coordinator	Mentors/homeroom teachers	Stipends for 2-hour training sessions ($1,250) (25 mentors at $50)	August	Mentors sign commitment forms
Hold meeting of students and mentors or make individual contact with students	Counselors/ assistant principal	Students/mentors/ homeroom teachers	—	August	Students return commitment form
Determine times and places that mentors will contact students	Mentors	Students	—	First week of school	Schedules turned in to assistant principal
Schedule and hold mentor meetings	Assistant principal	Counselors/ mentors/ homeroom teachers	Early release time once per month	Monthly, October–May	Minutes of meetings; summary of student attendance and grades
Reexamine attendance data	Counselors	—	—	Weekly by student; monthly for all	Graph attendance and grades each month as run charts
Plan celebration for mentors and students	Assistant principal	Students/mentors/ families/homeroom teachers	Budget for food, certificates, etc.	May	Progress certificates to students with targeted percent improvement

Note: SIT = School Improvement Team

helps the group break down major tasks into their component parts. Continue to probe by asking, "What would need to happen before that?"

These questions will guide the group to identify missing steps and create a sequence, so the list of steps will need to be reorganized many times. This makes an awfully messy planning chart. It saves a lot of work if you do the first column with stick-on notes. If you left something out or have things in the wrong order, it is easy to rearrange them. This can also be done in a Google doc and projected, but the hands-on approach seems to better engage participants initially.

When the sequence of steps or tasks seems complete, have the group work across the chart horizontally for each step. Identify the person responsible for each step and the people who will participate.

Let's imagine that Our Town School identified these goals:

1. Students will show improvement in reading and writing skills.

2. Students will demonstrate increased use of conflict resolution strategies, and incidents of violent behavior will decrease.

3. All students will apply computer skills in their work in all subjects.

The school would then need to develop four Action Plans: one for changes in reading, one for writing, one for conflict resolution strategies, and one for increasing use of technology. As the Shared Leadership Team compared those plans, they would look at the designated "persons responsible" to assure that a few people are not carrying the full load for everyone else. The information from these columns would also clarify roles and responsibilities for keeping the process moving along.

After designating the human capacity for each part of the plan, budgetary implications must be considered, as addressed in Chapter 8. "Time is money" also, so there's a close connection between these two columns. If release time is needed, there will be substitute costs. If compensation for time outside the contract day must be provided, that cost must be estimated. Timelines should consider the school calendar and capitalize on any staff development days or in-service time to carry out the school's plans for improvement. Existing resources must be clearly identified and scrupulously reallocated to match priorities. The three goals mentioned for Our Town School might be funded through a combination of federal Title funds, state basic education allocation, a Safe and Drug-Free Schools grant, and local technology levy. Without one "master plan" for school improvement, there might be multiple plans fragmenting the available resources.

Earlier in this chapter, I shared the story of a school leadership team's transformation as its members explored data about absenteeism and created the fishbone chart shown in Figure 9.1. Their decision to create one-on-one relationships for chronic absentees resulted in the Action Plan shown in Figure 9.10.

Note the careful breakdown of preparation steps that occur before any mentor relationships are established. Also note the specificity of the timeline. Activities are designated by month and sometimes by week. An implementation plan will never move along at exactly its planned pace and sequence. But unless the sequence is outlined, there will be no way to know how far behind we are or what to adjust. The challenge is to strike a proper balance between flexibility and evolutionary planning on the one hand and patience and perseverance on the other.

A most neglected but essential column is the last one, often given the heading Monitoring or Evaluation. It corresponds to the Evidence component of Figures 7.1 (p. 108) and 7.2 (p. 110). Too often, this column is simply used to check off completion of the activity. For example, "All staff attended a workshop on cooperative learning." This is inadequate because it does not verify whether anyone actually went back to his or her classroom and applied the knowledge and skills that were learned in the workshop.

Take another look at Figure 9.10 and notice the Monitoring column. You may realize that there are two different kinds of indicators listed. They identify evidence that the strategies are being done *and* that the goal is being met. Various documents will be presented and approved, schedules will be turned in, and minutes of meetings will be recorded. This is proof that the plan is being carried out. But the real proof will come when attendance and grades are graphed each month to demonstrate that the students are at school more and are learning more. This is evidence that the goal is being attained. Such evidence will help substantiate the title of this chapter—that *we can do something about it*—and double as evidence for Chapter 11 where we prove that we *did* make a difference.

Chapter 10

You Get More Excited About Data When . . . You Have Time to Deal With It

There's an old saying that time is money, and it's true in a number of ways. The difference is that there are ways to find more money, tough as they may be, but there is no way to stop the earth spinning around the sun and somehow gain any more than the allotted twenty-four hours per day. Chapter 8 was about saving resources by avoiding costly mistakes that sap money, energy, and morale. Chapter 9 continued to focus use of resources by sticking to aspects of problems that are within the reach of the school with its staff and stakeholders. This chapter is specifically about that finite resource of time and how to salvage it, repurpose it, prioritize it, and use it both efficiently and effectively.

KINDS OF TIME NEEDED

Chapters 4 and 7 outlined structures for using data collaboratively in the processes of schoolwide planning and instructional decision-making. The Shared Leadership Team needs to meet on a dedicated schedule of at least once per month for at least three hours to coordinate the data analysis, planning, and professional development activities that result in decisions about student achievement. The most frequent practice has been to provide substitute teachers so this team could meet during school hours. In some cases, the scarcity of substitutes and the staff members' preference to be in class with their students has led to a different format in which Shared Leadership Teams meet outside the school day and are compensated on an hourly basis or with a stipend similar to provisions for extra duties or sponsorships. Other schools have been creative in their scheduling so that planning times of team members are coordinated and meetings can begin during the last hour of the day—partly on school time and partly as additional commitment.

The Data Team will have variable needs for time, depending on when there are new data sources to analyze. Their time is often supported on an hourly basis as the Shared Leadership Team collectively determines needs and agendas, such as requests for preparing certain data displays. In some schools, a few key individuals are provided additional time by having one less teaching preparation (secondary) or being relieved of supervisory duties (elementary lunchroom, recess, etc.). Creative scheduling can also make it possible for members of a small Data Team to have a common planning period.

Teaching Teams need two kinds of time. First, at summer and/or semester breaks, they need time to handle the curriculum-related aspects of their work shown on Figure 7.6 (p. 125). They also need scheduled time of at least one hour per week—ideally, thirty minutes per day—to complete the ongoing cycles of planning, teaching, formatively assessing, and providing support. In some schools, one of the weekly meetings each month is focused on interventions for students and the Teaching Team is joined by other staff resources like the school psychologist, counselor, etc. These specialists rotate their schedules in order to meet with multiple Teaching Teams each week. Special education teachers are already embedded in Teaching Teams.

The collective bargaining agreement in some districts provides for a stated number of hours for individually directed professional development. This makes it possible for team members to "pay themselves" by identifying their work with the Data Team or Shared Leadership Team as their individual professional development—and it is one of the most powerful professional learning opportunities available.

In addition to the work of teams—Shared Leadership, Data, and Teaching Teams—there are times when all staff need to be engaged in a systemic view of the learning that is occurring in their organization, for both staff and students.

A SYSTEM LOOK AT DATA

Figure 7.6 described the work "in the trenches"—educators who serve students together and provide similar content participating in an ongoing cycle of planning, teaching, assessing, adjusting, and supporting students. But this authentic work in the trenches can also become work in silos—separating small teams from the big picture and sapping the culture of collective responsibility for all students that is so critical. While teachers may experience most of their time in school focused on their own teaching assignment and closest colleagues, students experience their time in school as one long journey that should be coherent and unified.

From time to time, everyone in the school—perhaps everyone in the district or K–12 strands of staff members—needs to look at data together, understand and appreciate each other's efforts, and surface concerns and ideas for the future. This book provides activities that range in time from twenty minutes to two hours and can be embedded in staff meetings—when those times have been repurposed. The overall district or large school view of all that's happening may take longer. Although Figure 7.6 made it clear that using data is a process, not a one-time event, many districts still find it useful to focus together once or twice a year—or even once every three years. Bernhardt (2015) presented four benefits of looking at systemwide results:

> First, schools look at what all types of data are telling them. They don't just cherry-pick data and draw conclusions from a few data points without studying the linkages among the different types of data. Second, all staff members become engaged in reviewing schoolwide data. This provides an opportunity for everyone to understand what has to change system-wide to get better results. Third, by starting with an independent review of data followed by a small-group review, staff members can validate with others what they see in the data . . . By going from small-group to large-group discussions, staff members build consensus on the implications for the continuous school improvement plan. Staff see a lot independently. Together, they see much more. Finally, with everyone committing to implementing one continuous improvement plan informed by a detailed shared vision, the focus on continuous growth for all students is clear to all. (p. 61)

The essential first step is to identify the specific purposes of convening to look at data. Any of the engagement activities presented in other chapters can be used to set the tone and change up the agenda in a data-focused professional learning opportunity. For example, the Motivation Continuum or the challenge to Monitor the Mission may build a commitment focus and counter the perception of a "compliance event" that some may have.

Figure 10.1 outlines a staff development activity that engages staff in discussion, empowers them to interpret what their data means, and allows them to express reservations about its use.

Preparing the Materials

Materials for the Carousel Data Analysis are data displays such as any of the figures in this book. For example, Figures 5.1 through 5.4 (pp. 65–68) provided visual images that illustrate the demographics of the district and the disparities in outcomes they experience. The data displays are enlarged to poster size so they can be displayed on the wall and discussed as a small group. They may be electronically projected if enough equipment is available. It is much more effective to keep the discussion focused in this way rather than providing paper copies of a packet of information to each individual or having everyone viewing the data on their individual devices. The data should be a shared focal point, with all eyes focused in the same direction. Each station would include the disaggregated data for a particular content area (reading, writing, math, etc.) and would incorporate available school-based data as well as test scores.

Figure 10.1   Carousel Data Analysis

Preparing the Materials

- Enlarged or projected copies of the data displays
- Discussion questions (see below) on flip chart paper
- Colored markers
- Post or project the data displays and post the questions at stations around a large room with blank wall space

Preparing the Participants

- Structure groups of 5 to 11 that cross department or grade-level boundaries
- Have groups designate a facilitator and recorder
- Colored marker travels with the recorder

Prompting Discussion

- What do these data seem to tell us?
- What do they not tell us? What else would we need to know?
- What good news is here to celebrate?
- What needs for improvement might arise from these data?

Using the Responses

Responses to Question 1

- Refine for use in Data Summary statements
- Use to help focus the priority goals

Responses to Question 2

- Shape the Study phase – identify data to analyze further
- Identify additional data that needs to be gathered
- Help determine sources of evidence for implementation and impact

Responses to Question 3

- Reinforce effort and celebrate progress
- Generate energy for ongoing effort

Responses to Question 4

- Use in focusing on priority goals
- Stimulate search for related, proven strategies

One or more stations could include nonacademic data—all the discipline, attendance, and other student-related data. Survey data from students could be at another location.

The room to be used should be a large room with plenty of blank wall space for posting (or projecting) graphs and recording responses to the prompts. This activity does work fine in a lunchroom or gym, because people can "think on their feet" and move about, which is an important way to release tension if this is an unfamiliar task.

The time needed is related to the amount of data ready for staff review and the number of staff members who will be participating. This activity generally takes about an hour and a half with a staff of fifty and fifteen data displays to consider. Participants would be divided into fifteen groups of three to four in each group. There would be fifteen stations to visit. At five minutes per station, the data review would take seventy-five minutes. Similar arithmetic will help you plan your time and groups.

Variations can be made for a group of 100. One is to have groups of seven or eight people. Another is to have two sets of data displays and operate two sets of stations. A third is to have larger groups and cluster several related data displays at each station.

Preparing the Participants

Groups should be structured before the event to help cross the natural boundaries of grade level or department that people drift into naturally. This structuring can be done in a straightforward manner just by posting rosters. Or a lighthearted approach can be used, such as putting colored dots on name tags or numbers on the sticks of lollipops or bases of ice cream cones.

Take the first fifteen minutes to explain the purpose of the activity and the reasons the participants have been placed in groups. The purpose is to give everyone an opportunity to view the data that represents their collective efforts. The participants are being asked to contribute to the interpretation of the data and provide input to complete collection of additional needed data. The groups are a way of encouraging new discussions with people they may not see often and sharing various perspectives. Their activity models the collaborative culture that looks at the "big picture" of the whole school (rather than how the department is doing), and they experience a sense of the collective responsibility that a school staff should share.

The numbers or color codes of the groups will help participants find the other members of their group and the station where they will start. Once they get located, they choose a facilitator and recorder for their group. Groups will have a designated time at each station. The task is to discuss the data that is shown and react to each of the questions. The recorder will write members' reactions on the flip chart paper that is posted. After the designated time, at a signal announced in advance, each group will move to the next station to review another type of data—taking their marker(s) with them.

In addition to the kinesthetic value of moving from station to station, another benefit is that each group reviews the reactions of other staff members, increasing the shared perceptions. A less interactive alternative is to have groups seated at tables and provide each table with a set of all the data displays for discussion. The same input may be provided, but the interaction of the groups with each other and the awareness of what other groups have said will be missing.

Prompting Discussion

The questions for reflection and discussion have been carefully worded. The first question does not say, "What do these data tell us?" but "What do these data seem to tell us?" People will see different things in the same data, and someone is sure to quote Mark Twain's comment, "There are lies, damned lies, and statistics." Words like *seem* or *appear* acknowledge that the conclusions may not be cut and dried.

The second question provides further acknowledgment that a single snapshot of data may not tell the whole story of what we need to know to make decisions. Asking, "What else would we need to know?" sends a clear message that these are not the only data we will ever see.

The third question, "What good news is here to celebrate?" highlights the positive results and reminds participants not to overlook the progress that is being made. Although student needs are urgent, we will not become more skilled or dedicated by focusing only on what is not yet done.

The last question raises awareness of the fact that these data will guide goal-setting, decision-making, and planning in the future. Including the word *might* reminds participants that these are tentative conclusions at this point.

Listening In

During the Carousel Data Analysis activity, groups are primarily self-directed, but some "listening in" to assess the quality of the dialogue is critical. This may occur by having a member of the Shared Leadership Team embedded within each group, or by having some facilitators moving about the room and observing the process. These leaders or facilitators need to be sensitized to comments that may be made and briefed on some strategies for guiding them in a productive direction. As Ruth Johnson (2002) pointed out,

> Inevitably, some of the discoveries that the school and district make regarding their beliefs, practices, and outcomes will be painful. The school community must be prepared to work through some hard times. Self-knowledge is the first step toward self-improvement. There will be conflict and debate, and some members of the school community will not be pleased with the data process. The knowledge, beliefs, values, and experiences that we bring to the table influence how data are interpreted. Others can interpret one person's analysis of the data picture very differently. Without opportunity for dialogue, problems and misunderstandings can fester. In the long run, the question should be: How can we use the data to build a common agenda for student improvement?
>
> If data regarding achievement of various groups of students are particularly disturbing, there will be lots of finger pointing, and the familiar excuses will be heard about why things are the way they are. The responsibility for poor achievement may be placed solely on students and parents and the conditions in which they live. Policies and practices within the school or district may be skirted, and there is likely to be an abdication of the school's responsibility for outcomes. Without thoughtful dialogue, the same old tired solutions continue to occur, such as adding on more programs rather than fixing core problems. (pp. 49–50)

As groups discuss the data before them, especially disaggregated data, facilitators should listen in to hear if comments are being made that reflect or convey stereotypes and low expectations. Statements like, "Well, what can you expect? All (such students) are always low performers and unmotivated," cannot be ignored. If they are not addressed, "silence is consent" and these beliefs go unchallenged and spread within the culture. The Carousel Data Analysis activity provides an opportunity to redirect such statements toward the "What else would we need to know?" question. Asking the speaker how we might follow up and check the accuracy of a negative statement conveys that it is not being accepted at face value, without creating an adversarial stance or passing moral judgment on the individual.

Using the Responses

The four reflection questions in Figure 10.1 have specific application for use as the school moves forward with its school improvement process. Responses to the first question "What do these data seem to tell us?" will be synthesized to form the summary statements under the graphs in the school portfolio. Reference to these summary statements is an important part of narrowing the focus to a few priority goals.

The next two questions—"What do these data not tell us? What else do we need to know?"—prompt further analysis and start the "snowball" rolling for data work. The needs for additional data also support indicators that may serve as the evidence of implementation and impact required by Chapter 11.

The third question, "What good news is here to celebrate?" focuses on positive accomplishments and highlights data the school will want to emphasize in both public and internal communications.

Answers to the last question identify possible "needs for school improvement." These needs will be verified through additional data work, and strategies will be selected to match.

STUDYING AND REPURPOSING TIME AVAILABLE

The most powerful way to cope with the dearth of time is a serious evaluation and redesign of the current time and practices for meetings and staff development. Learning Forward (Killion, 2013, 2016) provides a unique workbook specifically focused on establishing policies and parameters for use of time, analyzing current time usage by purpose, and comparing time working alone and in collaboration. These tools can be used by teams of educators, parents, and community members working together to examine the issue of time for collaborative educator professional learning. The procedure is not just to increase time *available* but to increase time in which educators are *engaged* in professional learning and collaboration among teams of educators who share common professional learning needs based on identified student learning needs.

With data in hand about all the time that is available, the tough decisions involve how to use it in different ways with different groupings of people and for different purposes. The technological options for information dissemination have multiplied, yet many schools remain in the pattern of having a staff meeting once a month that focuses on announcements and housekeeping. It's imperative that when people are brought together, there is a clear objective that can only be met through direct, timely interaction—that means collaborative work and building collective understanding. Figure 10.2 compiles strategies that schools and districts have used to repurpose time.

Figure 10.2 Finding Time

- Longer school day four days per week with time "saved" used on another day for professionals to meet, study, plan
- Extend each day of the week by 10 minutes for an early or late start or to provide a periodic release day.
- Extend the school day ½ hour on Monday, Tuesday, Thursday, Friday; on Wednesday staff are involved in professional development and dialogue from 8:00-10:30. Students arrive at 10:30 for modified day: thematic work, community activities, field trips, community assistance exchanges.
- Bank time by choosing one hour per week before or after school in study groups – compensated by districtwide professional development days.
- Consider the possibility of gaining time from scheduled lunch periods by reassigning staff supervision.
- Add minutes to beginning and end of four days – give ½ day off to students on fifth day.
- Same as above, but designate some staff to work with students on that half-day as an intervention/support strategy.
- Bank time by adding minutes per day – yields 1/w day for professional development per semester
- Cut down on passing time to build time available for professional learning one afternoon per week or month
- "School day" becomes "school week" with beginning and ending hours of each day flexible for schools.
- Extend to eight-hour workday for teachers, principals, and all others supporting teaching and learning.
- Extend school year to gain days.
- Extend the school year and "plant" planning days and professional development throughout the year.
- Use state staff development days to create time spread throughout the year.
- Come an hour early or stay an hour late – once a week over time – when district gives a workday you don't have to come. Documentation is necessary.
- Professional learning community meets before school.
- Professional learning community meets on a Saturday or after school, and this can replace a professional day. Pay for Saturday for team members' time.
- Meet beyond the "contract" day by being able to leave early on another day.
- Provide waivers for instructional contact hours.
- Handle administrative matters in writing to free up meeting time for staff learning.
- Reconsider the use of scheduled faculty meetings.
- Teachers from one grade level invite students in for "buddy work" with older kids, teachers from lower grade meet together; trade off the next week (or day).
- Students of teams of teachers do volunteer community work – frees that team of teachers for study and work together.
- Stipends from grants for release, or extra compensation.
- "Weed the garden" – decide what to stop doing without harming student learning in order to make room for best practices.
- Establish common formative assessments as the priority work for teacher requests related to time, clock hours and compensation.
- Hire floating substitute teachers to release entire grade levels or departments to work together.
- Troubleshoot related issues that may threaten or stall progress and consume precious time.
- Provide teachers with paid opportunities to work beyond the contract school day.
- Make common formative assessment progress a written priority in school improvement plans.
- Dedicate time at regular grade-level and department meetings to common formative assessments and related analysis and planning.
- Reduce the number of all-faculty meetings to once a month or less; allocate that additional time to be spent by grade-level and department meetings to implement common formative assessments.
- Provide a friendly staff competition with prizes for the most creative ideas on repurposing time.

Source: Adapted from Hord & Sommers, 2008 and Ainsworth & Viegut, 2006

Of course, whether time is added at a financial cost to the district—or time is repurposed by changing the schedule for students and their families—the public needs to understand the rationale and importance of this time. One principal uses the school newsletter to create transparency around early release days. A typical message reads "Thank you for your support in providing for your children's care on Wednesday afternoon. Their teachers will be conducting student progress reviews so we can be sure every child is receiving appropriate support for learning success." A district posted messages on the doors and school message boards reading "2,100 staff hours devoted to learning literacy strategies for your children." Signs in another district read, "Data Day Underway— we're studying the surveys you filled out for us." One of the best ways to safeguard the precious commodity of collaborative learning is to be proactive in communicating how it is being used and how that benefits students.

USING TIME WISELY

Even when every minute of time has been analyzed and focused on the priority work of the school, there will never be a moment to waste. Time must be used efficiently in terms of routines and processes, and it must be used effectively in terms of collaborative dynamics. Chapter 4 included the importance of using a standard format for setting agendas, taking notes that become minutes, and rolling the next steps section of those notes into the next agenda. Teams that have been diligent about maintaining those routines say that they had no idea they could accomplish so much in just forty-five minutes—they know right where to start, what to focus on, and leave with the next meeting already planned. Protocols like the Data Discussion Chart (Figure 4.4 [p. 61]) become second nature and help teams avoid distractions and use time efficiently. Useful protocols for various purposes are available online from the School Reform Initiative at www.schoolreforminitiative.org. The National School Reform Faculty (NSRF) also publishes protocols—some of which require attendance at NSRF trainings before use.

Time must also be used effectively—with explicit attention to the human dynamics that can enhance or inhibit the productivity of the team. The importance of collaborative work on a set of norms was introduced in Chapter 4. Many of the problems that occur in teams can be corrected with explicit agreements and a willingness on the part of each team member to hold him or herself accountable and accept reminders from colleagues. Figure 10.3 provides a collection of norm statements that teams have found useful. Some of them refer to procedures, some address interactions, and some describe the mindset that members pledge to employ when they work together.

Effective teams designate a member as norms observer and agree on strategies that will be used to maintain focus on the norms. They number and post the norms where they can easily be read by all—and the norms observer or any member can simply call the number of a norm to remind the group that they may be straying. Humor can be added with members being charged a nickel fine for breaking a norm—and all enjoying cookies

Figure 10.3 Team Norms

A Typical Set of Team Norms

- Come on time with materials and ready to serve assigned role.
- Follow scheduled rotation of facilitator, timekeeper, note-taker, and norms observer.
- Remain open-minded—withhold judgement and listen for understanding.
- Start each meeting with updates on next steps from last meeting.
- Stick to the agenda items determined at last meeting. Use a parking lot for other things that come up.
- Ask clarifying questions and pose new ideas.
- End each meeting with assigned responsibilities for next steps and agenda items for next meeting.

Examples of Other Procedural Norms

- Start and end on time.
- Plan and take breaks when necessary.
- Come prepared with agenda, data, materials, and assigned roles.
- Develop pre-planned agendas and come prepared.
- Define tasks and assign roles: note-taker, communicator, time-keeper, facilitator, data coordinator, snack-bringer.
- Start each meeting updating resolution or progress.
- Summarize with next steps, meeting date/agenda, assignments.
- Create a parking lot or use post-its to identify things to address in debriefing. Identify follow-up for parking lot items.
- Clarify tasks and assignments. Debrief tasks and parking lot at end of meeting.

Examples of Other Norms About Interactions

- Be respectful, listening to and valuing all viewpoints.
- Be actively engaged, contributing to discussions.
- Participate actively with all engaged in meeting.
- Be respectful and actively engaged.
- Limit sidebars and distractions with technology.
- Stay on task, avoiding distractions such as sidebars and cell phones.
- Be available to the team and limit distractions and sidebar conversations.
- Communicate honestly and maintain confidentiality for trust.
- Participate actively; listen and contribute; communicate openly.
- Share ideas honestly with all voices equal.
- Model use of data and best practice by providing evidence for claims.

Examples of Other Norms About Attitudes

- Value humor as a stress management tool.
- Be positive and keep a positive attitude about change.
- Don't take offense to ideas; be open-minded.
- Identify and avoid investing in issues outside our scope.
- Realizing we are all detail-oriented, we will designate a big picture thinker to force us to reflect and consider options.
- Maintain confidentiality until decision made to be shared.
- Present common front and messaging outside the group; be unified.
- As a team, we understand there will be conflict AND, in the interest of students, we will work towards resolution.
- Recognize and embrace unique differences to meet our common goal.
- We will come with an open mind and bring an appreciation for our different opinions.
- Keep our focus on the learner and work toward positive solutions.
- Share our challenges and celebrate our accomplishments.
- Foster trust by upholding confidentiality regarding students, colleagues, and our work.
- Foster a safe environment based on confidentiality and trust.
- Keep our focus on our learners and work toward positive solutions.

or donuts when the kitty is full enough. Positive reinforcement can be provided with applause for having completed an agenda in an efficient *and* effective manner. As teams grow together, they must become courageous enough to confront situations that threaten the productivity or student focus of the effort. They resolve not to keep recycling back to the same issues that waste time, energy, and goodwill. A quote from Nelson Mandela summarizes this chapter best: "We must use time wisely and forever realize that the time is always ripe to do right."

Chapter 11

You Get More Excited About Data When . . . It Shows You've Made a Difference

It's a cliché, but it's true. "Nothing succeeds like success." The phrase applies to hardworking adults as well as to challenged students. When teams look at data, become overwhelmed, and back away from taking action, they lose the opportunity to experience success and gain the satisfaction, momentum, and energy that comes from seeing they made a difference. When teams focus on a few priorities that arise from concerns in their data, identify powerful strategies to match those needs, and collect evidence of their results, they increase their sense of collective efficacy as well as the achievement of their students. This chapter focuses on these uses of data from Chapter 1:

- Making clear distinctions between inputs (by adults) and outcomes (for students)
- Using both objective and subjective (perceptual) data appropriately
- Gathering evidence of both implementation and impact of improvement strategies
- Taking the initiative to tell "the rest of the story"

The inputs by adults and the evidence of implementation relate to staff efforts. The outcomes for students are reflected in evidence of impact on students. Both kinds of evidence may come from multiple sources—and what they show tells the story of the school's efforts.

TENDING TO TEACHER EFFICACY

The work of Tschannen-Moran (2014) contributed to our understanding of teachers' need for a collective sense of efficacy in Chapter 3. She wrote further:

> This collective sense of efficacy is related to greater motivation toward school goals, greater effort, as well as greater persistence in the face of setbacks . . . teachers with stronger efficacy beliefs are likely to be more enthusiastic and more organized, and to devote more time to planning their teaching . . . [they] are less likely to become angry, impatient, or frustrated with a student who is having difficulty; they will stick with that student longer; and they will try more strategies to help the student to understand. . . . (p. 145)

It's a cycle. Describing a case study school, Tschannen-Moran (2014) stated, "There was a rise in the collective sense of efficacy among the teachers . . . as their level of trust increased and the school grew into a professional learning community. Trust bolstered the risk taking required in trying new teaching practices. This was rewarded with higher student achievement, which, in turn, raised the sense that the teachers could make a difference even among their most disadvantaged students" (p. 146). The previous chapter focused on use of norms and protocols to save time by resolving conflicts and making meetings more effective. This chapter emphasizes the importance of tending to teacher efficacy as an essential prerequisite for gaining commitment, assuring implementation of agreed-upon actions, and seeing the fruits of success that, in turn, sustain ongoing effort.

PRODUCING EVIDENCE OF IMPLEMENTATION

Many sound, research-based innovations have been initiated in schools, "tried" for a while, and then discarded because "they don't work" when there has been no way to know whether they have really *been* "worked." I have already stressed the need to select strategies that have documented data to back up their claims of improving student performance. But to get the same results, they have to be implemented in the same way in your school. A classic example is cooperative learning. Schools have a one-day workshop for staff on cooperative learning and assume teachers are then ready, willing, and able to apply this powerful approach in their classrooms. A year later, test scores are the same; just as many kids are getting Ds and Fs; and someone in a formal leadership role asks, "Are we doing cooperative learning?" Various people reply, "Oh, sure, I moved my desks into circles." "Well, of course, I do group stuff once a week." And a serious skeptic is bound to chime in, "And they're even harder to manage because they talk more now." The point of this example is not to evaluate cooperative learning but to emphasize that if you're going to choose a proven program, use it as proven, and prove you are using it—or don't blame the program for your lack of results.

Once a strategy has been identified and staff has made a commitment to learn and apply it, they must engage in a discussion of what it really looks like in action, how they will recognize it in their own work, and how the principal will observe it to provide reinforcement and support. They also must think about how these new practices or programs will show up in student work so that evidence of impact on learning can also be demonstrated (see section on generating evidence of impact).

Critical questions to address are these:

- What will implementation look like? Sound like?
- What will teachers be doing (and not doing)?
- What will students be doing (and not doing)?
- What evidence will be present in the classroom?
- How will this evidence be gathered and shared for celebration and support?

Some evidence of implementation will be classroom based and may be gathered by teachers and shared with each other in grade level and team meetings. For example, Figure 7.7 (pp. 130–131) provided a template for teachers to examine common formative assessments and other student work together. The work they bring may be students' responses to a schoolwide writing prompt. Or it might be a math problem-solving task including explanation of the approach students used to reach their answer. Teachers do a quick sort of the student work into three groups and then compare the characteristics of each group of student work to identify common challenges with which students are struggling. They also discuss what supports are needed by each group of students or individuals. This information is used to guide the next instructional steps and suggest flexible skill groups with specific objectives.

Classroom-Based Data Gathering

At an elementary school, teachers made a commitment to use monitoring notes to observe students' successes and struggles and use that information to group and regroup for differentiated instruction. The principal and staff discussed how the principal could support their efforts by providing feedback from informal observations. Figure 11.1 is an artifact from the principal's log of visits to classrooms to observe grouping and regrouping. This data was then reviewed by the staff at the next early release day. Teachers shared the challenges they faced with classroom management to be able to work with small groups, and gave each other ideas about selection of materials to support specific skills.

Teachers at another school studied their data on writing performance and realized that in order to discuss student work, they needed to emphasize the use of common expectations and editing marks. Figure 11.2 lists attributes they would stress during the year. Their principal regularly took home a few student draft books from a classroom, and reviewed them for

Teacher	When Groups Meet	How Often Groups Change	Assessments Used	Walk-Through Notes	Evidence
Figure 11.1 Grouping and Regrouping for Instruction					
Grade 3 Room 6	9:30–10:30	Change approx. 3 weeks	Running Records every 3 weeks; more often w/lower kids	5 Jan Yes Reading	Observation Planning sheet
Kindergarten Room 1	M/W 9:00–10:30 T/TH/F 9:00–10:30 12:00–1:30	M/W/F Regularly	RRR Monitoring notes Screening	16 Jan Yes Reading	Observation
Grade 5 Room 9	M–TH 9:30–10:30 F 10:00–10:30			17 Jan Yes Reading	Observation
Grade 1 Room 10	10:45–11:30 12:00–1:00	No group (daily)	Draft books	15 Jan No groups–sub Yes	Observation
Kindergarten Room 2	M/W 9:00–10:30			28 Jan Yes	
Grade 2 Room 8	11:00–11:30	Monthly	Oral reading	15 Jan Yes	Observation
Grade 1 Room 3	10:00–10:25 10:00–11:25	Every 3 weeks	RRR	21 Jan Yes	Observation
Grade 2 Room 5	10:45–11:30	Weekly	RRR Monitoring notes	23 Jan Yes	Observation
Grade 5 Room 11	10:00–10:25 10:00–11:30	Weekly	Monitoring notes	Weekly 15 Jan Yes	Planning sheet
Grade 3/4 Portable B	M/T/TH/F 2:30–3:00 W 11:00–12:00			10 Jan Yes Reading	Observation
Grade 4 Room 7	11:15–12:25	Every 2 weeks	Responses to guided reading	23 Jan One group w/ teacher and one with aide	Observation
Grade 4/5 Room 14	10:00–11:30	Every 2 weeks		6 Feb Groups listed with times on whiteboard	

evidence of using the date-topic-audience-purpose format, skipping lines to make revising and editing easier, and completing the planning stage of the writing process. Handwritten notes indicated the variety of planning tools he noticed, including lists, illustrations, beginning-middle-end reminders, and categories.

Schoolwide Data Gathering

A powerful method for gathering evidence of implementation of best practice, or specific new instructional strategies, or climate indicators, is

Figure 11.2   Gathering Data From Draft Books

Grade 2—January   Editing Marks

Room/Student No.	Drafts/Collection	Date: (DTAP)	Skip lines	Planning	Underline "SP"	Paragraph "P"	Circle Punctuation	Caret Insert	Cross-Out Line	Change Case Dbl Line	Other
A/1	Y	DTAP	Y	Y—list				Y	Y		
A/2	Y	DTAP	Y	Minimal							
A/3	Y	DTAP	Y	Y—pictures				Y	Y		
A/4	Y	D	Y	Y—web					Y		
A/5	Y	DT	Y	Y—web					Y		
B/1	Y	DTAP	Y	Y—categories	Y			Y			
B/2	Y	DTAP	Y	Y—B-M-E (beginning-middle-end)				Y	Y		"Things I know how to do well"
B/3	Y	DTAP	Y	Y—list					Y		
B/4	Y	DTAP	Y	Y—web				Y	Y		
B/5	Y	DTAP	Y	Y—B-M-E				Y			
C/1	Y	DTAP	Y	Y—boxes-sequence	Y	Y					"I can & am learning to . . ."
C/2	Y	DTAP	Y	Y—4-box	Y			Y	Y		" "
C/3	Y	DTAP	Y	Attempt							" "
C/4	Y	DTAP	With help	Minimal							" "
C/5	Y	DTAP	Y	Y—categories				Y	Y		" "

the "walk-through." Some authors use similar terms like "learning walk" and "instructional rounds" and focus on different purposes for taking a collaborative look at school and classroom practices. The process may be conducted by a team of external observers such as central office administrators, consultants, or technical assistance staff. Figure 11.3 might be used to guide such an overall view of the school and classroom environment and the roles of students and teachers.

The content and process can also be "owned" by the school staff as they identify desired characteristics from their new strategies, their mission statement, or attributes of schools they have studied who achieve high performance with similar students. Figure 9.6 (p. 163) illustrated a homegrown method of gathering data on five practices staff agreed to use consistently.

Figure 11.3 School Walk-Through Look-Fors				
SCHOOL WALK-THROUGH "LOOK FORS"	**Evident**	**Partially Evident**	**Not Observed**	**Not Applicable**
The Learning Environment – School				
Grounds and hallways are clean.				
Office staff is warm and welcoming.				
Student work is displayed and displays are created by students.				
Safety and evacuation plans are easily visible.				
The Learning Environment – Classroom				
Academic standards for the lesson are posted.				
Criteria for good work are prominently displayed.				
Students know routines for all parts of the day.				
A variety of types and levels of literature are available and attractively displayed.				
Different spaces or seating arrangements are provided for different learning purposes.				
Students as Learners				
Students engage in activities that require interaction and collaboration.				
Students can articulate what they are doing and what they are learning.				
Low-level recall questions and worksheets are minimized.				
Students write frequently about what they read, think, learn, and feel.				
Teachers as Learning Facilitators				
Teachers facilitate discussion and group work (goal is 50% or less lecture).				
Teachers engage all students in higher-order thinking and application of knowledge.				
Teachers vary work with individuals, small groups, and the whole group.				
Teachers provide graphic organizers and other tools to scaffold student learning.				
Teachers refer to plans and materials that colleagues have worked on together.				

An excellent resource on teachers' roles in classroom walk-throughs is provided by Kachur, Stout, and Edwards (2013). They defined these visits as brief, frequent, and informal with the purpose of gathering data on education practices and engaging in some type of follow-up. A particular focus and set of look-fors are identified, and the visits are repeated in order to record information over time. These authors prefer "teachers observing teachers [to] provide opportunities for the teaching staff to (1) note useful practices other than the ones they use; (2) ease the fear of trying something new; (3) feel motivated to improve their craft; (4) identify possible areas for their own professional development; (5) identify areas of practice for reflective dialogue with colleagues; and (6) accelerate improvement in student performance" (Kachur et al., 2013, p. 3). The book describes the use of teacher walk-throughs at forty different locations—elementary, middle school, and high school—with a range of demographics. A collection of observation forms (including software options) are included that match the areas of focus and specific look-fors of each site's model.

GENERATING EVIDENCE OF IMPACT

Traditional reports of school improvement have included descriptions of professional development provided, programs adopted, support staff hired, and materials purchased. All of these reflect the work of the adults in the organization. In some cases, the activities could take place and make no difference at all to the experiences and learning of the students. Evidence of impact ties the work to results for students. In order to demonstrate that impact, discussions in Teaching Teams and the Shared Leadership Team must address critical questions:

- How will we assess the critical skills in formative ways?
- How will we keep records of student status and progress?
- How and when will we share and compare our results?

Evidence of impact on student learning may be expressed in statements like these:

- The percentage of students proficient and above in ___ on the ___ improved from ___ to ___.
- Our mean score on the ___ improved from the ___ percentile to the ___ percentile.
- The number of students completing 80 percent of their assignments on time improved from ___ to ___.
- The average per student gain from fall to spring was ___ points.

Figures 11.4 and 11.5 provide examples of the link between strategic actions, evidence of implementation, and evidence of impact. Most of our work to increase student achievement will ultimately be judged by how our students perform on a state-mandated high-stakes assessment. But schools need "up close, in real time" evidence that they are making a difference. The number of middle school students correctly using nonfiction text forms and features provides this evidence of student learning that will, in turn and in time, translate into higher scores on the state test. The elementary report on its efforts to increase achievement in writing draws upon staff data from a coaching evaluation and student data on the state test.

USING DATA TO DEMONSTRATE THE DIFFERENCE YOU MAKE

The challenges faced by schools are real and are often not reflected in the public information releases of state test scores. Principals and teachers need the surge of energy that comes from knowing they made a difference,

---

Figure 11.4   Reporting Progress: Middle School Examples

School: Our Town Middle School	Strategic Plan Area: Reading	

Goal: Students will comprehend a variety of nonfiction texts, as measured by classroom assessment and 6% increase in state test scores.

Strategic Action	Evidence of Implementation	Evidence of Impact
• Schoolwide Read-Aloud using high interest, nonfiction text. • Teachers will emphasize text forms and features in content area textbooks and supplemental materials.	• Grade-level teams planned activities to accompany schoolwide Read-Aloud. • Teachers used strategic questions to monitor use of text forms and features.	• 70% of students correctly used the nonfiction text forms and features according to teachers' monitoring sheets. • WASL scores in nonfiction improved from 73% to 79% meeting standard.

School: Our Town Middle School	Strategic Plan Area: Writing	

Goal: Use research-based strategies to improve WASL writing scores by 5% per year and improve ITED by 3% per year.

Strategic Action	Evidence of Implementation	Evidence of Impact
• Teachers developed common rubric for writing in all content areas.	• All teachers trained in rubric on October 15 late arrival day. • Teachers analyzed the quality of a regular written assignment in teams on late arrival days in November and March.	• The quality of samples from regular written work improved from 39% getting 3's and 4's in November to 99% in March. • WASL scores improved from 62% meeting standards to 67% meeting standard.

School: Our Town Middle School	Strategic Plan Area: Learning Environment	

Goal: We will create a safe, supportive environment for learning by improving student conflict resolution skills and reducing playground incidents requiring referrals.

Strategic Action	Evidence of Implementation	Evidence of Impact
• Implement Second Step curriculum. • Train and use peer mediators.	• All teachers took Second Step training and are teaching the lessons. • 25 peer mediators have been trained.	• 79 conflict resolution reports were written and turned in by students. • Discipline referrals down by 10% from last year.

Figure 11.5 Reporting Progress: Elementary Writing

School: Sunnyland Elementary

Strategic Plan Area: Writing		
Goal: Teachers will develop competent writers who communicate effectively in a variety of genres.		
Strategic Action	**Evidence of Implementation**	**Evidence of Impact**
Teachers will provide regular demonstrations of written responses focusing on organization in a variety of genres.	Observable on chart paper in each classroom and teaching area.	33% increase in the number of students at standard in organization from fall to spring on the Sunnyland writing prompts; the 3rd grade writing score in organization increased by 13% from the previous year and the overall increase is 17%.
Teachers will score specific writing prompts 3 times each year using appropriate rubrics.	Copies of writing prompts and rubrics developed by grade level.	38% increase in the number of students at standard on all 6 traits from fall to spring on the Sunnyland writing prompts; the average per student gain from fall to spring was 0.82 points.
Teachers will be supported by a coaching model that focuses on organization in writing.	17 teachers and 3 coaches participated in 1:1 coaching.	On the coaching evaluation, 65% of the participants felt a single focus was helpful and 85% of participants felt they had increased their expertise in teaching writing.
Teachers will learn strategies for teaching organization in writing.	The building focus and the coaching focus was organization in writing.	On the coaching evaluation, 85% of the participants felt they had increased their expertise in teaching writing. 45% increase in writing scores on the WASL over the last three years.
Teachers will learn how to assess student writing for organization.	Writing prompts; rubrics developed by grade levels.	33% increase in the number of students at standard in organization from fall to spring on the Sunnyland writing prompts; the 3rd grade writing score in organization increased by 13% from the previous year; the average per student gain from fall to spring was 0.59 points.
Teachers will develop appropriate grade-level prompts and rubrics for organization in writing.	Writing prompts and rubrics developed at all grade levels.	33% increase in the number of students at standard in organization from fall to spring on the Sunnyland writing prompts; the 3rd grade writing score in organization increased by 13% from the previous year; the average per student gain from fall to spring was 0.59 points.
Teachers will attend district 3rd or 6th grade writing assessments scoring to learn about organization.	6 teachers attended the scoring and 1 Title I IA attended.	33% increase in the number of students at standard in organization from fall to spring on the Sunnyland writing prompts; the 3rd grade writing score in organization increased by 13% from the previous year; the average per student gain from fall to spring was 0.59 points.

and some begin to find their own ways to use data to document that reality. For example, a principal greeted my school visit with enthusiasm. "I'm so glad you came on a school visit today. What I'm excited to share with you is about *data*! The district data might look like our trend line is flat, but we know better . . . What I'm working with is 'what's happening in the classroom' data . . . We decided to quit worrying about all the challenges our kids bring, and focus on what we control— our own understandings about learning . . . As we worked on updating our strategic plan, we talked about what the evidence of impact on student learning would be, and we discarded most of the ideas we had that wouldn't contribute evidence."

The principal of a magnet school also decided to tell her own "difference" story. The staff serve a regular population and two special education programs that draw students in need of service from across the district. Students are very mobile, and it's difficult to determine the effectiveness of the school's efforts on a single test, at a single point in time, at one particular grade level, when the target population is constantly on the move. So the principal decided to "do her own data" and discover what she and her staff wanted to know. She began with the first kindergarten cohort to be served under the schoolwide Title I plan. Figure 11.6 illustrates her discovery that, of students who remained at the school, a greater proportion each year reached proficiency. By the time they were in fourth grade, almost everyone had closed their own gap and met the grade-level standards.

Challenges also faced another school where 61 percent of the students qualify for free and reduced lunch, and enrollment has grown about 20 percent over the past three years, even though 15 to 20 percent leave

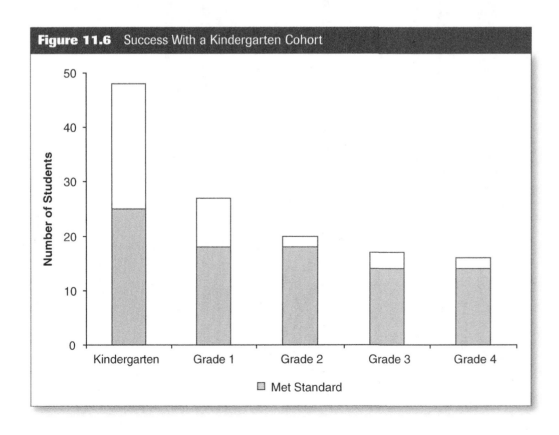

Figure 11.6 Success With a Kindergarten Cohort

	Figure 11.7 Success With Students Who Stay		
State Scores	Mean for Students 2+ Years	Mean for Students Less than 2 Years	Standard
Listening	401	305	400
Reading	398	359	400
Writing	9.4	7.6	9.0
Math	410	336	400

each summer and don't return for the next year. This issue of mobility also complicated interpretation and use of test results for decision-making and planning for instructional improvement. So in preparation for a recent School Board visit, the principal decided to discover what his staff might learn if they could account for the mobility factor. Figure 11.7 shows their findings that the means of state scores for students in the school two years or more essentially met or exceeded the score described as standard on the state test.

Digging out this data was labor-intensive without the data warehousing and analysis capacity the district was seeking to acquire. Staff members devoted hours of extra time to "mine and combine" multiple data sources by hand. It was well worth the effort—but not so they could use this evidence of effectiveness as a reason to quit working for equity. The presentation for the Board visit ended with a set of Future Directions, and first on the list was "Find a way to respond to the needs of our mobile population." And the principal celebrated with this follow-up e-mail to staff:

> Congratulations! We just received summaries of the fall reading scores for the district. Ours look very good. Kindergarten: 93% met standard compared to 73% district wide. First grade: 84% met standard, 90% district wide. Second grade: 84% met standard, 82% district wide. Third grade: 70% met standard, 72% district wide. Fourth grade: 73% met standard, 74% district wide. Fifth grade: 62% met standard, 78% district wide. As we look at these numbers, we need to remember that in fifth grade we only have 8 students that have been with us from kindergarten, and a 130% turnover rate. In fourth grade, our turnover rate is over 200%. We have the highest free and reduced lunch count in the district. SUPER WORK! We know that when students remain with us, they are very successful. Our job now is to figure out how we can bring all of the students that move into our building up to standard also. That is a task that the Leadership Team is addressing now and will be working with you on as we look ahead to next year.

State test scores are not the only measure of evidence of impact. Staff at a nearby high school had been working to increase the success of entering ninth graders. In an e-mail to staff, the principal noted that the number of freshmen failing three or more classes is down 6% from last year. Even more interesting, the number of freshmen failing any classes at all for the first semester has been reduced by 9% this year. . . . Interventions we have made this year (peer support at the beginning of the school year, community-building exercises during the opening days of school in all classes, special ed reconfiguration to provide increased support to teachers and students in classrooms, a greater focus on 9th grade challenges and needs, a common homework policy, beginning attempts to make connections across the 9th grade curriculum, a common writing rubric, introducing reading strategies into a number of classes across the content areas, etc.)—all may be having a positive impact on the lives and learning of our freshmen.

Evidence of impact can also be related to nonacademic goals for students. A school had been struggling to maintain the integrity of instructional time, while dealing with an array of discipline issues. Based on his informal data tracking, the principal was able to congratulate his staff with this message: "We only had 11 official office discipline referrals for February . . . This compares to 17 last February and 36 the previous year. The total for this year is now 133, compared to 204 at this time last year. That is 35% fewer than last year."

In another setting, the district charted the percentage of students meeting standards over a period of six years, disaggregated by socioeconomic status (SES). This one visual (Figure 11.8) provided the proof that their persistence in the early years paid off over time—and fueled their continued effort. The inescapable tension is the push-pull between the sense of urgency for students who can't afford to lose another day—and the reality that change only comes as the result of sustained and flat-out-stubborn refusal to give up.

REAPING UNEXPECTED BENEFITS

There's a fringe benefit to monitoring implementation, as one junior high school discovered. Teachers had been concerned about the low self-esteem and disengagement of some students and what they perceived as an overall lack of respect for diversity in the student population. Some of the teachers had been reading about student engagement in learning and a few others had attended a workshop on cooperative learning. They felt that use of cooperative learning might seem more engaging to the students and thereby might increase achievement. Social Studies teachers decided to work together and develop cooperative learning activities. Their goal was to have a cooperative learning activity every Thursday and see what would happen.

The data-gathering aspect of their project was overlooked at the time but emerged as an "aha!" for the entire school. After a month or so, the guidance counselor reported at a faculty meeting that for some reason, attendance in seventh and eighth grade was showing an increase and was higher on Thursdays than any other day of the week. He wondered if anyone was doing anything special on Thursdays. When the Social Studies

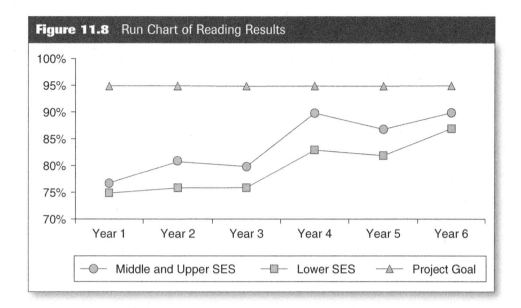

Figure 11.8 Run Chart of Reading Results

teachers mentioned their experiment, the language art teachers decided to test it further. They chose Tuesday as a day to use cooperative learning and consciously set out to have the counselor help them trace the attendance patterns. The staff had not yet determined the effects on student test scores, but they had certainly made an impact on student interest and attendance. They had also stimulated the growth of a community of learners in their school.

SPREADING A LITTLE CHEER

Becoming transparent about our work as educators—inviting colleagues or supervisors or outside experts to visit and observe us, displaying up close data about our personal endeavors—can be daunting. Even the most passionate people, committed to truth and proof, need celebrations and cheerleaders. Just as change for the sake of change is illogical, crunching data for the sake of spouting statistics is inappropriate. The underlying and overwhelming purpose of this book is to use data as *tools* to focus our efforts on the real *goal:* maximizing the success of our students. When benchmarks are reached or milestones achieved, call on the staff members who love drama, the former cheerleaders and the social organizers, and plan unique ways to celebrate!

In your study and analysis and planning, in your assessing and monitoring and celebrating, be guided by one teacher's version of a traditional cheer:

Give me a D! *D!*

Give me an A! *A!*

Give me a T! *T!*

Give me an A! *A!*

Who is it *FOR? KIDS!*

ONE SCHOOL'S STORY

After observing and talking with educators at a middle school, Noonan (2014) concluded that it can be "difficult to shift norms of professional learning in schools" (p. 151). Calvert (2016) agreed:

> Educators confirm that it takes time for new approaches to be shaped to fit individual contexts and begin to make a difference. Harnessing teachers who have operated as solo fliers into collaborative communities will not happen overnight. Teachers who have not been given much responsibility or agency in the past will have to learn to use them well . . . [Quoting a district leader] We expect change to be this massive, rapid thing . . . The truth is it takes time to build trust and to move the needle. It can take five to seven years. (p. 14)

Even that time span may be optimistic. Principal Darren Benson generously shared with me his ten-year "Memory Lane" chronicle of data use and change at Blaine Middle School in Washington State. For the purposes of reflection and growth, Benson has kept a running record of key data points, initiatives, and tipping points in the journey. Refer to Figure 1.5 (p. 17), and identify how each of the twenty high-performance data uses are embedded in this decade of work.

During Benson's first two years at Blaine, the school developed a new mission statement, while continuing an existing School Improvement process. Staff participated in Carousel Data activities, reviewing test data along with staff, parent, and student surveys, and created narrative statements about the data. Once they identified math as the most critical priority for immediate attention, seven barriers were identified for further research, and three of those became the focus of change efforts. Staff developed Action Plans that included implementation of Response to Intervention (RTI), heterogeneous grouping, teaming of teachers, and increased parent involvement. A morning Math Academy was initiated to provide math skill intervention and preteaching. Students who are in the Math Academy classes receive math skill support based on multiple assessments, and are given a double dose of time and instruction to help them increase their speed and comprehension of upcoming lessons.

In Year 3, strategies included Morning Math Academy for Math support and Enrichment for Reading, Heterogeneous Grouping with Double Dose Support; teaming by sharing students; and surveys of parents, students, and staff to shape continued refinement of the Math Academy design. Seventy percent of students stated that they understood math better than in the past because of Math Academy. By the end of the third year, Benson wrote this in the school newsletter:

> On the 2009 [state test], each grade has shown gains and middle school students have many accomplishments of which to be proud. In reading, 75% of sixth graders met or exceeded the state reading standard, a gain of 14% from last year; the seventh grade had 60% of its students pass . . . In eighth grade, 85% of the students met the state reading standard, up from 81.5% last year. In math, significant

gains were realized as well. Sixth grade made a 10% achievement increase from 45% to 55%; seventh grade students held steady at 55%, but increased the math achievement 10% from sixth grade to seventh grade. In eighth grade math, an 8% gain in math achievement . . . from 51% to 59%. Gains were also reported in writing and science, and parents were assured "We are continuing to take intentional and innovative steps to address academic performance . . . We will continue with Academy, Teaming, and heterogeneous grouping . . . adding a Core Extension class to address the needs of struggling readers."

Year 4 featured an in-depth analysis of all areas of Grade 6, 7, and 8 essential skills in Math and English Language Arts—in order to identify and focus on the most critical skill gaps that needed further intervention. Students and teachers were again surveyed, and a PM Reading Academy was added. New strategies were learned and implemented, including six-minute solution fluency practice, Read-Alouds with strategy discussions, remediation with previously taught strategies, extended work time for completing assignments that faster readers did during class, and prereading texts. Use of formative assessment was emerging as a more common practice for targeting specific interventions for individual students. Four years of hard work culminated in a major celebration! Blaine Middle School met annual yearly progress goals in all areas, stopping the slide into lower categories of state designation. This success motivated further effort.

Year 5 continued to provide double doses in reading and math through the Academy and Core Extension design. Heterogeneous grouping and teaming provided a class mix. Intervention opportunities and use of common formative assessments expanded. Collaboration was increased through coteaching to support special needs students in Grades 6 and 7. The school schedule was changed at eighth grade so that teachers could specialize in math or science. Collaborative work and common assessments were expanded from Math and English Language Arts into Science. At the end of Year 5, Blaine Middle School celebrated again! Blaine Middle School was designated as a School of Distinction—among the top 5% most improved schools in the state!

A tipping point occurred in Year 6 when the 5 Dimensions of Teaching and Learning (5D) from the Center for Educational Leadership (CEL) was chosen as the instructional framework to provide a common language for instruction and focus of professional development. The fall preconference with teachers became more meaningful, as teachers chose their own area of focus to work on. Feedback from peers and administrators was couched in the common language. Teachers and administrators used a Lesson Study Observation format and received clock hour credits for engaging in a book study focused on Learning Targets—an area from the dimension of Purpose for which staff data indicated greatest need.

Another tipping point began in the summer after Year 6 and emerged as a strong and successful focus in Year 7. Staff representatives attended AVID training and shared key learnings with the rest of staff, who then adopted it as a core professional development focus for everyone. From this base came two strands of Action Plans: schoolwide strategies focused on organizational strategies and note-taking skills for students, and individual professional growth plans for teachers based in the 5D instructional framework.

During Year 8, professional learning communities got more involved in data collection, and data analysis processes were formalized to add more consistency and specificity to the RTI provisions for struggling students. Data Snaps were used to analyze practices in the school. One such Data Snap revealed that 77 percent of the students were "mostly" or "always" using their planners to keep track of homework and other important school-related information.

Two tipping points occurred in Years 9 and 10. In ongoing collaboration with Western Washington University, teachers were now working consistently in content-related professional learning communities. And Data Snaps were conducted frequently, focused on Student Engagement (another of the 5D) with emphasis on increasing student talk and shifting teacher questioning.

In these two years, staff reviewed and specifically identified initiatives that were being sustained from previous years: Morning Math Academy and Reading Enrichment, formative assessment and targeted student interventions, Career and Tech Ed and Spanish electives, Core extension with focus on reading improvement and math enrichment, coteaching, and intentional student placement to support students with special needs. In addition, some strategies were listed for "fine-tuning": systems focus, content-area professional learning communities, Data Snaps of schoolwide practices, and feedback cycles for every staff member. Teachers also worked together in cohort professional learning communities, based on their year in the teacher evaluation process. In their meetings, these cohort groups shared ideas related to their chosen focus area from the evaluation criteria and/or their cycle of inquiry. The newly emerging practice at this stage was vertical articulation of curriculum, resulting in development of Grades 6 to 8 unit maps.

In discussion this spring, Benson mentioned this:

> The way we talk to each other has changed—it is more solution-focused. We set a foundation, provide opportunity for dialogue, and develop training and expertise in each other. We don't have the grants any more, but the structures and norms are in place. With the most recent shift to another state assessment based on Common Core State Standards, we can't "YET" say that we have 80% or more of all our students passing every part of the state tests. But we can say we have professional learning structures in place; highly trained, caring, motivated staff; and a Growth Mindset that will help staff and students increase their performance over time. This is underway—as evidenced by the 2015–2016 state assessment data which shows a growth from year one to year two in 8th grade math of 8% more students proficient or above, and an 18% growth in students proficient in 6th grade from year to year two. Additionally, the cohort of 7th graders showed a growth of 13% more proficient since they were in the sixth grade. In English/Language Arts, we saw a similar trend from year one to year two: grade level growth of 2% in 6th grade and 18% in 8th grade. Seventh graders showed

a 6th to 7th student cohort growth of 6% more proficient in ELA. Scores in Science also increased with 16% more students proficient or above in 2016 over 2015. In summary, we are striving to live our mission, which asserts that, "**We believe** in creating a safe, caring, and respectful environment so that **ALL students can learn**. **We are dedicated** to cultivating academic **persistence** and **excellence** in our students. **We believe** this will empower them to **grow** as learners and influence positive change **in our community and beyond**." (emphasis his)

Blaine Middle School has used multiple kinds of data in multiple ways to initiate, evaluate, refine and sustain, or replace new practices on behalf of student achievement. The early gains they were able to document fueled ongoing commitment and energy for effort. As Benson stated, they are not "there" *YET*—but they can clearly see and celebrate that they are making a difference.

Chapter 12

You Get More Excited About Data When . . . You Have Appropriate Support

In its brief, powerful one-page stance on the achievement gap, the Center for Educational Leadership (CEL, 2016b) summarized that "the teacher is the most influential factor on student learning, and students must experience quality teaching consistently from year to year and from classroom to classroom to attain and sustain high levels of achievement." Individual teachers, principals, or schools do not have that full scope of influence, so the role of the school district becomes the focus of this chapter.

A common complaint at the school level is aimed in that direction. "They just don't support us." The comment leaves district leaders dumbfounded. They are not intentionally neglectful. In fact, they can make a list of things they've done to support schools, including the grants they've written and the professional development programs they've initiated. Perhaps—like beauty in the eye of the beholder—"appropriate" support is defined by its effect on those for whom it's intended. Support is "inappropriate" when, though well-intended and perhaps even "research-based," it does not match or respond to the needs of those to be supported. Some of the main areas of support addressed here include design of systems for professional learning and curriculum development, modeling use of data and continuous improvement, dedication of time and control over time, and technology tools and support. If support is focused on changing the structure of schools, then providing more professional development in traditional ways, and rewriting curriculum without a clear and close focus on the classroom environment and the instruction provided by the teacher, and generating policy and technical assistance will not extend to reach the desk of the student.

TOUCH THE TALENT IN THE TRENCHES

Consider how it would look if you introduced the "desk" of the student into your next districtwide meeting, regional conference, or state workshop. Literally place a chair at center front of the room, label it "Student," and ask all present to visualize a specific student as though he or she is present in the room. If the group is not too large, an even more powerful approach is to ask each person to think of a student in whom they have made significant investments already—perhaps a child they worked with passionately and persistently all this year who now moves on to another grade or school, or perhaps a child within their personal sphere whose school experience matters deeply to them. Write the child's name on a stick-on note, and come forward and attach it to the chair. Now everyone in the room has a student in focus.

Now ask the common introductory question of what roles are represented in the room: teachers, principals, central office coordinators, superintendents, board members, university staff, regional coaches or directors, state department staff, and so on. As each role is identified, identify a representative of that role to come to the front of the room. Then stand aside, and ask them to arrange themselves in a row starting with the student and moving outward to the right. They will eventually end up with the teacher in closest contact to the student chair, and all other roles farther and farther away. It is interesting to watch as the state superintendent—or even the district superintendent—acknowledges that she or he can not influence the experience of that student except by working with and through the entire line.

If comfortable, take this a step further, and tie a length of nylon clothesline to the chair before you begin. Once the lineup is ready, ask the person farthest from the chair—who is sometimes perceived as the most powerful—to pick up the string and "push the rope." Nothing will happen to the chair. Ask every person to pick up the rope and pull in the same direction—and the chair will move.

Whether this human demonstration is useful or not, the point is that we must respect the talent in the trenches—where the work is really done. Touching that talent in the day to day means being present in the schools—and not from a deficit-based perspective. Don't just go to the classroom or grade that may be struggling the most, to document or even to "help." Go to the classroom of the master teacher and be awed.

DELIVER ON RECIPROCAL ACCOUNTABILITY

The term *reciprocal accountability* was defined by Richard Elmore (2002b) in this way: "Accountability must be a reciprocal process. For every increment of performance I demand from you, I have an equal responsibility to provide you with the capacity to meet that expectation. Likewise, for every investment you make in my skill and knowledge, I have a reciprocal responsibility to demonstrate some new increment in performance" (p. 5). Applying this principle to schools and districts, he continued,

> When you begin to describe the organizational conditions under which professional development actually contributes to instructional capacity in schools, you begin to describe an organization as it rarely exists.

> Such an organization would only require teachers to learn new skills and knowledge if it were prepared to support their practice of these skills in real classrooms, providing experts to work with teachers as they master these skills and adapt them to their students' responses to new practices and materials. It would be an organization that offered consistent messages to principals, teachers and students about what goals are most important and what resources are available to support the work of meeting them. It would be an organization in which administrators, at the school and system level, think their main job is to support the interaction of teachers and students around the mastery of specific content. And, it would be a system in which no judgments about performance, of teachers or students, are made without first ensuring that the conditions for high performance have been met; a system in which no one is expected to demonstrate knowledge and skill that they haven't had the opportunity to learn. (p. 25)

Tschannen-Moran (2014) has reminded system leaders of what happens when reciprocal accountability is not modeled from the district or school level: "When school leaders unveil a new vision or change initiative . . . and then do not follow through, or change course again, or do not uphold the principles of their own program, it is worse than if they had not begun in the first place. The 'flavor of the month' syndrome creates cynicism and damages trust, rather than leading to positive, sustainable change" (p. 26). The underlying test of appropriate support involves considering every district initiative and being completely honest in answering these questions: How big a change is this from current practice? How thorough is our analysis of the knowledge, skills, and follow-up teachers will need? How complete is our plan for meeting those needs? Does it include the peer coaching that Joyce and Calhoun (2016) found necessary to raise the probability of long-term implementation from 5 to 10 percent of trained participants to 90 percent and higher?

REDESIGN PROFESSIONAL DEVELOPMENT FOR LEARNING

Following up on the concept of reciprocal accountability, Elmore (2002b) emphasized that

> this kind of difficult, contingent, and uncertain *learning* is best done in close proximity to the work itself. And the work of schools is

instruction. Teachers acquire different values and beliefs about what students can *learn* by observing their own students and students like theirs in other settings, *learning* things that they, the teachers, might not have believed possible. Teachers and administrators *learn* how to connect new knowledge and skill to practice by trying to do specific things in the classroom and by asking themselves whether there is evidence that, having done these things, students are able to do things they were not able to do before. School administrators and teachers *learn* to change the conditions of work by trying new ideas in the context of specific curriculum content and specific instructional problems, grade-level conferences and observations around particular problems of math or literacy instruction, for example. System administrators *learn* to change structures and resource-allocation patterns by observing what effective practice in schools looks like and trying to figure out how to support it. (p. 30, emphasis mine)

Redefine

A first step in redesigning professional development is to refocus on the *learning* that results, as emphasized by the italics in the Elmore's quote just given. Calvert (2016) stressed the "term professional learning because it recognizes teachers as agents of their growth and emphasizes that learning is an experience driven largely by the learner. The degree to which a teacher acts with agency in professional learning depends on a number of factors including both a teacher's internal traits, such as the motivation to engage in professional learning, as well as a school's structural conditions for professional learning, including the degree to which the system involves teachers in decisions about what and how they learn" (p. 2).

Listen

Calvert (2016) continued: "In addition to analyzing data, visiting classrooms, and reviewing school and system goals, leaders must cultivate an environment of continuous learning that engages teachers in their professional learning at every step of the way. They must understand the tangible, but enormous, value teachers place on being listened to and involved meaningfully as well as the benefits the school community enjoys when teachers are intrinsically motivated to pursue their continued development" (p. 2) In this context, "listened to" means more than circulating a survey about topics for workshops in the coming year. It means face-to-face conversations informally as district leaders visit schools. It also means providing a formal structure for teacher voices, such as a district professional learning team. Figure 12.1 contrasts the conditions that do and do not support teacher agency (Calvert, 2016). Since teacher agency is key to professional learning, these columns might also be titled "Inappropriate Support" and "Appropriate Support." One entry in the category of district planning is that a district team comprises at least 50 percent practitioners—meaning those directly practicing the art and science of teaching and learning.

Figure 12.1	Conditions That Do and Do Not Support Teacher Agency	
System Conditions	**Professional Development Lacking Teacher Agency**	**Professional Learning Supporting Teacher Agency**
School approach to professional development	• Planned by administrators, often delivered by external vendors • Driven by constraints of current scheduling • Doubts about whether professional development is working • One-time workshops without follow-up	• Teachers plan and present professional learning • Educators engage in learning communities based on mutual trust and expertise • Professional learning happens during the school day and everyone engages in cycles of learning
Reason for teacher participation	• Compliance: to earn credits or carry out existing policies • Compulsion or external pressure to achieve a score, satisfy someone else's objective, or to receive external rewards	• Intrinsic desire to improve teaching and learning and connect with colleagues • Internal motivation to master one's craft, to be accomplished, to prepare students for the future
Source of solutions to learning challenges	• Assumption is that the source of expertise and solutions comes from outside the school	• Look internally first for the source of expertise to solve problems
Topics and skills addressed	• Little input from teachers • Potpourri of topics chosen by system leaders and principals based on multiple, often competing, objectives • Decisions about what teachers need to know are made by the central office and school administrators • Topics are often unrelated to teacher and student learning	• Teacher-identified learning objectives • Based on data (including observations) • Focused on teachers' and students' continuous growth • Topics address specific classroom challenges • Teachers decide what they need to learn
Role of teachers	• Implementers, recipients of information, deliverers of content	• Planners, designers, advisors, presenters, implementers, evaluators, decision makers
Collaboration	• School leaders predetermine topics for collaboration • Teachers do not choose which team(s) they will join • Norms and protocols are set outside of the group and may or may not be accepted by group members • Groups may include non-teachers whose primary role is to supervise the group's interaction	• Teachers determine topics based on students' and teachers' needs • Teachers may choose to join teams with common goals and interests • Teams determine norms and protocols • Teams are responsible for working within their established norms and protocols, though non-teachers may participate as team members without a supervisory function
Format	• Form of learning is not personalized • Sit and get • Teacher watches presentations, listens, takes notes, sometimes engages in small group discussion	• Format based on teachers' learning needs • Grounded in adult learning research • Collaborative, constructivist exchange
Tone of learning activities	• Checking the boxes; passive, inauthentic interaction • Unclear purpose • Loses focus, gets off track, devolves into staff meetings or complaint sessions • Evaluative	• Goal-oriented • Professional • Clear agenda and meaningful protocols • Interpretive, solutions-oriented

System Conditions	Professional Development Lacking Teacher Agency	Professional Learning Supporting Teacher Agency
District plan and priorities for professional learning	• Driven by administrators and school board • Plan executed by central office • Focus on state and district mandates and program implementation • Excludes monitoring and feedback of effectiveness	• Educators examine data and determine priorities • District team comprises at least 50% practitioners • Plan to monitor implementation and impact • Established feedback loops

Source: Reprinted with permission of Learning Forward, www.learningforward.org. All rights reserved.

Diagnose

The ultimate purpose of listening more intentionally to teachers (and all employee groups) is to diagnose skill needs. Louis, Leithwood, Wahlstrom, and Anderson (2010) found that district leaders in higher-performing settings

> understood that the reasons for differences in student performance, or in implementation of district initiatives, were particular to the setting. Similar problems . . . might result from different contributing conditions in different schools. Therefore, standard solutions were considered unlikely to apply in all situations. Leaders in these districts engaged school staff members in collaborative inquiry about the unique circumstances affecting student learning or teacher performance in their schools. They then tailored district support for improvement based on the analysis of school-specific needs rather than relying primarily on centrally determined interventions based on categorical differences among schools and their students . . . One-size-fits-all policies will not build confidence, and will be less likely to encourage schools to be reflective about their own capacities for redesigning their organizations to meet very local needs. (pp. 212, 215)

Thus, one source of diagnostic information for district planning is the work of schools as they create their own data summaries and select strategies to meet their students' needs.

Another source for diagnosis is teacher reflections when they look at student work together. Chapter 7 described the work of Teaching Teams, and Figure 7.7 (pp. 130–131) concluded discussion of student work with this question: "Based on how our students learned, what do *we* need to learn?" Key points from these discussions can be compiled and shared in the district's professional learning team.

Additional information for diagnosing professional learning needs may be gathered through frequent classroom walk-throughs, as described in Chapters 9 and 11. When these visits are grounded in an instructional framework (e.g., Marzano, Danielson, 5 Dimensions of Teaching and Learning [5D]), common language facilitates collaborative discussion so that patterns of effective practice and problems or gaps in practice can be recognized.

A potentially valuable legacy that may be salvaged from the wreckage of No Child Left Behind (NCLB) is the use of rubrics in teacher evaluation processes. When these rubrics are grounded in a research-based instructional framework and developed carefully, they can provide clear road maps of growth in instructional practice as a teacher enters and increasingly masters the teaching profession. As teachers use their rubric for self-assessment of strengths and targeted areas for growth, they can form learning groups and identify their needs for very specific, strategic support. Figure 12.1 emphasizes that topics should arise from teacher-identified learning objectives, data, and specific classroom challenges.

The Shared Leadership Team can also assist in diagnosing needs. For example, at Robbinsdale Cooper High School in Minnesota, a group of teacher leaders identified knowledge and skills needed to strengthen their professional learning communities (Kind, 2014). Those needs included the following:

- Writing Formative Assessments—Alignment with summative; variety of assessment modes
- Writing Summative Assessments—Alignment with standards, course and unit objectives and learning targets; variety of assessment modes and higher thinking skills; writing quality criterion-based rubrics
- Using Assessment Data—How to display data visually; timely response; appropriate feedback; self-assessment and reflection strategies for students; tools for students to monitor progress
- Grading—Common understanding of criteria; common weighting
- Learning Targets—Writing clear learning targets

These examples of teacher learning needs arose after professional learning communities were already in place, illustrating the importance of diagnosis not just at the beginning but *during* implementation of anything new. For instance, Chapter 5 described a medium-sized school district that was midway into the second year of implementation of a new math program when teachers were complaining and frustrated, and instructional coaches were noting wide variations in implementation. A schedule of focus groups was set up so that teachers had a choice of several times and places to meet with grade-level colleagues from other schools. Focus group questions included the following:

- What aspects of implementing [the program] are going well or best for you?
- What do you observe about your students' experiences and reactions in this approach?
- In general, what are your biggest concerns about using [the math program] right now? What specific aspects of implementing [the math program] are problematic for you at this time?
- What kind of help do you need to continue to be more effective in your use of [the program]? What would support look like?

When the responses were compiled, there were some common themes at all grade levels, but the specific kinds of support requested were very different. This "implementation check" allowed district resources from curriculum and professional development departments to be timely and tailored for each grade-level group in response to the stated needs.

Deploy

One way to support teacher agency is to recognize and draw upon expertise that already resides within the district. Dale Hair (2016), a senior consultant on the Learning Forward staff, identified what she wished she had learned sooner: "It's not about the wisdom *you* bring to the group, but the wisdom *within the group* that you unlock so that they can become learning leaders for themselves" (p. 19). After diagnosing needs, the next questions should be these: Who are our resident experts? How can we deploy them in response to these needs (without totally depriving students of their expertise in the classroom)? After the full cast of internal experts has been reviewed, then it becomes appropriate to ask, "In what areas or roles do we need external support?" *In*appropriate support is the all-too-common knee jerk "let's bring in a consultant" response to identified needs. Figure 12.1 points out the importance of teachers planning and presenting professional learning; looking internally first for expertise; and increasing the roles of teachers as planners, designers, advisors, presenters, implementers, evaluators, and decision-makers.

Differentiate

The question about resident expertise reminds us that across a district and even within a school, practitioners represent a range of experiences from preservice education and learning on the job. When a new expectation or action is being explored, the knowledge and skills should be clearly identified, but it should not be assumed that everyone is starting from scratch. The question of who needs "basic" training versus an "advanced" review and refinement is critical to show respect and trust in the professionals. One-size-fits-all approaches are demoralizing to teachers and waste time, energy, and money.

Professional learning for implementation must include the levels of follow-through necessary to result in classroom use. An "overview" during the rush of August in-service can be useful to create momentum and signal importance but is not sufficient to ensure that students throughout the school will benefit. Planning for learning must include ongoing and multiple exposures with content-specific examples and practice with feedback through arrangements such as use of video, instructional coaching, or professional learning communities.

Differentiation will require a variety of opportunities, so all of the possible venues for professional learning should be considered, not just the two or three days designated as "PD days" in the master calendar—for example, staff meetings, common planning times, grade/department/team meetings, early/late dismissals. Then decide which of these possible times and places best fit the purpose of introducing new knowledge and which opportunities make it possible to coordinate practice with feedback and coaching. A twenty-minute segment of a staff meeting can accommodate a mini-lesson or video clip of a concept or teaching strategy. But for coaching to occur, students must be in session and the coach or observer must be made available. Finally, double-check the overall professional learning plan for the year and ensure that more time is dedicated to practice than to sit-down inputs.

The analysis of best venues and time frames allows for another important dimension of differentiation. An important variable in a teacher's ability to incorporate new instructional strategies is their understanding of application to the specific curriculum content for which the teacher is responsible. Especially at the secondary level, it's important that instructional strategies be discussed, tried, and analyzed with colleagues who share similar teaching assignments. In small high schools, there are often "singletons"—teachers who handle all the art, or music, or some other discipline, and feel they have no colleagues. It could be argued that teachers can be clustered in various ways to have common ground (e.g., performance arts have a common need for performance assessments more than written), but when a teacher *feels* isolated, that teacher is far less likely to risk contributing ideas in discussions that seem unfamiliar. An important way that districts can differentiate and provide content-related applications is to connect with other districts and create electronic networks for these teachers with unique assignments. Owens and Strahan (2016) described such a networking project in which two-teacher teams in different districts created their own interaction plans including at least two full-day "live" classroom visits to each other, with virtual follow-up sessions on a regular schedule.

District leaders should also respond to a unique challenge in terms of data use at the high school level. Louis et al. (2010) noted that teachers need assistance for accessing, interpreting, and making use of evidence for their decisions about teaching and learning: "Increased support will be especially important for secondary school staffs, where state testing data is typically more limited, and data must be examined at the department, as well as the school and grade levels" (p. 216).

Integrate

Previous discussion of differentiation included diagnosing needs, deploying internal expertise, differentiating formats and venues for professional learning, and providing for unique school and individual teacher needs. Implied in that discussion—but stated more explicitly here—is that collective professional learning and collaborative practice and feedback should be integrated into the cycles of school improvement and professional learning communities at all levels and as "the way we do things here."

Discontinue

In order to provide the space and time for true professional learning, it must also be stated explicitly that already-full plates must be cleared. Authentic listening to teacher voices will help identify those well-intended supports that are no longer needed or are missing the mark. Wise district leaders know that when the horse is dead, dying, or just bucking and twisting, it may be time to dismount and look for a different way to reach the destination.

MODEL USE OF DATA FOR CONTINUOUS IMPROVEMENT

This chapter has introduced the concept of reciprocal accountability in quotes from experts. It might be paraphrased as "don't ask someone to do something without giving them the tools they need." To take even more liberty, reciprocal accountability may include "hold yourselves accountable in the same way you expect us to be accountable." Part of that exercise would be to model use of data and planning for continuous improvement in every department of the district (central office). How often do your district leaders gather data about the impact of their work on the schools? How do they diagnose whether their services are truly supportive—in actuality and/or perception? When do central office leaders talk about the improvement goals they have set and strategies they will use to become more effective in their use of resources so that a higher proportion of budgets can possibly be directed to the core mission of teaching and learning? In short, the cycles of work shared in Chapters 4 and 7 related to Shared Leadership Teams and Teaching Teams have corollaries at the district level. One way to provide appropriate support is to demonstrate the same commitment to continuous improvement.

REVISIT CURRICULUM ROLES

Chapter 7 described how Teaching Teams work with their curriculum standards: analyzing them for leverage, endurance and readiness, rigor and vocabulary; checking their specific responsibility in the vertical scope and sequence; and chunking the content into units and a time sequence (Figure 7.6 [p. 125]). For each unit, their work included reviewing data, designing performance tasks or assessments, planning instruction, analyzing common assessments, and providing interventions and enrichment. All of this work was grounded in and performed with specific grade-level or content-alike colleagues—at the school level.

Figure 12.2 provides a look at the relationship between district and school-level work, with data on student performance as the driving force. Ovals at the beginning and end highlight the focus on student data. Diamonds represent questions that must be explored at the system level. Shaded boxes represent activities at the district level, in support of and alignment with the white rectangles that represent aspects of school focus. For example, budget considerations often guide a rotating cycle of program review and textbook and materials adoption. But the first diamond raises a question of "what is needed most for student learning" versus "whose turn is it next"? If the answer to the question is no, then the cycle may need to be revised in order to prioritize based on student learning needs. Using math problem-solving as an example, based on a pattern of student struggles, that first question relates to having processes in place to address the need. At the district level, there must be a process or forum in which to address needs as they arise. At the school level, data suggesting a student achievement need should be reflected in the school's improvement goals and plans.

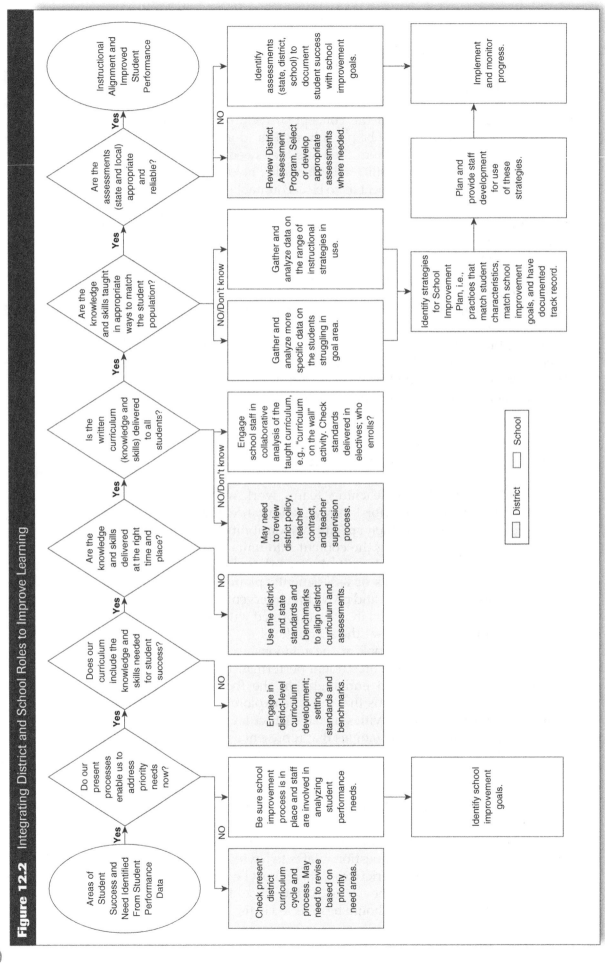

Figure 12.2 Integrating District and School Roles to Improve Learning

When Teaching Teams analyze student results, they may discover that the curriculum they are following does not include problem-solving as early or with as much emphasis as newer standards and assessments may require. Or the real problem may be that the written curriculum is not actually being delivered. Most math programs include problem-solving as a thread through all units and all grade levels. But it may be given short shrift due to time constraints or teacher preferences for one-right-answer computation. A "curriculum on the wall" activity would start with teachers working by grade level to identify the main topics, units, or skills they teach along with time allocations, then cluster them in an affinity process. This may provide a more useful picture than starting with the written curriculum guides. If math problem-solving *is* adequate in the curriculum and the curriculum *is* being taught, the next consideration may be the methods that are used and the characteristics of the student population. Further study at the school level would include gathering information on how problem-solving is taught. Student performance data would be analyzed further to identify the students who are having difficulty and see if they have common characteristics that might provide clues about prior knowledge, learning style, or other barriers to learning that may be present.

School-level attention would be directed toward strategies that match their students' needs and have been proven to increase achievement of these skills. Once these strategies are selected, the Shared Leadership Team would develop plans that include professional learning so teachers can utilize the strategies effectively. Meanwhile, the district curriculum process would also include scrutinizing the assessments that were the source of the student performance data. The district purpose is to analyze the degree to which existing assessments accurately ensure the learning expectations and determine whether other types of assessment will be needed to measure all of the expected learning, provide ongoing information about student progress, and make decisions to strengthen the instructional program.

DEDICATE TIME

Chapters 4 and 7 described the structure and work of the Shared Leadership Team, Data Team, and Teaching Teams at the school level. Chapter 10 described time requirements for these ongoing groups and their tasks, as well as periodic whole-system looks at the results of their overall collective efforts. In particular, Figure 10.2 (p. 179) provided thirty-three suggestions for ways to find the necessary time. The first role of the district is to support and coordinate the designation of appropriate times for these activities. The second is to *dedicate* the time—which means allowing nothing short of a true emergency crisis to take away that time. One district assured its schools that professional development days would be held harmless from district mandates so that they could utilize the time to implement the steps articulated in their school improvement plan. School X had recently made a major investment in classroom technology, but students were not benefiting because every time the technology training had been scheduled, the district hijacked the professional development day for some other purpose. So School X postponed implementation and rescheduled the training coordinator. Shortly thereafter, they received notification that the curriculum department had written a literacy grant and been awarded funds for training in writing strategies. Without apology, they were informed that the district professional development days would now be focused on writing. Such experiences not only inhibit the implementation of change, they destroy trust and system coherence. In this case, support in writing was not the appropriate support for School X.

TAILOR TECH SUPPORT

The needs of schools for access to data and the time and technical assistance to use it are clear. Data Teams at individual schools need the help of a District Data Team. This group would include district staff with responsibility for curriculum, assessment, professional development, and technology as well as representation of principals and teachers to connect district and school efforts. Responsibilities of the District Data Team include identifying common sources of data for use by the district and by all schools, making it usable, and developing the capacity of principals and teachers to make use of it.

In *The Art of Coaching Teams*, Elena Aguilar (2016) described the overload that can occur when teachers are asked to learn new attitudes, new content, and new structures all at the same time. Our minds have a limited amount of cognitive energy at any given moment and must sort out which stimuli will get a response. A common example of this overload is when teachers are asked to embrace greater use of data, learn the functions of a data system, and interpret data all in the same setting. These sessions are often led by facilitators who know more about (and are more enthused about) the capacities of the technological tool than the readiness level of their participants and the actual and most immediate uses of the tool they will employ. Technical support should employ the concept of "just-in-time-training," scaffolding learning through a sequence of shorter introductions with opportunities to practice, not just observe.

Hord (2009) affirmed that "reviewing, studying, and interpreting data is the foundation of professional learning communities. Someone must be responsible for organizing the various sources of data in formats that are user-friendly. This can be a formidable job for smaller districts and schools with limited personnel. Eventually, all teachers should learn how to do this task so that they have ready access to current data" (pp. 42–43). The time frame of "eventually" is pertinent. In the meantime, the District Data Team will help to scaffold learning at the school and classroom level. For example, the Data Team in one district began by surveying principals and gathering the "what I wish I could do with data" list to inform selection of an electronic data warehousing system. As the system was being implemented to make student data available at the teachers' desktops, their role included planning and delivering professional development tailored for various groups of users. While that individual capacity was being developed, the data warehousing system enabled them to create user-friendly reports that they placed in the hands of principals and teachers so they could see what they would be able to produce for themselves and learn how to use them. This group also developed a Data Handbook for schools that included a timeline of the district-based and school-based assessments and data-related activities for each month of the year. This referenced specific score reports that would come from state and district tests and other sources, and explained the purpose and audience for each type of report.

Reporting specifically on patterns in high-data use schools, Louis et al. (2010) noted that "data use was often the focus of professional learning community initiatives. Districts contributed by offering training in the use of curriculum-linked classroom assessments, school-wide data analysis events, coaching of teacher teams (grade or subject teams, professional learning community groups), and the purchase and training in the use of data software" (pp. 192–193). Identifying challenges faced when increasing data use, the authors further "observed tensions in some schools between traditional norms of decision-making (reliance on established expertise) and the recent move toward decisions informed by evidence. The tension was especially notable in settings where districts mandated the use of computer-based data management systems to record (and potentially retrieve and use) many forms of assessment information, student characteristics, and program placement data (e.g., by grade, classroom, sub-group population) over time. Teachers talked about data overload, emphasizing the time required to enter information into these systems as well as the time and expertise required to retrieve and interpret it. It often remained unclear what purposes these systems were to serve" (pp. 193–194).

This book has addressed twenty ways that teams in schools should be *using* data—employing verbs like reviewing, analyzing, making decisions, and planning. Training and technical support should focus first on these *uses* of the data, rather than on the data entry itself—especially when switching to a new system.

TEST DATA WAREHOUSES

The recent proliferation of electronic data systems has provided school districts with a range of choices, not limited to Skyword, Canvas, Learning Management Systems, Infinite Campus, eduCLIMBER, and many others. Purchasing decisions are made at the district level and must be guided by the needs of potential users.

Shop

The earlier section described how a District Data Team started by gathering a "wish list" from users. Others would contribute technical requirements. Following are some of the attributes that should be investigated:

- Usability or user-friendliness—Who are the users? What do they know how to do with it? What do users want or need to do? What is the general background of the users? Can users easily accomplish their intended tasks at acceptable speed?
- Documentation and supporting materials available—Are they clear and easily understood in plain language?

- Recoverability—What errors do users most frequently make? How can they recover their work?
- Compatibility with existing systems
- Flexibility of training and support options—Adequate support for skillful, confident use; ability to access training in increments over time
- Capacity for multiple simultaneous users
- Accessibility—Is the system available to all users, including those with special needs, at home, or work via web-based interface?
- Scalability—Can the system continue to respond quickly with an increasing number of users?
- Ability to customize—How much can the vendor conform to district specifications?
- Rollover of existing data—How will student's academic history remain intact and archived year after year?
- Report creation—Ability to aggregate and report data on demand by student group, content standards, school, grade, etc.
- Real-time, dynamic data transfer—Interactive system with continuous change and updates as data are entered
- Access portal for parents and students to view real-time performance data
- Language translation
- Costs for standard system, customization, and service

In addition to whether the system will create the kinds of reports requested, Rankin (2015) pointed out that the design of the reports can make or break its users' ability to understand the data, draw accurate conclusions, and respond appropriately. Design elements should include summaries or averages to allow comparisons, a way to track gaps and whether they are narrowing or widening, clear labels in the visual versus set-out legends and keys, and use of color to distinguish sections and levels of performance.

Verify

Questions about features and capacity of electronic systems will almost always be met with affirmative, assuring responses by the seller. Insist on talking with people who are already using the product. Ask them the same set of questions and verify that the product is operating "as advertised."

It's also important to verify that the functions of the system will match the philosophy of the district. For example, an electronic grading system that automatically calculates an average of all entries is not compatible with a standards-based grading philosophy that weighs most recent scores as more accurate representations of the student's learning. With more than forty programs currently available (Guskey & Jung, 2016), careful research should yield a result that will match—or customize to match—the uses of data and grading policies adopted by the district. Technology should be a tool to accomplish essential tasks—not a tyrant that dictates practice.

Compare

Comparing available systems with each other and the above criteria are aspects of the selection process. Districts should also compare their desires for use with available state data dashboards. Rothman (2015) reported that forty-three of fifty states received waivers under NCLB, through which many developed or refined their data tools at the state-wide level. Their intent is to provide "an array of indicators in a transparent way so school staffs, parents, and public officials know each year how schools are performing . . . They [dashboards] can include measures of school operations and practices so schools know what to address . . . they also enable districts to add real-time measures, such as grades and attendance rates, to supplement the state data" (p. 30). If the state data system is well-developed and adaptable for district purposes, time and energy may be conserved.

Support

As noted earlier, appropriate tech support is provided in segments based on specific functions that users will implement in real time. And among the criteria for a data warehouse system are flexibility of training and support options. If vendors are only going to be available for consultation and support at initial installation, it should raise second thoughts about the purchase.

I recently overheard teams at tables discussing their electronic systems. They used the same system, but their comments were very different. One statement was "I just love I.C. Every time I use it to make a report, I say 'I SEE!'" because I can really get a visual of what's happening. At another table, the comment was "I just call I.C. IC-ky! We can't get anything out of it." Such different attitudes toward the same system raise questions about how training and support was provided. Whatever tool is chosen, the district needs to make its own decisions about the scope and sequence of capacity-building for each user group.

PROTECT DATA SECURITY AND PRIVACY

One of the ways school teams have begun to focus on data is creating "data walls" that provide posted information about student performance. They provide a focal point visually and are interactive — often using stick-on notes that can be moved around to form groups or relocated when students improve. This beneficial practice has come under fire in some settings because of privacy concerns. If the "data wall" is in a faraway, locked location, it loses its function as a constant focus of attention. If it's located in a setting accessed by parents or others, it becomes "insecure" as a holder of individual student information.

Educators must be sensitive to three categories of data (Slaven, 2015). *Personally identifiable information* includes an individual student's name, name(s) of parent(s) or guardian(s), home address, and personal identifiers like a social security number or student ID number. These are the same kinds of data that represent possible sources of identity theft in the public marketplace and require the most attention in terms of privacy and security. *De-identified data* reflect individual students but the personal details have been removed. De-identified data can be used for research and compiled into aggregate data about groups of students, but does not inform personalized instruction. *Aggregate data* is used to monitor progress of groups and compare performance based on group characteristics such as race and income. Aggregate data may seem very safe, but if any group does not contain a sufficient number of students, it does not adequately protect individual identities. Teachers, parents, and even students themselves need personally identifiable information. Researchers need complete data sets in order to conduct the kinds of studies that inform best practices and planning as described in earlier chapters. But marketers do not—and that has raised great concern in recent years. Large-scale data breaches like those at Sony, Target, and Home Depot have frightened consumers—especially parents who finally realize that when they use their iPhones to add money to their child's lunch account or check on homework, their own device makes a data system vulnerable. A few years ago, a multistate data collection project funded in part by the Bill and Melinda Gates Foundation created inBloom, a promising tool that enabled participating schools and districts to collect and aggregate a wide range of student data and store it on a cloud-based server (Michelman, 2015). Parents raised so many concerns about lack of controls on participating educational technology companies that the project was abandoned. As of June 2015, 182 pieces of legislation had been introduced in forty-six states. Only twenty-four of those were signed into law in twelve states. Legislative efforts have continued at the state and federal level. There *is* a federal law—the Family Educational Rights and Privacy Act of 1974 (FERPA). In one aspect, it requires that schools receive written permission from legal guardians before they release information from student records. However, regulations that have been updated by the Education Department allow schools to release records, without permission, to "school officials with legitimate educational interest; schools to which a student is transferring; appropriate officials for audit or evaluation purposes; appropriate parties in connection with financial aid to a student; organizations conducting certain studies for or on behalf of the school; accrediting organizations; to comply with a judicial order or lawfully issued subpoena; appropriate officials in cases of health and safety emergencies; and state and local authorities, within a juvenile justice system, pursuant to specific state law" (Michelman, 2015, p. 2). Of course, FERPA predated statewide longitudinal data systems that can collect everything from eligibility for free and reduced-price school meals to daily attendance and had no way to make clear whether individual information like academic work habits and attitudes count as part of a student's formal education record, which may follow him or her for a lifetime.

Real harm can occur (Barnes, 2015). In 2013, the Electronic Privacy Information Center filed a complaint with the Federal Trade Commission against a company that asked students for sensitive data including sexual orientation, religion, political affiliation, and medical information. The company claimed this would help provide students with scholarships and financial aid but did *not* communicate that it was disclosing this information to its business partner, which in turn, sold the student data. In a 2013 court case, Google admitted that it read e-mails it had accessed through Google Apps for Education and used the information to serve targeted ads to students.

Barnes provides two important cautions. First, local officials should be particularly careful of anything that seems too good to be true—like "freemium" ed tech services. A careful reading of "privacy" policies reveals that companies offering free on-line platforms often disclose student records they collect to nameless third-party affiliates and business parties. Second, educators should prioritize privacy-enhancing technology such as an online platform that permits students to access practice exercises without providing personally identifiable information or companies that permit students and educators to download student files and automatically removes the files from company records when the online course is completed.

Unfortunately, some of the proposed solutions seem just as scary. Biometric scanners such as fingerprint, iris scan, or voice recognition could certainly speed up the lunch line, but more immediate and familiar actions are probably in order (compiled from Johnson, 2013; Michelman, 2015; and Student Data Principles Coalition, 2015):

1. Work with your district's technology department to require the use of programs and products that take privacy and security seriously and facilitate security audits of networks by independent contractors.

2. Ensure that your district's Internet Acceptable Use policy lists current rules, such as requiring parental permission before posting student work on the website and keeping students' last names, e-mail addresses, or other identifying information off school web pages.

3. Ensure that district publications provide clear and concise information about collection and use of student data as required by FERPA.

4. Teach all staff and students about use of strong passwords—unique for each application, frequently changed, and never shared.

5. Use screensavers and device log-in screens that automatically kick in so screens of data are not left visible while unattended.

6. Assure that technology staff can remotely locate, control, and even erase contents of school-owned portable devices, especially those used off-campus.

7. Emphasize wariness—not responding to social engineering hacks that "phish" for personal information and never opening unexpected e-mails.

8. Create good backup provisions for district systems and insist that everyone who uses their own device backs up regularly onto the school server or purchases and uses large-capacity external hard drives.

9. Teach students how to protect their data—embedding clear, frequent lessons about protecting your online information and reputation in the curriculum.

10. Create a policy and protocol for overseeing the district's process of sharing data with legitimate entities and purposes.

11. Review policies for provisions related to collection, use, and safe-guards of data *as well as* removal of data and destruction of old devices.

12. Establish a system of governance that designates rules, procedures, and the individual or group responsible for decision-making regarding data collection, use, access, sharing, security, and the use of online educational programs.

13. Include a policy for notification of any misuse or breach of information and available remedies.

14. Provide and publicize a central point of contact where students and families can go to learn of their rights and have their questions answered.

SUPPORT PRINCIPALS

Principals are a key linkage between the district and the school and teachers, so all of the actions recommended so far that support teachers provide support to them as well. But their roles are unique, and they also should receive specific support. School leadership plans will include intentional change, and the supervisors of principals should talk them through challenges of initiation and be ready to support them when they encounter pushback.

Sometimes principals report to line supervisors who approve their school plans and write their formal evaluations but also receive directives from central office staff administrators regarding use of the curricula, instructional framework, assessments, and technology. The superintendent's cabinet should review expectations set for principals from all departments and clarify a big picture of their work that recognizes and supports their full range of responsibilities—and reduces them if necessary.

Principals also need opportunities to learn with colleagues. Such avenues may include classroom learning walks at each others' schools, role-playing challenging situations with staff or parents, and having school improvement leadership days where representatives from school teams present to each other and share ideas.

Rimmer (2016) emphasized "differentiated support to principals" as one of the avenues for developing principals into equity-centered instructional leaders and described three important structures for such support:

The whole group structure is quite conducive to presentation sharing and discussion of research and information. It is also during whole group sessions that leaders can focus on building knowledge and skills, group learning and dialogue. A second . . . is one-on-one coaching. Coaching facilitates differentiation by providing the opportunity for principals to take the knowledge and skills learned in the whole group sessions and focus collaboratively with a coach on their own strengths and areas of focus, and go deeper in their own learning as it applies to their specific needs and context. This coaching is strengthened by the use of qualitative and quantitative, disaggregated student and school performance data, as well as data from classroom observations and student work. Finally, grouping leaders in small groups by area of focus (i.e., creating a learning-focused culture, analyzing disaggregated data, looking at student work, etc.) can serve as another effective strategy for building leaders' capacity in very specific skill areas and differentiating support. (p. 14)

ONE DISTRICT'S INSIDE-OUT STORY

In Bigfork, Montana, they seem to have figured out the district–school relationship—not as top-down or bottom-up but as inside-out. Decision-making processes start where the students are—"inside" the classroom and move "out" via teachers to whole-school to district policy. The pattern of relationships in the district is not viewed as vertical or hierarchical but as horizontal or flat and collaborative regardless of position power. Principal Brenda Clarke shared this with me first, and then said, "But you might not believe me, so you should talk to our superintendent also." Turns out Matt Jensen was a student teacher, teacher, assistant principal, and principal in the district before moving up—oops, out—to superintendent. That may be why he sees himself on the same plane with all the other roles.

When I asked about use of data, the principal replied

I'll be blunt—we trust our teachers to do the responsible thing as far as data and intervening with kids. They know best, they're the ones in the classroom. It's organic. All students take the [diagnostic assessment] fall, winter, and spring on computers, and it gets harder the better they do. As an initial screener, it provides a benchmark of whether students are at, above, or below grade level. That information is taken back to the classroom teacher and intervention team—but it is not the sole basis for planning. The classroom teacher's feedback and any other classroom assessment that's available is used to determine whether the screening assessment is accurate. If lots of students in the same classroom have struggled, the help is moved "inside" the classroom. Students are not pulled out during core instruction but may be given a double dose if they are even farther behind.

A harder task was finding more frequent assessments to give every three weeks. The district didn't take that over—we looked for what we needed. An example from this year was that we looked at our data and found a large number of first graders needed to be served. It was hard to schedule, so the intervention team AND grade level team looked at it together. They found a phonics screener to use, and all the teachers in Grades 1–3 found the holes that were common to a lot of kids. We worked together to strengthen instruction around those gaps. We've been working with the district on what kind of system to hold the data in, but we're very cautious because of privacy/security issues around data-sharing. We have HPTs—high-performance teams—that are like professional learning communities. Every two weeks, we have early dismissal and work on things like the data warehouse system requirements. Each HPT has a representative to Forum, which meets once a month, after school for an hour, with all of the administrators. We tell the district what we need through the Forums.

We don't just look at test scores but other kinds of data—especially discipline data. We use the counselors a lot in classrooms and have a Student Assistance Program because we believe that social and mental well-being comes before academic success. Test scores won't happen if kids aren't taken care of.

The principal was right—it did sound a bit like the teachers bossing the administrators around, or maybe a little too good to be true, so I also interviewed the superintendent. He began with "She was accurate. That's exactly right" and continued:

We began with high performance teams before professional learning communities became popular. We stole the model from Toyota—their belief system that the people closest to the problem know best how to fix it. That's one of our pillars: we trust teachers—they are white collar professionals that deserve that type of trust. For everything about curriculum and instruction (C&I), we rely on classroom teachers. It's humbling for me to remember every day that the farther you get away from the kids, the less you know about specific solutions. We consider everything that's not C&I as just managerial detail and we handle it so they stay focused—things like bell schedule, etc. We put together the 180-day calendar the best we can and don't commit-tee it. The trade-off is that we trust YOU on the classroom level.

Some of the decisions we make administratively have included the staff in the past and taken time from their other C&I work (calendar, schedule, etc.). There are also administrative decisions made that impact their planning like how we triage our schools' students' needs. We have decided to serve youngest students first and reading before math. Ultimately, we try to make decisions that will define the boundaries and allow teachers to do what they do best, teach.

Every two weeks we have early release so there's two hours for the collaborative work. At one point in time, we used a form to fill out about use of the time, but we found people were just jumping through hoops and it was killing progress. So instead of forms, we [administrators] set aside our time during those meetings and just float in and out. At first it was awkward, but it does change the energy. They get used to it and if it's the alternative to filling out forms, they said ok. Now they don't skip a beat. One day the high school principal had a question for a team and he came in and sat for

15 minutes and then left because they never asked him anything. The Instructional Forum meets for an hour at a time and there's no compensation—it's come through some rough times but now teachers are happy to give of their time for the greater good of the district.

Another belief pillar is that everything happens from a relationship with somebody. The teacher has to establish relationships before laying academic expectations on students. Stand in the hall and greet kids by name when they approach the classroom. High school teachers are visible every passing period, talking to kids. So as administrators, we try to do the same with staff. It's a challenge at some times of the year, but all administrators are present to greet teachers, talk to them and stop by classrooms to be with them, not observe them.

An example of data and relationships working together is recess supervision. Half the data on office referrals was directly from recess or hang over from recess. Aides were there but didn't know the identities and who shouldn't be playing together today, etc. When teachers took over, the referral rate went down and we gained more learning time. The administrator proposed it but invited teachers to propose a different solution if they wished. After a month, they came back and said it was working for students and they could rotate two of three teachers per grade, cover for each other and also maintain teacher presence with the students. So that's what we do now.

In the past when we discussed data with the staff, it was more centered at the administrator to teacher level. These were good conversations, but limited. Since our students rely on a team for support, many people on that team were missing out on important information. Now we have more teacher to teacher conversations, and the results are way better. However, because these conversations are deeper, they are tougher. Recommending changes in practices, reviewing data, and evaluating programs can feel personal at times and that is something we are learning to work through. Some of this is challenging to work through without being offended or taking things too personally. The main message the administration wants to share is an encouragement for growth. We know we are doing things now that will end up changing later, and we know that is part of the process. Our staff should look forward to opportunities to make adjustments, not feel bad for doing something 'wrong.' Mrs. Clarke says it best "when we know better, we do better."

Another pillar of practice with data is that these are OUR kids and we are together responsible for their progress. We are resources for each other. So we are very careful never to break out the data in a way that isolates any individual teacher. We break it down by grade level, share at grade level, intervene at grade level. We say "Our third grade kids are missing . . ." but we don't say which classroom is better than another. As a result of working together, we now have clear processes in place to provide both academic and behavioral interventions. [See Figures 12.3 and 12.4.] The bottom line is that teachers from other districts want to come to Bigfork because we are respected as the professionals and our district thinks its job is to help teachers help kids.

Both the principal and superintendent commented that their story would not be complete without the voices of teachers. Jensen described Amy Bessen as the person responsible for either creating or assisting in the creation of several middle school math assessments that help place students. In addition to teaching middle school math, she also provides intervention time, and she has had a lot to do with an incredible year of growth in middle school math achievement. As part of the intervention and the Forum, she has used her energy and knowledge to push the groups to define goals and a clear path to get there:

> One of the key things is knowing that we all have the same goal and agenda in our school district. Everyone (teachers, admin, aides, etc.) has the students and what is best for the students as the top priority and number one goal. I think this makes the hard and tough conversations a bit easier. At no point during data conversations does it feel focused on the teacher. It is always focused on the students and how we can better serve and meet their needs. What I'm doing is probably still a good teaching technique; however, it may not be working for these students. When that conversation is about meeting students' needs and not what teachers are doing right or wrong, then it shows our priorities are aligned for kids. It has helped me feel comfortable to try different techniques and strategies.

> I also think the way our district uses multiple tools to get student data and find how to better serve needs has been great. The [benchmark] assessment can show a student is struggling, but it isn't going to show what that foundational gap or hole is. Once [the assessment] identifies a student, he or she is given additional assessments and conversations with teachers occur. Often when a student demonstrates a lack of understanding in a standard, there is something foundational missing that can be addressed and retaught that will help everything fall into place . . . we look for the deeper root. We can give formative assessments and find and meet the root issue. This can occur in whole class teaching and intervention instruction as well.

> Looking at data can be hard, but being in a school where administrators demonstrate their trust in their staff through making all data conversations focused on students makes it easier. We all have the same goal and are always trying our best to support students to be and feel successful.

Bridget Martel provides another teacher voice and in-depth description of teacher reactions to increased use of data. Her superintendent

Figure 12.3 Response to Intervention Process—Academic

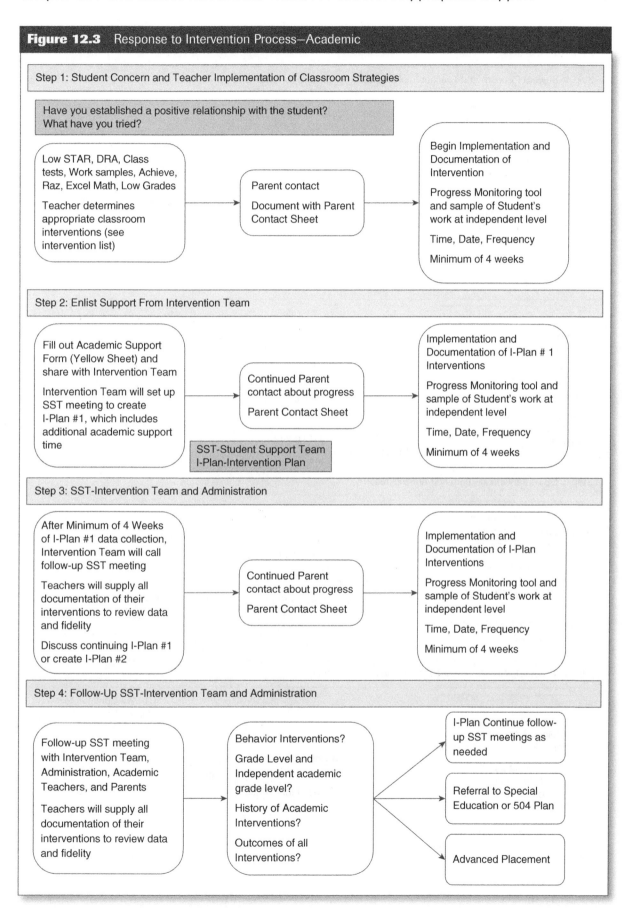

Step 1: Student Concern and Teacher Implementation of Classroom Strategies

Have you established a positive relationship with the student?
What have you tried?

Low STAR, DRA, Class tests, Work samples, Achieve, Raz, Excel Math, Low Grades

Teacher determines appropriate classroom interventions (see intervention list)

Parent contact

Document with Parent Contact Sheet

Begin Implementation and Documentation of Intervention

Progress Monitoring tool and sample of Student's work at independent level

Time, Date, Frequency

Minimum of 4 weeks

Step 2: Enlist Support From Intervention Team

Fill out Academic Support Form (Yellow Sheet) and share with Intervention Team

Intervention Team will set up SST meeting to create I-Plan #1, which includes additional academic support time

Continued Parent contact about progress

Parent Contact Sheet

SST-Student Support Team
I-Plan-Intervention Plan

Implementation and Documentation of I-Plan # 1 Interventions

Progress Monitoring tool and sample of Student's work at independent level

Time, Date, Frequency

Minimum of 4 weeks

Step 3: SST-Intervention Team and Administration

After Minimum of 4 Weeks of I-Plan #1 data collection, Intervention Team will call follow-up SST meeting

Teachers will supply all documentation of their interventions to review data and fidelity

Discuss continuing I-Plan #1 or create I-Plan #2

Continued Parent contact about progress

Parent Contact Sheet

Implementation and Documentation of I-Plan Interventions

Progress Monitoring tool and sample of Student's work at independent level

Time, Date, Frequency

Minimum of 4 weeks

Step 4: Follow-Up SST-Intervention Team and Administration

Follow-up SST meeting with Intervention Team, Administration, Academic Teachers, and Parents

Teachers will supply all documentation of their interventions to review data and fidelity

Behavior Interventions?

Grade Level and Independent academic grade level?

History of Academic Interventions?

Outcomes of all Interventions?

I-Plan Continue follow-up SST meetings as needed

Referral to Special Education or 504 Plan

Advanced Placement

Figure 12.4   Response to Intervention Process—Behavior

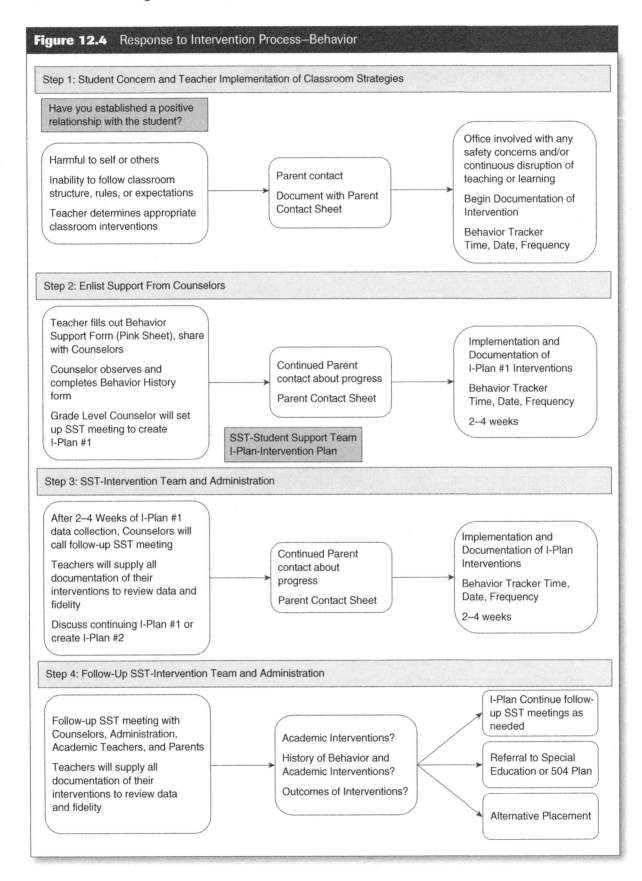

Step 1: Student Concern and Teacher Implementation of Classroom Strategies

Have you established a positive relationship with the student?

Harmful to self or others

Inability to follow classroom structure, rules, or expectations

Teacher determines appropriate classroom interventions

Parent contact

Document with Parent Contact Sheet

Office involved with any safety concerns and/or continuous disruption of teaching or learning

Begin Documentation of Intervention

Behavior Tracker Time, Date, Frequency

Step 2: Enlist Support From Counselors

Teacher fills out Behavior Support Form (Pink Sheet), share with Counselors

Counselor observes and completes Behavior History form

Grade Level Counselor will set up SST meeting to create I-Plan #1

Continued Parent contact about progress

Parent Contact Sheet

Implementation and Documentation of I-Plan #1 Interventions

Behavior Tracker Time, Date, Frequency

2–4 weeks

SST-Student Support Team I-Plan-Intervention Plan

Step 3: SST-Intervention Team and Administration

After 2–4 Weeks of I-Plan #1 data collection, Counselors will call follow-up SST meeting

Teachers will supply all documentation of their interventions to review data and fidelity

Discuss continuing I-Plan #1 or create I-Plan #2

Continued Parent contact about progress

Parent Contact Sheet

Implementation and Documentation of I-Plan Interventions

Behavior Tracker Time, Date, Frequency

2–4 weeks

Step 4: Follow-Up SST-Intervention Team and Administration

Follow-up SST meeting with Counselors, Administration, Academic Teachers, and Parents

Teachers will supply all documentation of their interventions to review data and fidelity

Academic Interventions?

History of Behavior and Academic Interventions?

Outcomes of Interventions?

I-Plan Continue follow-up SST meetings as needed

Referral to Special Education or 504 Plan

Alternative Placement

described her as "an incredible asset to our school and very knowledge-able about current intervention practices and the story of our journey to this point. There is not another opinion I would trust more than hers." So this is her perspective on the journey and a tipping point that changed the mood into motion:

Everything that both Matt [superintendent] and Brenda [principal] shared is absolutely true. However, it didn't happen as easily as it reads. It was a journey, that's for sure. Teachers are a unique group of people. We put our "all" into our students—and part of that "all" includes our hearts. Hearts and data often don't mix too well! So, when this idea of using data to drive instruction was intro-duced, we were all on board. Especially me—when I was first hired by this district, I was hired to be on the intervention team. It was all about the data! We loved it! It made sense—in the logical parts of our brains. Then, when we actually saw the data on the screen, our emotional brains kicked in. When we saw the gaps that data was reporting, we did what every single teacher would—and will continue to do—we got emotional, we got offended, we got defen-sive. We wanted students to be retested, we wanted to dig up daily work, we wanted the district to find a different assessment—a BETTER assessment because the data we were reading was TOTALLY wrong. We questioned norms, we questioned how the questions were stated in the test, we questioned the environment the students were tested in, we questioned absolutely everything. Then we got kind of angry. BUT . . . never, EVER did the Administration foster those emotions in us. Never, EVER did our Administration associate OUR performance with the students' per-formance on the screeners. This data never, EVER came up in performance reviews. Never, EVER did the Administration imply that we (the teachers) were responsible, liable, or "in trouble." It was quite the opposite. When we had discussions about the data, they always started the conversations with "This is not about your teaching . . ." or "This is not about a teacher . . ." Our Administration allowed us to be emotional about this process. They allowed us to vent freely, to speak openly both in a group session and in private. They didn't do the talking, they listened.

While we were emotional through this process, we are also a healthy group of teachers. We were bound and determined to fix this—even if we put it as "we're going to prove those tests wrong". . . The "young" teachers went to their college portfolios; us "old" teachers went digging into the archives, and we all were on our computers researching. Brenda approached us when she learned of a Reading Specialist who was doing some training in our area. This specialist was booked but agreed to meet us, in a private setting, on a Sunday. We had a teacher from each grade level ready and willing to go—with notebooks in hand full of notes taken at our grade-level "venting session" ready to ask questions—maybe about the inaccurate screener or if this "data driven instruction" was really just another fad.

A crazy thing happened on that Sunday! We were collectively inspired! We listened to some pretty compelling information—not just about the students in our classrooms but rather the students in our state. Then—students in our nation. Same gaps, different teachers. It WASN'T just us!! Next, she showed us some tools. And the crazy thing is we already HAVE the tools in our school!! We have a teacher on our team who used to be the special education director. As tools were presented, she'd say, "We have that!" It's just that with the staff changes, not all of us knew about them. We couldn't flip past the "venting notes" fast enough! We started making notes of who was going to get what and when. We determined the best time that we could all meet, the next DAY, and develop a unified process to move forward. We determined which tool we would use and when/how we would administer it. We created a deadline and then scheduled a meeting to review what we learned about our students. Once we got our information, we began to design our instruction to meet those gaps. Now the tools that we chose to use within our grade level will be used on a regular basis to measure progress as well as drive instruction.

There are a few keys in this process, I believe: the trust the administration has in the teachers, the communication that occurs in the structure of the way our school operates with HPTs and Forum, the safety within our school culture to be heard, and the belief that EVERY student that walks our hallways is taken care of academically and emotionally. Looking back, I can actually sum it up to one "key"—relationships!

Roland Barth (1990) described these relationships as service and support. "When the central office runs a service agency for principals, then principals are able to set up service agencies for teachers, and teachers for children. The chain of command can then become a chain of support."

Chapter 13

Get More Excited

The two prior editions of this book were titled *Getting Excited About Data*. Lots of data-related activity has occurred in the meantime, as summarized in Chapter 1. This new edition is *Getting **More** Excited About **Using** Data*—not merely more data, definitely not more tests, by all means not more mandates but more authentic and meaningful ways to use data for purposes that matter to us in our own settings. I truly believe that skillful use of data has the power and potential to move us toward this result: Students achieve more, *and* educators feel more comfortable, competent, and confident. The important questions now are these:

What do *you* believe at this point?

What have *you* learned?

What next steps are *you* ready to take?

REVIEW AND REFLECT

In Chapter 1, you learned how high-performing schools use data and how it connects to student achievement. You may have marked the text or margins with your own analysis of which data practices are strongly in place in your setting and which need attention. Go back and review those notes as we get ready to celebrate successes and entertain some specific next steps. You may want to create two columns for your examples of "YES!!!" and "OOPS" reflections.

In Chapters 2 and 3, we took a deeper look at how No Child Left Behind (NCLB) affected trust and morale and how important it is to rebuild teachers' sense of efficacy and feelings of safety. You may have learned more about how underlying beliefs about assessment, student capabilities, and school potential determine how willing educators are to learn new practices and how much they will invest in change. Those chapters focused on cultural conditions surrounding use of data. You now have strategies at your disposal to confront and overcome fears about using data. Flip back through those pages, and consider the culture of your school or district. What's positive? What needs to be addressed? Add those thoughts to your notes from Chapter 1.

You learned about structures for collaboration in Chapter 4 and the processes they use in Chapter 7. How representative and functional are the Shared Leadership Team(s) and Data Team(s) in your school and district? Have Teaching Teams been intentionally formed and focused on analysis of standards, development of common assessments, and collaborative planning for instruction and interventions? Jot down a few of your observations.

Chapter 5 focused on the faces of our students and the whole child realities of their school experience above and beyond test scores. You are now more aware than ever of how much we need to connect numbers to knowledge of our students so we can promote achievement for all. Equity issues affect attendance and discipline and academic opportunities. Perceptual data can bring diverse voices into the conversation. Using your learning from Chapter 5 and Johnson's tool in Figure 9.2, are there issues related to culture and equity that need to surface in your school and district?

Technical considerations were explored in Chapter 6 about accessing data and in Chapter 12 about electronic capacity. What did you learn that identifies the kinds of support you need to pursue for yourself, your school, your district? Add those notes to your reflection list.

In Chapters 8 through 11, you learned about the importance of using data to develop plans that conserve resources and how to gather data about your own programs and practices before developing Action Plans. Many ideas were presented about creating time to consider data and act on it productively through effective and efficient meetings. Chapter 11 provided a range of strong examples of evidence-gathering to check whether those plans are being implemented, and whether they are making a difference for students. What did you note to reaffirm? And to tackle?

CHOOSE YOUR NEXT STEPS

Keep those reflections on your learning in mind as you consider the possible next steps suggested here. But first take one more look at your notes. If you're like most of us, your list of the positives needs to be amplified because we tend to forget the things that went well and focus on those that frustrated us. Bulk up that "YES!!!" column. Now consider the list of things you've noted that may need attention. It's probably longer and may seem impossible. Tackling all of it probably is. That's why all those items are just possibilities right now. Some of the steps below will help you narrow your focus and establish your starting point.

1. <u>Define your sphere of influence and leverage points.</u> The most powerful professional learning " . . . occurs in real time around real problems in real schools involving real people who actually have to make decisions about what to do on a day-to-day basis" (Elmore, 2005, p. 25). Those "real people" are you. You may be the district administrator, the principal, a team leader, or an individual classroom teacher. You control your own attitudes and practices, and you touch the people around you. Your sphere of influence begins "next door"—whether it is your fellow teacher or the next department down the hall at the central office. Your sphere of influence is both horizontal and vertical. If you're a teacher, your sphere of influence touches the principal. If you're the principal, your sphere of influence includes every department at the district level that affects your school. Review the lists you made and consider which of those will resonate with the "next door" and the "one up" edges of your sphere. Mark them as possible leverage points for pursuing use of any of the remaining suggestions.

2. <u>Identify and celebrate strengths.</u> Chapter 1 outlined twenty uses of data, and you have just reflected on their status in your setting. Make an explicit note about when and how you will celebrate things that are going well and progress that you are making. If you are a principal, you have a unique platform so you can make a concrete plan and proceed to publicly celebrate with staff. In any role, you have power in conversation and interaction. Practice starting your advocacy for the new with affirmation of the present using starters like "I was thinking back and realized that we've . . . " or "When I think about how well we're doing ___, I wonder if we're ready to . . . " In addition to public collective celebration, privately celebrate your role in the successes. You were either a leader or a supportive team member and follower and helped move those things forward. Take personal pride in your contribution and renew your hope, energy, and determination.

3. <u>Give a quiz to check shared understanding of your school's reality.</u> This activity could be introduced with this question: What if we did just a little quiz to see how much shared knowledge we have about our school—and maybe see how much is accurate and what might be assumptions? Figure 13.1 could be used in a group setting.

Figure 13.1 Data Awareness Questionnaire

1. _____ % of the students in our school were successful meeting standard on their most recent assessment of reading skill.
2. The aspect of reading that was problematic for the most students was _____.
3. _____ % of students in our school successfully met standard on their most recent writing assessment.
4. The most common area(s) of difficulty in writing tasks is/are _____.
5. _____ % of students in our school are taking and succeeding with the level of mathematics needed for the next stage in their future.
6. The area of most critical needs for increased achievement in mathematics is _____.
7. _____ % of students in our school enjoy being at school and feel their work is interesting and important.
8. The main subgroups in our student population are _____ and a comparison of their performance would show that _____.
9. To get the answers to these questions, I would _____.
10. I have discussions about questions like this with _____ (whom) at _____ (when, where).

Provide each person with their own copy and give them quiet time to think about and jot down their *predictions*—predicting is safe because it doesn't imply that this is a right-or-wrong test of something they should already know (even if we think they should). Assure them that their sheets will not be collected. Then facilitate sharing and comparing of answers. Have a designated facilitator in each group capture the range of responses and comments to be compiled with all the other groups so they are really anonymous. The facilitator may have the "answer key"—a summary of data available to then compare and note where there were gaps in knowledge and understanding.

4. Create a data summary to build shared knowledge. Figure 13.2 could be provided for a follow-up discussion after the quiz above. It provides a template to summarize the last year's or the past three years' data in simple sentences. Reading, Writing, Math, and Science are mentioned specifically because they are now tested in most states. Any of the headings can be modified to fit your context. If you don't have access to all of the data, fill in what you can and begin asking school or district leaders about where other data is available. Keep this data summary somewhere handy—hard copy or electronic—so you can model referring to it in other settings.

Figure 13.2 Summary of School Data

Summary of Data for _____ School _____ Date _____

Student Learning Data – write separate sentences for each demographic group in each area

Reading

Writing

Math

Science

(Other areas as data available)

Non-Academic Student Data – write sentences for each demographic group in each area

Discipline

Attendance

Graduation

Survey Results

Staff Data

Experience

Certification & Degree Majors

Professional Development Participation

Survey Results

Parent/Community Data

Demographics

Communication

Participation

Survey Results

5. <u>Come bearing data.</u> The importance of norms and protocols was emphasized in Chapters 4 and 10. A well-known and widely used set of norms for collaboration was developed by Garmston and Wellman (2013, p. 31) and includes the following:

    -   Pausing
    -   Paraphrasing
    -   Posing questions
    -   Putting ideas on the table
    -   Providing data
    -   Paying attention to self and others
    -   Presuming positive intentions

    The authors emphasize how establishing the norm *that* we use data is essential as and before the skills of *how* to analyze and use the data can develop. Be the person who establishes the norm by bringing data—perhaps starting with a first draft of the summary you began with Figure 13.2. Garmston and Wellman also pointed out the importance of talking about data in a depersonalized way, saying *"the* data" and *"this* information" rather than appearing to point fingers with phrases like *"your* scores."

6. <u>Be ready with data questions.</u> Even if you don't have data to bring, come prepared with some of the question stems provided in this book or create your own good, open-ended questions as you would when coaching or stimulating substantive student discourse. Here are some additional examples:

    -   *So when we say we believe or will . . . , do we have evidence this is really happening?*
    -   *What's the baseline data for this so we can measure progress?* Many schools have things they are already working on that may have been determined at the local school level or may indeed have been driven by some other process such as a district strategic plan or state initiative. They may have been developed based on participants' perceptions, and this is an opportunity to backtrack and decide what evidence to monitor. This is not to discount the importance of perceptual data as discussed in Chapter 5 but to create a means for checking its validity and/or actually monitoring that those perceptions change over time.
    -   *When we say that, I wonder what's coming from our data and what might be coming from assumptions we've made in the past.* Note the respect and presumption of positive intent implied by "wondering" and "in the past."
    -   *Hmm . . . it seems like we keep coming back to this issue again and again. What data are we using—or could we use—to ground our next discussion?*

    Yes, become the pest that always brings up "the *D* word." When that shift becomes a predictable pattern, others will begin to anticipate it and start to think about data sooner *themselves.*

7. <u>Pick a protocol, and apply it in search of data.</u> Each chapter includes some formal protocols, question or sentence stems, or informal energizers to stimulate involvement. Pick any one or use those seeds to generate your own better creative idea. For example, the cause-and-effect diagram (Figure 9.1) can be used to unpack a whole range of issues. And it can be used for individual reflection as you analyze factors to find your own leverage point, or with two or three colleagues, as well as in a team or staff setting.

8. <u>Reinterpret past failure to build future success.</u> As you created your reflection notes on what you learned here, you may have experienced that pit-of-the-stomach clench, remembering "We tried so hard on that." Fullan (1993) and others have identified the implementation dip as a predictable phenomena of a change effort. Something new is initiated with enthusiasm and energy, and there is upward movement toward the goal. Then we become tired, realize it's going to be harder than we thought, and get distracted by yet more "new things" coming along, causing a dip in the trajectory. When the focus is maintained and support is continued, people can push through the implementation dip and advance well beyond that first plateau. The first strategy for coping with the implementation dip is to know about it and expect it and—when it hits—help people understand what's happening and that it's natural to get stuck. Figure 13.3 provides a tool for such analysis (based on Kegan & Lahey, 2001; Wood, 1989).

Part I helps participants clarify the characteristics of the change that was intended. Confirming the reasons for the change, its purpose, and intended outcomes reconnect the school to its mission and goals and concern for students as the impetus. Discussion of the impacts that were foreseen and who would be most affected reminds everyone that consideration was given to the realities of change. (In Chapter 7, the leadership of School B intentionally created opportunities for those who would be most affected by aspects of block scheduling to serve on the committees that would resolve these issues.) At the same time, this discussion begins to create awareness of "blind spots" that were overlooked. At this point it's important to restrain the group from leaping directly to the last step in Part III and making quick decisions about how to "fix" the first few things that are missing. It's essential to spend time on Part II and discuss success as well.

Part II helps tired, disillusioned people see that there are implementation successes. At least some things are going well for some people. These need to be publicly identified and honored. Evidence of success renews hope and energy and should be celebrated. Even more important, we must assure that any revisions we make do not *undo* the aspects that are working effectively.

Figure 13.3   Implementation Analysis

Part I: Initiation			
What was the change?	**What was its purpose, desired outcomes?**	**What were the expected/anticipated impacts?**	**On whom? (how many, specific)**

Part II: Implementation Successes			
What is going well? (being implemented, aligned with purpose)	**For whom? (how many, specific)**	**What is the evidence? (of implementation, alignment with purpose)**	**Which strategies that worked well should be maintained?**

Part III: Implementation Challenges				
What is problematic?	**For whom? (how many, specific)**	**What is the evidence?**	**What are the competing priorities or unmet needs? (specific, by name or group)**	**What strategies shall we revise or add?**

In Part III, the problems of implementation are identified and its sources are clarified. Specific, concrete data on who is adversely affected or is resisting implementation is critical. Sometimes the unrest of a very small group is being overgeneralized to "everyone thinks this was a terrible idea." Seek actual evidence of the problem. "Kids can't sign up for electives and they won't have enough credits to graduate" must be pursued in terms of which students, how many, what credits they may be lacking, and so forth.

Just as we want to keep the strategies that worked and generated success, we must identify the things we tried that weren't so useful. The fourth column is particularly important to avoid blaming and casting judgment. Most of us have wants and needs that compete with other wants and needs within ourselves or within the organization. What looks like resistance may be a legitimate struggle to balance this conflict. Understanding what is missing for some may result in small alterations or additional individual support, rather than premature abandonment of the entire effort. Unless all agree that it's **totally** broke, fix it and sustain the effort. Above all, don't do a knee jerk based on emotional stress and take a yes or no vote about whether to continue. First, focus on *why* and *how* the effort might be refined and rejuvenated. Albert Einstein is quoted as saying, "It's not that I'm so smart, I just stay with problems longer."

9. <u>Analyze your school's plans to make sure they can generate evidence.</u> As Sagor (2000) pointed out, "Many teachers now ask, 'Am I making any difference?' Regardless of all the negative pressures on teachers, the sheer nobility of the work keeps many dedicated educators on the job, but only so long as they can get credible answers to the 'efficacy' question . . . Fortunately, evidence has shown that teachers who elect to integrate the use of data into their work start exhibiting the compulsive behavior of fitness enthusiasts who regularly weigh themselves, check their heart rate, and graph data on their improving physical development. For both teachers and athletes, the continuous presence of compelling data that their hard work is paying off becomes, in itself, a vitally energizing force" (2000, p. 6). Figure 7.5 and multiple examples in Chapter 11 provide ideas for matching evidence to goals and assuring that implementation actually happens and students benefit.

10. <u>Push one promising practice and see what it will yield</u>. Perhaps your Teaching Team is stuck and "just doesn't know what else to try." Or perhaps your team has formed the bad habit of just brainstorming ideas without checking for evidence that those ideas really work. Consider the proven strategies in Figure 8.3, and select one that group members find interesting enough to learn and try. It may perk things up, increase student interest, and in turn show more positive results.

11. <u>Tap into a personal passion and pursue it with data.</u> Look back over your notes, and find a data use that needs a push *and* matches a passion of yours. It may be an equity issue arising from discipline data. It may be your passion for literacy in the content areas underlying concern about technical reading and writing. It may be your passion for your colleagues—seeing their discouragement and wanting to rekindle their excitement. If you are not an administrator, you may be thinking you don't have position power. Remember what we have learned about the downsides of pushing change through power and policy. The resulting culture of compliance is not what you want to develop anyway. Just engage your own best self because you have more potential to change things than you think. Let your passion empower you to fight for what's right—but pick your battles, gather your data, and strategize first with someone you trust. Don't run away from conversations that need to happen, even if you're not sure how to have them. Try this: "I'm not feeling quite comfortable with the direction this conversation is taking and it's so important—and you're so important—that I want to handle it carefully. Could we come back to it in a day or so?" Work on building a relationship with one of those people you've considered resisters. Everyone has a backstory. Respect that we all struggle and take hope.

12. <u>Pick a coach or colleague as traveling companion on your journey.</u> It can be scary to step out alone. Whether your organization provides you with an official, formal coach or not—cultivate a relationship with someone who is willing to help you clarify your thinking. A lifetime can be devoted to fine-tuning coaching skills and I do not diminish the repertoire of attributes and strategies acquired by someone like Judy Heinrich. I was about thirty years into my career when a grant from the Bill and Melinda Gates Foundation provided the opportunity to be coached for two hours a month for two years. Judy listened with patience as I described recent actions and upcoming challenges. She probed with precise questions that helped me stay in touch with my own personal core values, build my confidence, and clarify next steps I would take. If I pressed **really** *hard*, she would suggest a move I might consider but always insisted that I have the answers within myself. She employed a stubborn use of wait time to make me think through the skills I've learned, strategies that worked in the past, personal issues that might be driving my reactions, and synthesize a solution of my own.

If you don't have this wonderful benefit, find someone willing to learn along with you, someone who will accept this request: "I just want you to listen and ask me questions. Help me sort out what's facts and feelings and where my feelings might be coming from, so I can get back to the facts to choose next steps." It won't be ideal, might start out clunky, but both of you will grow and learn together. You can start by asking each other the simple questions:

- **What's working?** How do you know? To what do you attribute that success? How are you celebrating that? How will you keep that going?
- **What's stuck?** What's your evidence (the facts)? Why do you think that is happening? What might do you do next? What support do you need? How can I help?

13. <u>Take the next step.</u> You've reflected on new learning and on your own situation. You've identified your sphere of influence and considered some companions to support you. But none of it will happen if you don't take that first step. Be explicit. You may need to literally fill in these blanks: Tomorrow I will talk to ____ about ____. I will bring this data—or this question—or suggest this activity. And I will follow up again on ____ to keep the momentum going.

ROCK YOUR WORLD

This book described conditions that were cultural and technical and systemic related to use of data for student improvement. A shift in any of those conditions can have a ripple effect in the organization, and any individual can help to make shift happen. If several people make shifts, regardless of their role, the ripple effect can rock the boat. Archimedes' famous quote has been translated as "Give me a lever and a place to stand and I will move the world." You have a place to stand. It is in whatever place you find yourself—in the role where you contribute to the collective effort on behalf of boys and girls and young men and women. You have a lever. It is data, along with a whole tool kit full of ways to engage with it. So you can move your world. Push.

References and Suggested Readings

Aguilar, E. (2016). *The art of coaching teams: Building resilient communities that transform schools.* San Francisco, CA: Jossey-Bass.

Ainsworth, L. (2003). *Power standards.* Englewood, CO: Lead + Learn Press.

Ainsworth, L., & Viegut, D. (2006). *Common formative assessments: How to connect standards-based instruction and assessment.* Thousand Oaks, CA: Corwin.

Association for Supervision and Curriculum Development. (1995). Strengthening student engagement: ASCD's strategic plan. *Educational Leadership, 53*(1), 89–104.

Association for Supervision and Curriculum Development. (2015a). *Comparison of the No Child Left Behind Act to the Every Student Succeeds Act.* Retrieved April 13, 2016, from http://www.ascd.org/ASCD/pdf/siteASCD/policy/ESEA_NCLB_ComparisonChart_2015.pdf

Association for Supervision and Curriculum Development. (2015b). *United States whole child snapshot.* Retrieved April 13, 2016, from http://www.ascd.org/ASCD/pdf/siteASCD/wholechild/snapshot/2015/2015-us-ascd-whole-child-snapshot.pdf

Association for Supervision and Curriculum Development. (2015c). Research alert: What data tools do teachers really want? *Educational Leadership, 73*(3), 8.

Association for Supervision and Curriculum Development. (2015d). Tell me about . . . an obstacle you've encountered in using data. *Educational Leadership, 73*(3), 90–92.

Bailey, K., & Jakicic, C. (2012). *Common formative assessment: A toolkit for professional learning communities at work.* Bloomington, IN: Solution Tree Press.

Barnes, K. (2015). The challenges of data privacy. *Educational Leadership, 73*(3), 40–44.

Barth, R. (1990). *Improving schools from within: Teachers, parents and principals can make the difference.* San Francisco, CA: Jossey-Bass.

Bernhardt, V. L. (2015). Toward system-wide change. *Educational Leadership, 73*(3), 56–61.

Brennan, D. (2015). Creating a climate for achievement. *Educational Leadership, 72*(5), 56–59.

Bromberg, M. (2013, December 17). *Proficiency is a floor, not a finish line.* Retrieved May 9, 2016, from https://edtrust.org/the-equity-line/proficiency-is-a-floor-not-a-finish-line

Bryk, A. S., & Schneider, B. (2003). Trust in schools: A core resource for school reform. *Educational Leadership, 60*(6), 40–45.

Calvert, L. (2016). *Moving from compliance to agency: What teachers need to make professional learning work.* Oxford, OH: Learning Forward and NCTAF. Retrieved May 23, 2016, from http://nctaf.org/wp-content/uploads/2016/03/NCTAF-Learning-Forward_Moving-from-Compliance-to-Agency_What-Teachers-Need-to-Make-Professional-Learning-Work.pdf

Camera, L. (2016, January 13). Achievement gap between white and black students still gaping. *US News*. Retrieved May 9, 2016, from http://www.usnews.com/news/blogs/data-mine/2016/01/13/achievement-gap-between-white-and-black-students-still-gaping

Center for Educational Leadership. (2012). *5D+ Teacher Evaluation Rubric*. Retrieved May 19, 2016, from http://tpep-wa.org/wp-content/uploads/CEL-5D+-2.0-with-Observables.pdf

Center for Educational Leadership. (2016a). *5D+ Teacher Evaluation Rubric* (Version 3). Retrieved December 8, 2016, from http://info.k-12leadership.org/5d-teacher-evaluation-rubric?_ga=1.204336086.736822517.1463437450

Center for Educational Leadership. (2016b). *CEL's stance on the achievement gap.* Retrieved July 18, 2016, from https://www.k-12leadership.org/about-us

Danielson, C. (2011). *Framework for teaching evaluation instrument*. Retrieved May 19, 2016, from http://tpep-wa.org/wp-content/uploads/the-framework-for-teaching-evaluation-instrument-2011.pdf

Datnow, A., & Park, V. (2015). Five (good) ways to talk about data. *Educational Leadership, 73*(3), 10–15.

Dyer, K. (2016). Learning-focused feedback. *ASCD Express, 11*(16). Retrieved May 8, 2016, from http://www.ascd.org/ascd-express/vol11/1116-dyer.aspx?utm_source=ascdexpress&utm_medium=email&utm_campaign=Express-11-16

Elmore, R. F. (2002a, January/February). The limits of change. *Harvard Education Letter: Research Online*, p. 3.

Elmore, R. F. (2002b). *Bridging the gap between standards and achievement: The imperative for professional development in education.* Albert Shanker Institute. Retrieved August 27, 2016, from www.Bridging_Gap.pdf

Elmore, R. F. (2005). Building new knowledge: School improvement requires new knowledge, not just good will. *American Educator, 29*(1), 20–27.

Fullan, M. (2003, January). *Leading in a culture of change*. Handout. Keynote Presentation. Spokane, WA.

Fullan, M., & Hargreaves, A. (1991). *What's worth fighting for in your school.* Toronto, Ontario, Canada: Ontario Public School Teachers' Federation.

Fullan, M. (2004). *Leadership and sustainability.* Thousand Oaks, CA: Corwin.

Fullan, M. (2009). Have theory, will travel. A theory of action for system change. In A. Hargreaves & M. Fullan (Eds.), *Change wars* (pp. 275–293). Bloomington, IN: Solution Tree Press.

Fullan, M. G. (1993). *Change forces: Probing the depths of educational reform.* New York, NY: Falmer.

Fullan, M. G. (1999). *Change forces: The sequel.* Philadelphia, PA: Falmer.

Garfield, C. (1987). *Peak performers: The new heroes of American business.* New York, NY: Avon.

Garmston, R. J., & Wellman, B. M. (2013). *The adaptive school: A sourcebook for developing collaborative groups* (2nd ed.). Lanham, MD: Rowman & Littlefield.

Goodman, B., & Hein, H. (2016). Research says/looking at student work yields insights. *Educational Leadership, 73*(7), 79–80.

Goodwin, B. (2015). Mindsets are key to effective data use. *Educational Leadership, 73*(3), 78–79.

Guskey, T., & Jung, L. (2016). Grading: Why you should trust your judgment. *Educational Leadership, 73*(7), 50–54.

Hair, D. (2016). Advice from learning professionals. *JSD, 37*(3), 19.

Hattie, J. A. C. (2009). *Visible learning.* Thousand Oaks, CA: Corwin.

Hattie, J. A. C. (2012). *Visible learning for teachers: Maximizing impact on learning.* London, England: Routledge.

Haycock, K. (2016, February 23). *Prepared testimony: ESSA implementation in states and school districts: Perspective from education leaders.* United States Senate

Committee on Health, Education, Labor and Pensions. Retrieved May 9, 2016, from https://edtrust.org/press_release/prepared-testimony-of-kati-haycock-ceo-the-education-trust-for-the-senate-health-education-labor-and-pensions-committee

Hiebert, J., & Stigler, J. (2004, Fall). A world of difference: Classrooms abroad provide lessons in teaching math and science. *Journal of Staff Development*, p. 15.

Holcomb, E. L. (2001). *Asking the right questions: Techniques for collaboration and school change* (2nd ed.). Thousand Oaks, CA: Corwin.

Hord, S. M. (2009). *Professional learning communities: Educators work together toward a shared purpose—improved student learning.* Retrieved May 26, 2016, from http://www.plcelearning.com/DL/Hord.pdf

Hord, S. M., & Roussin, J. L. (2013). *Implementing change through learning: Concerns-based concepts, tools, and strategies for guiding change.* Thousand Oaks, CA: Corwin.

Hord, S. M., Roussin, J. L., & Sommers, W. A. (2010). *Guiding professional learning communities: Inspiration, challenge, surprise, and meaning.* Thousand Oaks, CA: Corwin.

Hord, S. M., Rutherford, W. L., Huling-Austin, L., & Hall, G. E. (1987). *Taking charge of change.* Alexandria, VA: Association for Supervision and Curriculum Development.

Hord, S. M., & Sommers, W. A. (2008). *Leading professional learning communities: Voices from research and practice.* Thousand Oaks, CA: Corwin.

Johnson, D. (2013). Power Up! Updated rules for securing data. *Educational Leadership*, 71(3), 82–84.

Johnson, R. S. (2002). *Using data to close the achievement gap: How to measure equity in our schools.* Thousand Oaks, CA: Corwin.

Joyce, B., & Calhoun, E. (2016). What are we learning about how we learn? *JSD*, 37(3), 42–44.

Kachur, D. S., Stout, J. A., & Edwards, C. L. (2013). *Engaging teachers in classroom walkthroughs.* Alexandria, VA: Association of Supervision and Curriculum Development.

Kamm, C. (2010). Accountability and the data teams process. In *Data Teams the Big Picture* (pp. 157–176). Englewood, CO: The Leadership and Learning Center.

Kegan, R., & Lahey, L. L. (2001). *How the way we talk can change the way we work: Seven languages for transformation.* San Francisco, CA: Jossey-Bass.

Killion, J. (2013). Establishing time for professional learning. *JSD*, 34(4), 22–28.

Killion, J. (2016). Establish time for learning: Finding time to collaborate takes creativity and commitment. *JSD*, 37(3), 26–31.

Kind, J. (2014). United we learn: Team effort builds a path to equity and alignment. *JSD*, 35(1), 46–50.

Learning Forward. (2011). *Standards for professional learning.* Retrieved May 28, 2016, from http://learningforward.org/standards/data#.V0nmU_krLIU

Leithwood, K., Harris, A., & Strauss, T. (2010). *Leading school turnaround: How successful leaders transform low-performing schools.* San Francisco, CA: Jossey-Bass.

Lezotte, L., & Jacoby, B. (1990). *A guide to the school improvement process based on effective schools research.* Okemos, MI: Effective Schools Products.

Louis, K. S., Leithwood, K., Wahlstrom, K. L., & Anderson, S. E. (2010). *Investigating the links to improved student learning final report of research findings.* Learning from Leadership. Wallace Foundation. Retrieved May 25, 2016, from http://www.wallacefoundation.org/knowledge-center/Documents/Investigating-the-Links-to-Improved-Student-Learning.pdf

Marzano, R. J. (2003). *What works in schools: Translating research into action.* Alexandria, VA: Association for Supervision and Curriculum Development.

Marzano, R. J. (2007). *The art and science of teaching: A comprehensive framework for effective instruction.* Alexandria, VA: Association for Supervision and Curriculum Development.

Marzano, R. J. (2015). *The Marzano compendium of instructional strategies*. Retrieved April 15, 2016, from http://www.marzanoresearch.com/online-compendium-product?utm_source=MR_2016_Compendium_April&utm_medium=Email&utm_campaign=64MEE

Marzano, R. J. (2016). High Reliability Schools webinar. Based on *A Handbook for High Reliability Schools*. Retrieved April 13, 2016, from File:///C:/Users/Owner/Desktop/HRS-Survey_Marzano.pdf

Marzano, R. J., Pickering, D. J., & Pollock, J. E. (2001). *Classroom instruction that works: Research-based strategies for increasing student achievement*. Alexandria, VA: Association for Supervision and Curriculum Development.

Marzano Research Laboratory. (2012). *The Marzano Teacher Evaluation Model*. Retrieved May 19, 2016, from http://tpep-wa.org/wp-content/uploads/Marzano_Teacher_Evaluation_Model.pdf

McLeod, S. (2011). *10 reasons your educators are resisting your change initiative*. Retrieved May 26, 2016, from http://blogs.edweek.org/edweek/LeaderTalk/2011/05/10_reasons_your_educators_are.html

McWilliams, L., & Patton, C. (2015). How to share data with families. *Educational Leadership, 73*(3), 46–49.

Michelman, B. (2015). Locking the cloud: Student data collection and privacy safeguards. *Educational Leadership, 21*(3), 1–7.

Moss, C., & Brookhart, S. (2012). *Learning targets: Helping students aim for understanding in today's lesson*. Alexandria, VA: Association for Supervision and Curriculum Development.

Nielsen, K., & Pitchford, B. (2010). Data teams as professional development. In *Data Teams The Big Picture* (pp. 179–190). Englewood, CO: The Leadership and Learning Center.

Noonan, J. (2014). In here, out there: Professional learning and the process of school improvement. *Harvard Educational Review, 84*(2), 145–161.

O'Neill, J., & Conzemius, A. (2005). *The power of SMART goals: Using goals to improve student learning*. Bloomington, IN: Solution Tree Press.

Owens, B., & Strahan, D. (2016). Expanding excellence: Teachers cross district lines to learn with peers. *JSD, 37*(3), 20–124.

Phi Delta Kappa. (2015). *The 47th Annual PDK/Gallup Poll of the Public's Attitudes Toward the Public Schools: Testing doesn't measure up for Americans*. Retrieved May 28, 2016, from http://pdkpoll2015.pdkintl.org/wp-content/uploads/2015/10/pdkpoll47_2015.pdf

Rankin, J. (2015). How report design makes or breaks data use. *Educational Leadership, 73*(3). Bonus content on-line. Retrieved June 4, 2016, from http://www.ascd.org/publications/educational-leadership/nov15/vol73/num03/How-Report-Design-Makes-or-Breaks-Data-Use.aspx

Reardon, S. F. (2013). *The widening income achievement gap*. Retrieved May 9, 2016, from http://www.ascd.org/publications/educational-leadership/may13/vol70/num08/The-Widening-Income-Achievement-Gap.aspx

Reform Support Network. (2012). Targeting growth: Using student learning objectives as a measure of educator effectiveness. Retrieved May 28, 2016, from https://www2.ed.gov/about/inits/ed/implementation-support-unit/tech-assist/targeting-growth.pdf

Rimmer, J. (2016). Developing principals as equity-centered instructional leaders. *Essential approaches for excellence and sustainable school system transformation*. The Equity-Centered Capacity Building Network (ECCBN). Retrieved May 10, 2016, from https://capacitybuildingnetwork.org/article9

Rothman, R. (2015). What data dashboards can do. *Educational Leadership, 73*(3), 28–32.

Sagor, R. (2000). *Guiding school improvement with action research*. Alexandria, VA: Association for Supervision and Curriculum Development.

Shannon, G. S., & Bylsma, P. (2003) *Nine characteristics of high-performing schools*. Olympia, WA: Office of Superintendent of Public Instruction.

Slaven, C. (2015, July). *Understanding student learning: The need for education data*. Alliance for Excellent Education. Retrieved May 24, 2016, from http://all4ed .org/reports-factsheets/educationdata

Scudelia, C. (2016). Administrators' impact on teacher intrinsic motivation. *ASCD Express*, *11*(18). Retrieved May 26, 2016, from http://www.ascd.org/ ascd-express/vol11/1118-scudelia.aspx?utm_source=ascdexpress&utm_ medium=email&utm_campaign=Express-11-18

Sparks, S. D. (2013). Improvement science seen as emerging tool in K–12 sphere. *Education Week, 33*(6), 6.

Sparks, S. D. (2015). Studies probe how schools widen achievement gaps. *Education Week*. Retrieved May 9, 2016, from http://www.edweek.org/ew/ articles/2015/10/07/schools-help-widen-academic-gaps-studies-find.html

Sterrett, W. L. (2012). From discipline to relationships: What can school leaders do to support teachers in building stronger relationships with students? *Educational Leadership, 70*(2), 71–74.

Student Data Principles Coalition. (2015, March). 10 foundational principles for using and safeguarding students' personal information. *Data Quality Campaign*. Retrieved July 10, 2016, from http://dataqualitycampaign.org/resource/ student-data-principles

Tomlinson, C. A. (2014). The bridge between today's lesson and tomorrow's. *Educational Leadership, 71*(6), 10–14.

Tschannen-Moran, M. (2014). *Trust matters: Leadership for successful schools* (2nd ed.). San Francisco, CA: Jossey-Bass.

U.S. Congress, Every Student Succeeds Act. (2015). Retrieved May 22, 2016, from https://www.congress.gov/bill/114th-congress/senate-bill/1177/text

Varlas, L. (2002, Winter). Getting acquainted with the essential nine. *Curriculum Update*, pp. 4–5.

Wheelock, A. (2002). Foreword to Johnson, Ruth S. (2002). *Using data to close the achievement gap: How to measure equity in our schools*. Thousand Oaks, CA: Corwin.

Wiliam, D. (2011). *Embedded formative assessment*. Bloomington, IN: Solution Tree Press.

Wood, F. H. (1989). Organizing and managing school-based staff development. In S. D. Caldwell (Ed.), *Staff development: A handbook of effective practices*. Oxford, OH: National Staff Development Council.

Index

A SAGE Publishing Company

CORWIN HAS ONE MISSION: to enhance education through intentional professional learning.

We build long-term relationships with our authors, educators, clients, and associations who partner with us to develop and continuously improve the best evidence-based practices that establish and support lifelong learning.

Solutions you want. Experts you trust. Results you need.

Author Consulting

Author Consulting

On-site professional learning with sustainable results! Let us help you design a professional learning plan to meet the unique needs of your school or district. www.corwin.com/pd

Institutes

Institutes

Corwin Institutes provide collaborative learning experiences that equip your team with tools and action plans ready for immediate implementation. www.corwin.com/institutes

eCourses

eCourses

Practical, flexible online professional learning designed to let you go at your own pace. www.corwin.com/ecourses

Read2Earn

Read2Earn

Did you know you can earn graduate credit for reading this book? Find out how: www.corwin.com/read2earn

Made in United States
North Haven, CT
03 January 2025

63905474R00154